Discretionary Power of Public Administration

STUDIES IN POLITICS, SECURITY AND SOCIETY

Edited by Stanisław Sulowski
Institute of Political Science of the University of Warsaw

VOLUME 14

PETER LANG
EDITION

Leszek Leszczyński / Adam Szot (eds.)

Discretionary Power of Public Administration

Its Scope and Control

PETER LANG EDITION

Bibliographic Information published by the Deutsche Nationalbibliothek
The Deutsche Nationalbibliothek lists this publication in the Deutsche Nationalbibliografie; detailed bibliographic data is available in the internet at http://dnb.d-nb.de.

Library of Congress Cataloging-in-Publication Data
A CIP catalog record for this book has been applied for at the Library of Congress.

The publication was financially supported by Maria Curie-Sklodowska University and National Science Center in Poland (Narodowe Centrum Nauki) within research grant DEC-2013/11/N/HS5/04212, entitled: "The influence of judicial decisions on the discretionary power of public administration in the law application processes".

ISSN 2199-028X
ISBN 978-3-631-67468-0 (Print)
E-ISBN 978-3-631-72454-5 (E-PDF)
E-ISBN 978-3-631-72455-2 (EPUB)
E-ISBN 978-3-631-72456-9 (MOBI)
DOI 10.3726/b11220

Peter Lang Edition is an Imprint of Peter Lang GmbH.

Peter Lang – Frankfurt am Main · Bern · Bruxelles · New York · Oxford · Warszawa · Wien

This publication has been peer reviewed.

www.peterlang.com

Table of content

Introduction

I. Public administration in modern states is perceived as an organisation of a special kind which acts on behalf of a state as well as for its sake, but also for units subjected to state powers. Hence, a projection is brought into life of a way in which a society is to function, which is drafted and favoured by a centre of the political power. The activity of public administration is geared towards taking most efficient actions within their legal boundaries and accounting for socio-political conditions.

Activities of public administration organs are being assessed through elaborate control and supervision systems, which frequently builds their vested interest in the content of decisions being made. Simultaneously, processes of administrative decisions occur in situations with potential conflicts of interest.

A legislator provides public administration organs with an appropriate range of competence in order to facilitate best possible fulfilment of their tasks. Additionally, they are granted administrative powers, i.e. a possibility to decide unilaterally about a content of a legal relation between themselves and subjects from outside the administration realm. Imperative forms of administrative actions remain an indispensable element for humans to function within a society organised in a state despite numerous attempts at finding new ways and methods for meeting needs of the society and its members.

A legislator also provides public administration organs with some decision latitude in order to facilitate efficient fulfilment of their tasks and to adjust activities they undertake to individual cases and needs that may change in a dynamic social context. Decision processes feature (or at least may feature) other sources of latitude that do not stem from legislator's conscious actions, which also contributes to a current depiction of public administration's decision latitude. Hence, some aspects of this latitude might slip away from legislator's control. In turn, this adds up to the acute problem of the range of discretionary powers that public administration organs exercise in connection with making individual decisions that may affect citizens' rights and obligations. Furthermore, the said problem is inextricably connected with limits of such latitude and making sure that these limits are not crossed, and finally with the supralegal context in which public administration functions as well as administration's vested interest in the content of decisions being made.

II. This publication aims at presenting numerous expressions of public administration's prerogatives within the processes of law implementation. It is also to present a complexity of factors that may affect the range of these prerogatives as well as public administration's reasoning (narrowing or directing its discretion). Finally, the study is to present a complexity of forms and procedures for control of decision latitude that is actually exercised by the public administration (these are defined as internal control maintained by the very administration in addition to external control maintained by independent organs and institutions, including courts of law and other subjects, e.g. the society and its representatives).

Continental legal culture as well as the theory of law and administrative proceedings make the starting point for deliberations by all authors of those papers. Representatives of Polish legal studies (theory of law, administrative law and administrative proceedings) as well as legal practitioners (in particular, judges of administrative courts) have been invited to contribute their relevant research and adjudication experience to this monograph. Furthermore, the team of authors includes representatives of other systems and legal cultures (common law), which has granted some comparative perspective.

The majority of analyses made within respective parts of this monograph are of a universal character (pertaining to the theory of law). Any references to solutions from specific legal systems are merely exemplifications and they constitute some background for discussions of a more general nature.

The monograph is divided into four parts pertaining to various aspects and manifestations of discretionary powers of the public administration. The first part has been devoted to issues of a general nature pertaining to various ways of perceiving and defining the notion of administration's discretion as well as its boundaries. The next part deals with problems of public administration organs using decisional freedom in the processes of law implementation; it also refers to the range of control over these processes that is exercised by independent courts. The third part is devoted to selected problems of the theory of law which *inter alia* refer to law interpretation, including the influence of a precedence on shaping administrative decisions in the continental legal culture, processes of communication and mediation, as well as axiological limits of public administration's discretion. The last part focuses on specific legal problems that occur in various legal systems and cultures.

We are fully aware that the issues referred to in this book that are connected with both theoretical and practical aspects of shaping public administration's discretionary powers, the way that organs use their decision latitude, and finally the forms and methods for controlling such latitude hardly exhaust the topic and merely form a starting point for further discussions. At the same time, we hope to receive critical feedback on points made by respective authors, which will contribute to broadening the range of study in this respect.

III. This monograph was created in result of research conducted in the Chair of Theory and Philosophy of Law (Maria Curie-Sklodowska University, Lublin, Poland) and in the framework of research project granted by the Polish National Science Centre [Narodowe Centrum Nauki] on the basis of decision No. DEC-2013/11/N/HS5/04212, entitled: "The influence of judicial decisions on the discretionary power of public administration in the law application processes" ["Wpływ orzeczeń sądowych na dyskrecjonalną władzę administracji publicznej w procesach stosowania prawa"].

Academic Editors:
Leszek Leszczyński
Adam Szot

Part I

Małgorzata Jaśkowska
(Associate Professor, Cardinal Stefan Wyszynski University in Warsaw, Poland; The Supreme Administrative Court of Poland Judge)

Discretionality, Margin of Decision and Administrative Discretionary Authority – an Attempt at Terminological Clarification

Abstract: The article is aimed at systemizing the terminology related to the discretionary power of public authorities, given the scope of the concepts covered by it. It constitutes a proposal of a specific understanding of the concepts of discretionality, margin of decision and administrative discretionary authority.

Keywords: discretionality, margin of decision, administrative discretionary authority

1. Introduction

In the literature of administrative law the terms discretionality (*dyskrecjonalność*), discretionary authority (*uznanie*) or margin of decision (*luzy decyzyjne*) are frequently used as synonyms, and no regard is given to their internal differentiation[1]. Other authors, however, assign different meanings to these terms[2]. A number of causes for the absence of synonymity are given. References are made to the

1 The terms of "discretionality" and "discretionary authority" are treated as referring to the same concept by, amongst others, in P. Król, *Uznanie w tworzeniu prawa administracyjnego* [in:] K. Ziemski, M. Jędrzejczak (eds.), *Dyskrecjonalność w prawie administracyjnym*, Poznań 2015, the "Prawo" series No. 188, p. 29 et seq.; Whereas in D. Gregorczyk, *Dyskrecjonalność administracji jako gwarancja realizacji zasady demokratycznego państwa prawnego, ibid.*, p. 87, author equates "discretionality" with the "margin of decision".

2 Such an argument is presented in M. Jaśkowska, *Uznanie administracyjne a inne formy władzy dyskrecjonalnej administracji publicznej*, [in:] R. Hauser, Z. Niewiadomski, A. Wróbel (eds.), *System Prawa Administracyjnego* Vol. 1, *Instytucje prawa administracyjnego*, 2nd Ed., Warszawa 2015, pp. 318–323; I emphasised this already in the first edition of the above paper (M. Jaśkowska, *Uznanie administracyjne a inne formy władzy dyskrecjonalnej administracji publicznej*, [in:] R. Hauser, Z. Niewiadomski, A. Wróbel (eds.), *System Prawa Administracyjnego* Vol. 1, *Instytucje prawa administracyjnego*, 1st Ed., Warszawa 2010, pp. 298–303).

linguistic understanding of the terms, their etymology or designed purpose, and it is emphasised that some of them have been created for the purposes of the theory of law while others are applied within a given branch of law. This paper is an attempt to elaborate on and substantiate a concept covered by the latter line of argument, whose outline I have presented in my earlier publications[3]. This is because in my opinion if one applies these terms as carrying different meanings, one will obtain tools useful for attaining varying research objectives, in the area of both the general theory of law and its specific branches, including the science of administrative law. In this way, one also may underscore the similarities and differences between actions of individual types of public authorities, taken in different forms and areas. This is of significance for a review of such actions. The use of a defined term can simultaneously emphasise a range of considerations, effectively preventing many misunderstandings. From the perspective of the science of administrative law, a discipline I represent, and given the scope of review, and in particular the judicial review, it would therefore be desirable to achieve a certain level of terminological cohesion in this regard. This is true because, as Langrod has noted, the role of the judicature and legal science is to standardise certain general terms, which can be used for the purposes of developing their own vocabulary and uniform institutions, especially given that the proprieties of a technique (in our case, administrative law) reinforce the appeal for distinguishing the terms, which are consequences of the genesis, development and purposes of this branch of law[4]. Such arguments, in turn, support – which I will try to prove below – a given way of understanding the terms I propose.

At the same time, however, since the terms refer to law, I treat them as legal concepts, created within the sphere of the science of administrative law. On the other hand, I do not see a necessity to express the terms in definitions that would be acceptable for the legislator. Such a definition could be needed, but only in respect of administrative discretionary authority, because of the fact that this concept restricts the availability of judicial review and administrative courts ability to decide a case on its merits. Conversely, the other terms, such as discretionality or margin of decision, do not require a legal definition[5]. Given the above, I treat my approach to the subject principally as a research proposal.

---

3 Ibid.

4 J.S. Langrod, *Instytucje prawa administracyjnego. Zarys części ogólnej. Reprint*, Kraków 2003, pp. 372–374.

5 Therefore, contrary to arguments presented in K. Ziemski and M. Jędrzejczak, *Pojęcie dyskrecjonalności a pojęcie luzów decyzyjnych*, [in:] *Dyskrecjonalność w prawie administracyjnym*, op. cit., p. 13, I do not think the legislator's inability to adopt an

2. The notion and scope of discretionality

As a starting point for further discussion, I adopt the legal understanding of the notion of discretionality or, to be more precise, discretionary authority since I apply this notion not to all subjects of law, but only to those equipped with sovereign decision-making powers. Looking from the perspective of the science of administrative law, I am most interested in such forms of discretion that concern public authorities constrained by law but do not apply directly to a recipient of the authorities' actions, who may do anything that the law does not forbid. This does not mean I underestimate the sphere of the individual's rights and freedoms but results from the fact that discretionary powers of public authorities can limit the sphere of such rights and freedoms and therefore require to be discussed in a more detailed manner. Furthermore, the notion of discretionality relates to the situation where an issue has been presented to an entity exercising sovereign powers in order to be resolved in a way that is not rigidly determined by provisions of law[6]. This interpretation of the term is a consequence of a certain genesis and development of law, and has been shaped in the language of law by a number of factors, including Poland's accession to the EU and the ensuing wider interest in the European law[7]. The above interpretation differs from the common – and purely linguistic – meaning of the Polish adjective "dyskrecjonalny" that is equivalent to "poufny", which can be translated into English as "confidential"[8].

Considering the above, I assume that discretionality, or more precisely discretionary authority, has a very wide subjective and objective scope as a notion. In the subjective meaning, such authority may be exercised by any subject of the law attributed with a sovereign decision-making power. At the same time, the subjective scope is not only wide but also internally diverse. It extends to executive, judicial and legislative bodies[9]. Due to their role and constitutional position within a state, the widest extent of discretionary authority is afforded to lawmakers. Still, also this

---

unambiguous definition of discretionality (which is a consequence to the lack of a definition accepted by a majority of the scholarship) is a substantial defect.

6 Cf. S. Dubisz (ed.), *Uniwersalny Słownik języka polskiego A-J*, Wyd. Naukowe PWN, Warszawa 2008, p. 747, which defines "discretionary" as "something left for someone's discretionary recognition, free assessment, unspecified, unrestricted by any regulations".

7 As indicated by K. Ziemski i M. Jędrzejczak, op. cit., p. 15.

8 M. Bańko (ed.), *Słownik języka polskiego, t. 1, A-Gar*, Wyd. Naukowe PWN, Warszawa 2007, p. 426.

9 Such a wide subjective meaning is proposed in B. Wojciechowski, *Model zakresu swobody interpretacyjnej prawa administracyjnego, rozdz. X* [in:] L. Leszczyński, B. Wojciechowski, M. Zirk-Sadowski, *System Prawa Administracyjnego, t. 4, Wykładnia w*

category is internally diverse. This is because the legislative model of lawmaking differs from the legal and administrative models. As Ziemski and Jędrzejczak emphasise, the lawmaking power of executive bodies is always a derivative of the relevant power of the legislative branch. The executive's powers to create general and abstractive norms are thus similar to processes of enforcing the law. There are also material differences between the models of issuing individual normative acts[10]. Consequently, a wide area of discretion is not always a derivative of a body's rank. This is because a minister who issues an executive regulation has less discretionary authority that a local government body adopting spatial planning acts or local bylaws. However, the legal scholarship in particular emphasises the role of judicial discretionality[11]. It has been noticed that the application of law by courts affects the former's characteristics because the judicial autonomy and independence is what differentiates courts from executive bodies. The characteristics of law influences the subject-matter scope of discretionary authority enjoyed by a given body and the body's relationships with other subjects of law. On the other hand, the role and position of executive bodies is different and depends on a constitutional model, and is shaped by such phenomena as centralisation or decentralisation. At the same time, diverse bodies exercise public administration functions. Since public tasks are being privatised and their performance tends to be linked with certain obligations of public law, a new category of entities has emerged: they are given wide discretionary authority even though they do not perform, as a rule, any functions of public entities. This can be observed, for instance, in entities obliged to perform the duty of granting access to public information under the Access to Public Information Act of 6 September 2001[12]. Pursuant to Article 4 (1) (5) of this Act, the category of entities obliged to disclose public information includes also entities that represent other persons or organisational units which perform public tasks or holding public property, as well as legal persons in which the State Treasury, units of local government and those of business or

---

prawie administracyjnym, Warszawa 2012, p. 462. However, the author restricts the objective scope of this meaning solely to the application of law, ibid., p. 464.

10 K. Ziemski, M. Jędrzejczak, op. cit. pp. 18–19.

11 B. Wojciechowski, *Dyskrecjonalność sędziowska. Studium teoretycznoprawne,* Toruń 2004, pp. 16–17, H. Duszka-Jakimko, "Dyskrecjonalność i model argumentacyjny w stosowaniu prawa we współczesnym pozytywizmie prawniczym", Opolskie Studia Administracyjno-Prawne VI, Opole 2009, p. 138, Z. Czarnik, *Prawotwórcza rola sądu a dyskrecjonalność sędziowska, w; Dyskrecjonalna władza sędziego* [in:] M. Dębiński, R. Pelewicz, T. Rakoczy (eds.), *Zagadnienia teorii i praktyki,* Tarnobrzeg 2012, pp. 13–20.

12 Uniform text in the Journal of Laws of 2015, item 2058, as amended.

professional self-governing organisations have a dominant position within the meaning of competition and consumer protection laws. Paragraph 2 of the said article imposes the obligation to disclose public information on those of labour union organisations and employers' organisations that are "of a representative character" within the meaning of the Act on the Social Dialogue Council and other institutions of social dialogue of 24 July 2015[13], and on political parties.

The objective scope of discretionary authority is also wide and internally diverse. The above is true in particular of the sources of such authority. This is due to the fact that understood objectively, discretionary authority relates to any possibility of making a choice, which may be shaped by a range of different factors. This may be the social context of the law, the characteristics of the legal language, features of a given branch of law, nature of the process of application of law, in other words factors independent from the legislator, but also the factors that depend on the legislator such as the manner in which legal rules and normative acts are formulated, development of special structures referring to non-legal criteria or creation of discretionary competences. What matters is thus a defined concept of a policy that governs the creation and application of law as well as the technical and legal measures used[14]. All those factors affect the object and internal diversification of discretionary authority. Such authority may hence apply to the creation, application, enforcement or review of the law. It may be referred to all branches of law, or only to a selected branch such as administrative law.

At the same time, the objective scope of discretionary authority can be characterised by both internal similarities and differences. Entities exercising such authority take governing and unilateral actions, while the sources and stages of proceedings that serve the purpose of making a proper selection are actually similar. However, certain differences between the making and application of law appear against this background; similarly, there are differences between the judicial model and executive models of applying law (the latter being typical for administrative bodies). This is because the lawmaking process involves an attempt to adopt a general and abstractive norm with a future effect, whereas the application of law aims at resolving an existing dispute or forming individual rights and duties of subjects of the law. For this reason, discretionality of the legislative is extremely wide but also objectively (thematically) diverse. Three aspects of such discretionality are discerned. The first one is freedom to decide whether or not

13 Journal of Laws, item 1240.

14 Re. sources of margin of decision, please cf. L. Leszczyński, *Zagadnienia teorii stosowania prawa. Doktryna i tezy orzecznictwa*, Kraków 2001, pp. 41–45. In my opinion they may also be applied to the notion of discretionary authority.

to issue an act (the making of new laws is optional), known as the lawmaking discretion, which includes an assessment of the purposefulness and necessity of introduction of a new legal regulation. The remaining two are determination of the timeframe for issuing a new regulation and the freedom of determining the substantive content of a legal act[15].

On the one hand, courts and administrative bodies also apply the law in a similar way: the decision-maker (a competent state body or other entity authorised by law) determines positive or negative legal consequences of certain facts on the basis of applicable legal norms, in a way that is binding on particular entities[16]. The process results in an individual and specific norm that determines the recipient's behaviour by indicating the consequences of the facts of a case[17]. On the other hand, internal diversity also appears here. This diversity results from the fact that administrative bodies operate in different spheres, both externally, vis-a-vis entities that are not subordinated within an organisational structure, and internally, vis-a-vis subordinated entities and bodies, and this affects the scope of their obligations. Legal basis of an action and a degree of specificity of a legal norm are shaped differently in either of the above spheres[18].

The judicial model, on its part, is external as it covers entities that are not subordinated within an organisational structure. Moreover, as a rule courts review only legality, while administrative bodies assess both legality and purposefulness. At the same time administrative bodies do not have the attribute of independence. Because of this, their application of law is substantially influenced by the structural features of administrative law as norms of this law constitute a certain type of a peremptory norm (*jus cogens*) that determines a duty to take certain actions, and determine – at least generally – the legal situation of subjects of a legal relationship[19].

According to Jakimowicz, the differences between discretionality of courts and that of administrative bodies result from the fact that the two types of discretionality rest with different branches of government; because of this, grounds for their

---

15 P. Król, op. cit. p. 31 et seq.

16 D. Tykwińska-Rutkowska, *Stosowanie prawa administracyjnego* [in:] E. Bojanowski and K. Żukowski (eds.), *Leksykon prawa administracyjnego. 100 podstawowych pojęć*, Warszawa 2009 pp. 401–403.

17 Cf. L. Leszczyński, *Stosowanie i wykładnia prawa administracyjnego, rozdz. I* [in:] *System*, op. cit., vol. 4, p. 4, or W. Gromski, A. Bator (ed.), *Wprowadzenie do nauk prawnych. Leksykon tematyczny*, Warszawa 2010 pp. 300 and 309.

18 M. Jaśkowska, *System*, op. cit., pp. 230–232.

19 J. Filipek, "Elementy strukturalne norm prawa administracyjnego", ZNUJ DCXVII, *Prace Prawnicze* Vol. 99, Warszawa Kraków 1982 pp. 30–31.

actions and scope of discretion are different, too. In this respect, a model of applying the law and procedural rules are both different[20]. Ziemski and Jędrzejczak also note this, arguing that despite similarities and a resembling model of application of law, courts have much narrower discretionary authority. This is because courts adjudicate in respect of already existing legal situations while administrative bodies in principle operate with the intention to achieve a future result (in a creative manner)[21]. In the case of judicial administrative proceedings, additional differences appear in respect of evidentiary proceedings and, as a rule, the cassation-type model of adjudication.

However, the argument that courts, as opposed to administrative bodies, have much narrower discretionary authority in the area of application of law, cannot be accepted in its entirety. The accuracy of the above contention depends on a point of view. In some aspects, courts enjoy greater freedom because they are independent. As far as courts are concerned, different objects of discretionary authority intersect with each other since both processes overlap in a setting of judicial activism, despite the differences between the processes of creation and application of law[22]. This activism is an inherent feature of all kinds of actions taken by the judicature. It entails a situation in which "a judge takes a decision that is not determined by provisions of law, making an election that it is their own choice and not a choice made directly by the legislator"[23]. This may be the result of axiological considerations, as it was in the judgment of the Provincial Administrative Court (*Wojewódzki Sąd Administracyjny*, WSA) in Wrocław from 25 June 2014, case no. I SA/Wr 432/14[24]. In this judgment the Court invoked extraordinary circumstances of the case and opposed formal adherence to the law as leading to injustice.

In the judicial application of law, activism can manifest itself in the phenomena of judicial lawmaking and precedent. They are linked to each other since a law-making judgment accompanied by strong reasoning[25] may function as a

20 Cf. W. Jakimowicz, *Wykładnia w prawie administracyjnym*, Kraków 2006, pp. 328–338.

21 K. Ziemski, M. Jędrzejczak, op. cit. pp. 17–18.Also cf. W. Jakimowicz, op. cit. p. 331.

22 D. Dąbek, *Prawo sędziowskie w polskim prawie administracyjnym*, Warszawa 2010, pp. 192–193, cf. also B. Banaszak, M. Bernaczyk, *Aktywizm sędziowski we współczesnym państwie demokratycznym*, Warszawa 2012, in particular pp. 45–46, where the authors emphasise the characteristics of activism that exist in the Constitutional Tribunal.

23 L. Morawski, "Zasada trójpodziału władzy. Trybunał Konstytucyjny i aktywizm sędziowski", *Przegląd Sejmowy* 2009 Vol. 4, p. 65.

24 OSP 2016 Vol. 2 item 12, commentary by A. Gomułowicz.

25 Cf. L. L. Leszczyński, *Dyskrecjonalność a jednolitość stosowania prawa. Rola argumentu per rationem decidendi*, [in:] W. Staśkiewicz, T. Stawecki (eds.), *Dyskrecjonalność*

precedent, potently influencing other judicial rulings[26]. However, precedents are not an expression of lawmaking activities. This is because they do not create new legal rules or principles, but use and acknowledge existing jurisprudence and follow a certain line of reasoning[27]. In the case of activism, we deal with an argumentative form of application of law, balancing of legal and non-legal arguments, the ability of correcting law through interpretation, or establishment of new rules[28].

According to Morawski, judicial creation of new legal rules and principles is driven by the textual accessibility of law, conflicts between its principles and norms, absence of legal regulations and simultaneously imposed state obligations to perform a number of welfare or political functions[29]. In addition, Gomułowicz points to errors in lawmaking that cause major legal loopholes (axiological and structural) and errors of the axiological and praxeological nature, and also the legislator's inability to quickly correct defective laws[30]. Dąbek takes a similar position, referring to defects of law, legal loopholes, the necessity to make assessments in the process of application of law, indeterminate phrases or general clauses, a need to resolve conflicts between legally protected interests – also by way of a constitutional review of statutes performed by courts, as well as the requirement to take into account rapid changes of social realities that are insufficiently addressed

---

w prawie. Materiały XVIII Ogólnopolskiego Zjazdu Katedr Teorii i Filozofii Prawa. Międzeszyn k. Warszawy, 22–24 września 2008r., Warszawa 2008, p. 145.

26 M. Zirk-Sadowski, *Precedens a tzw decyzja prawotwórcza*, "Państwo i Prawo" 1980 Vol. 6, p. 73.

27 Here, an argument made as part of a line of judicial reasoning can be treated merely as a type of interpretation of law, and in fact a sum of interpretative acts, cf. E. Bojanowski, *Utrwalona linia orzecznictwa (kilka uwag na marginesie orzecznictwa sądów administracyjnych),* [in:] J. Supernat (ed.), *Między tradycją a przyszłością w nauce prawa administracyjnego: Księga jubileuszowa dedykowana Profesorowi Janowi Bociowi,* Wrocław 2009, p. 52, or sometimes be construed more extensively, as a form of factual precedential reasoning, see A. Jakubowski, S. Gajewski, *Argument z linii orzeczniczej w orzecznictwie sądów administracyjnych,* Warszawa 2015, p. 47–50; or even from the lawmaking perspective, as a source of normative reconstruction of one's own ruling, cf. L. Leszczyński, *Interpretacyjna rola kryteriów otwartych i innych decyzji stosowania prawa, rozdz. VII,* [in:] *System, op. cit. Vol. 4,* pp. 351–352.

28 L. Morawski, *Główne problemy współczesnej filozofii prawa. Prawo w toku przemian,* 4th Ed., Warszawa 2005, p. 288.

29 L. Morawski, "Zasada trójpodziału", op. cit. pp. 66–68, L. Morawski, *Czy sądy mogą się angażować politycznie?,* "Państwo i Prawo" 2006 Vol. 3, pp. 16 et seq.

30 A. Gomułowicz, *Aspekt prawotwórczy sądownictwa administracyjnego,* Warszawa 2008, pp. 34–36, 56 and 120.

by the legislator[31]. Lemańska, on the other hand, approaches to activism from a positive perspective, linking the phenomenon with the requirement to ensure uniform jurisprudence, protect constitutional principles and fill the gaps in legal and administrative regulations, which can be done, for instance, by self-imposition of certain rules within the public administration system[32].

In addition to the above, the concept of wide discretionary authority of administrative bodies will gain significance if one takes into consideration the various forms in which the administration system operates. As Błaś emphasises, widest discretionary powers originate from those norms of administrative law that administrative bodies apply in practice not as administrative decisions (acts of applying the law) but as material and technical or social and organisational acts. Therefore, it is necessary to perform a more in-depth analysis of the forms that do not involve decision-making; this will prevent such forms from being used in an overly extensive way, whether in order to avoid review, or to obtain extensive freedom for administrative bodies[33].

The aforementioned notion of discretionality, because of its wide scope, may constitute a useful research tool whenever a discussion concerns the choices made by entities included in different categories of public authorities or those related to different types, spheres or forms of action. This makes it possible to comprehend common mechanism and values underlying such mechanisms and allows for emphasising the differences that appear between the two. It also provides an opportunity to evaluate such similarities and differences from the perspective of division of powers, constitutional role of an entity and the nature of its activities.

3. The notion and scope of the margin of decision

Another justification concerns the introduction of the notion of the margin of decision. This refers to the relationship between law-applying and lawmaking entities. Leszczyński sees them as a manifestation of discretionality, which is

31 D. Dąbek, op. cit. pp. 323, 329 et seq., pp. 356, 362 et seq., p. 372 et seq., pp. 706 and 708.

32 J. Lemańska, *Tak zwane prawo sędziowskie w systemie źródeł prawa administracyjnego,* [in:] J. Zimmermann, P. Dobosz, *Źródła prawa administracyjnego. Konferencja z okazji 100 Rocznicy urodzin Profesora Jerzego Stefana Langroda, Uniwersytet Jagielloński-23 kwietnia 2004r.* Kraków 2005, pp. 69–71 and 77.

33 A. Błaś, *Jednostka wobec dyskrecjonalnych uprawnień administracji publicznej* [in:] E. Ura (ed.), *Jednostka wobec działań administracji publicznej. Międzynarodowa Konferencja Naukowa (Olszanica 21–23 maja 2001r.)*, Rzeszów 2001, p. 26–27.

associated with flexibility in the application of law[34]. At the source of this notion of flexibility lie two types of causes, which are partly beyond the control of legislators, and partly introduced as deliberate legal structures. The first type stems from the imperfections of the language in which the legislation is formulated and also the inability to regulate all characteristics of a social relationship. The second type, such as the intentional use of imprecise concepts, or the option to choose administrative discretionary authority as a legal effect, is deliberately introduced by the legislator. There may also be a margin of decision, which is a mixture of these two types. By accepting Leszczyński's notion in this respect, I shall discuss the margin of decision, subjectively, in the context of public administration (in its broad sense) and, objectively, in the context of the application of administrative law externally, with regards to organizationally non-subordinated entities. In this respect, the margin of decision is liked both to the application of substantive and procedural law. When the authorities make a decision to apply law, they follow legislation, which is the basis of both their actions and the content of their decisions. Thus, in this case, to apply law is to simultaneously follow it[35].

The notion of the margin of decision has subjectively and objectively a much narrower scope than the notion of discretionary authority. The margin of decision is only a part of this power. At the same time, it refers to the administrative model of the application of law[36]. What links the possibilities of choice in the case of the margin of decision is the fact that it refers to the activities of an authority in the process of applying law in the area of external administration. At the same time the process of applying the law is not homogeneous. It is made up of the following actions: (1) Determining what provision is applicable and determining its meaning in the language of the norm applied, (2) assuming certain facts to be proven on the basis of evidence obtained and the accepted theory of evidence, and putting these facts in the language of a norm applied, (3) subsuming the accepted fact as proven in the light of legislation used and (4) bindingly determining legal consequences of a fact accepted to be proven in the light of legislation used[37].

---

34 L. Leszczyński, *Dyskrecjonalność a jednolitość stosowania prawa,* op. cit. p. 137, cf. also L. Leszczyński, *Stosowanie i wykładnia prawa administracyjnego, rozdz. I* [in:] *System* op. cit. vol. 4, p. 28 et seq.

35 L. Leszczyński, *Stosowanie i wykładnia prawa administracyjnego, rozdz. I* [in:] *System* op. cit. vol. 4, p. 5.

36 On this type cf. L. Leszczyński, ibid, p. 14 et seq.

37 Cf. J. Wróblewski, *Sądowe stosowanie prawa,* Warszawa 1972, pp. 50–57. However, this source refers the nature of activities performed rather than the sequence of events; cf.

Taking all of the above into consideration, the margin of decision can be varied in nature. This is due to the fact that it refers to various phenomena. A selection may concern either validation rules, or facts relating to reality and their assessment, language, or the intended impact, or its aim. All this influences the criteria used when making decisions. And so validation arrangements performed by the administrative bodies functioning under written laws begin by searching for valid legal provisions that make up the source of the reconstruction of the norm. At the same time, it must be stressed that these authorities have a smaller degree of independence. They also lack traits of activism, they rarely indirectly apply legal provisions and they find using analogy generally inadmissible[38]. On the level of the interpretation of law, steps are taken towards the determination of meaning of a legal text. At the same time, the accepted paradigm of the interpretation that assumes the order of applying the interpretation's specific types, as well as the acceptance, or not, of the notion of the immediate understanding of a legal text, can be of importance here. Also, in the administrative application of law, what is being stressed is a diminished independence of the interpretation, basing it predominantly on linguistic rules, referring to the political context more frequently, and less so to argumentation[39]. At the same time, however, the administration is heavily dependent on the approved axiology that functions in the social reality. This is why the search for values which can serve as a foundation for the applicable law and the acts of the application of law is so significant for the development of the science of administrative law[40]. For a lawyer, however, they must always be based on legal norms. Incidentally, values can result from these norms in a direct or indirect way and, considering the fact that public authorities are bound by law, create an axiological context that determines the activities of the administration. The normativisation of these values can be performed simultaneously in a number of different ways: through the adoption of a preamble of a legal act, through the analysis of the provisions of positive law or through highlighting the

---

L. Leszczyński, *Zagadnienia teorii stosowania prawa*, op. cit. pp. 62–63, idem, *Stosowanie i wykładnia prawa administracyjnego, rozdz. I* [in:] *System*, op. cit. vol. 4, p. 38 et seq.

38 Cf. L. Leszczyński, *Podstawa decyzji stosowania prawa administracyjnego. Ustalenia walidacyjne. Rozdział II* [in:] *System*, op. cit. vol. 4, esp. pp. 66, 70, 80–87, 100 et seq., 104, 117 et seq.

39 Cf. L. Leszczyński, *Stosowanie i wykładnia prawa administracyjnego, rozdz. I* [in:] *System*, op. cit. vol. 4, pp. 45–46, and M. Zirk-Sadowski, *Pojęcie, koncepcje i przebieg wykładni prawa administracyjnego, rodział III* [in:] *System*, op. cit. vol. 4, pp. 133–140.

40 This is stressed by J. Zimmermann, *Wprowadzenie* [in:] J. Zimmermann (ed.), *Wartości w prawie administracyjnym*, Warszawa 2015, pp. 11–12.

protective function of law[41]. In the area of administrative and legal regulations, the following points are treated as the manifestation of the relationship between legal norms and other normative systems, in which the values accepted by these systems are reflected:

1. The formulation of general rules (legal principles) referring to particular values, which make up the basis for assessments related to the interpretation and application of law,
2. The inclusion of particular axiological assumptions to the set of legal norms by using vague expressions, including general clauses that use notions requiring a referral to moral and political indications or assessments,
3. The inclusion of a clear reference to a system or set of values in the provisions regulating a particular type of behaviour[42].

The most visible manifestation of the inclusion of a system of values is the reference made by the legislator to a particular set, as indicated in para. 3. An example of this is the reference to the Christian set of values in the Broadcasting Act of 29 December 1992[43] (Article 4 (10), and Article 21 (2) (6). An important role in the process of reflecting values in the decision-making process is also played by rules. Treating them as an interpretative argument entails a public perspective and leads to the use of axiological, non-system criteria[44].

Recognising values can also happen through the inclusion of particular axiological assumptions to the set of legal norms through the use of various types of vague notions[45]. Depending on their type, these notions determine a larger or smaller scope of the discretion of law-applying authorities to which the legislator refers in order to make the activities of administration more flexible. At the

41 Cf. J. Boć, P. Lisowski, *Normatywizacja wartości w prawie administracyjnym* [in:] ibid, pp. 27–35.

42 Z. Kmieciak, *Skuteczność regulacji administracyjnoprawnej*, Łódź 1994, pp. 121–122.

43 Consolidated text in the Journal of Laws of 2015, item 1531, as amended.

44 This is stressed by L. Leszczyński, *Wykładnia systemowa przepisów prawa administracyjnego, rozdz. V* [in:] *System*, op. cit., vol. 4, p. 242.

45 Their importance is also stressed by B. Majchrzak, according to whom researching the axiology of substantive law basically focuses on the principle around three structures of provisions: those containing vague notions, which means they do not have a clear, strictly defined content; legal definitions placed within a normative text; and task norms defining tasks and lines of action of particular entities, cf. B. Majchrzak, *Badania podstaw aksjologicznych prawa materialnego w zakresie jawności i jej ograniczeń* [in:] Z. Cieślak (ed.), *Jawność i jej ograniczenia*, vol. II *Podstawy aksjologiczne*, Warszawa 2013, pp. 76–77.

same time, pluralism of values is written into administrative law, and so they may stand in conflict[46]. Solving these conflicts also entails the assessment possibilities, as it requires the prioritisation of values and adopting set rules of conflict[47]. The choice can be made by the legislator, or it can be transferred to the law-applying authorities. It can be also specified by creating mechanisms ensuring the appropriate standard of legal determination, which makes the concept of procedural justice a reality[48]. The method of settling such conflicts is therefore determined by an additional axiological aspect, which must be taken into account when formulating the duties of public authorities.

The margin of decision also relates to the second stage of applying law, i.e. recognising facts as proven and putting them in the language of a provision applied. Here we have both the assessment of the actual state and an operation of a linguistic nature. This type of activity covers in part legal reasoning, and in part cognitive reasoning[49]. They both entail large-scale assessment possibilities. The source of these assessments is both the normative way of naming particular facts and the possibility to freely assess evidence attributed to decision-making entities[50]. This principle stems from Arts. 7 and 77 of the Code of Administrative Procedure[51]. However, the process of establishing facts is institutionalised and limited by rules of evidence to a large degree[52]. Putting the assessment into the language of the applied norm is connected to the use of value assessments and notions.

The margin of decision also refers to the third stage of applying law. Here we are also dealing with a certain degree of discretion, which is present when subsuming a fact regarded as proven and expressed in the language of a used norm under the applied legal provisions. This is all regardless of earlier validation choices, whose aim is to determine the applicable law. In some cases, validation determinations

46 M. Krawczyk, *Aksjologiczne uwarunkowania władztwa administracyjnego* [in:] *Wartości w prawie administracyjnym*, op. cit. p. 127.

47 Cf. J. Boć, P. Lisowski, op. cit. p. 39.

48 Cf. Z. Kmieciak, op. cit., p. 124.

49 L. Leszczyński, *Stosowanie i wykładnia prawa administracyjnego, rozdz. I* [in:] *System*, op. cit., vol. 4, p. 40.

50 L. Leszczyński highlights the presence of axiological elements in the process of determining facts, L. Leszczyński, *Zagadnienia teorii stosowania prawa*, op. cit. p. 68 et seq., idem, *Stosowanie i wykładnia prawa administracyjnego*, op. cit., pp. 41–42.

51 Act of 14 June 1960, Code of Administrative Procedure, consolidated text in the Journal of Laws of 2016, item 23.

52 This is pointed to by K. Pachnik, *Ocena dowodów w polskich procedurach sądowych i administracyjnych*, Siedlce 2015, p. 13 et seq. Pachnik also stresses certain model principles of assessing evidence, p. 206 et seq.

can require the verification of indirect application of legal provisions[53]. Consequently, we deal here with a choice of certain rules of inference, e.g. *per analogiam*, argumentation and rules of conflict.

The margin of decision also refers to the final stage of applying law, i.e. determining the legal consequences of the norm applied. They are linked to the involvement of open criteria, which, in the case of constrained decisions, may entail, for example, the option to moderate sanctions, or, in the case of discretionary decisions, give the authority the power to decide on the determination. In the latter case, the margin of discretion of the law-applying entity is the broadest. It is, however, limited by the consequence selection directive.

Regardless of the internal differentiation indicated above, I believe that the notion of the margin of decision, as a narrower type of discretionary authority that administrative authorities are entitled to in the process of applying law, can be useful from a methodological point of view. This is because it enables the determination of an authority's margin of discretion vis-a-vis an important sphere of public authority activities and, at the same time, it highlights its similarities and differences. This can be of huge importance in terms of formulating the criteria the administrative bodies should follow in the process of decisions made, and also in terms of review criteria of such processes by administrative courts. At the same time, it can be useful for demonstrating these fields of administrative activities, which have so far remained beyond the interest of administrative law. There is a lack in literature of detailed, analytical considerations indicating the specifics of individual types of the margin of decision. This lack is not filled by theoretical and legal considerations. The type of margin of decision that especially requires analysis is the one connected with the application of various types of vague notions, including general clauses. This is because vague notions are not of homogenous nature, but are internally differentiated[54]. Therefore, despite the fact that they always contain a certain degree of margin of decision, their reference point is different. General clauses especially grant a large degree of discretion to law-applying authorities. These clauses often refer to an assessment system, or norms of a non-legal nature, which makes the text of a legal act more flexible,

---

53 L. Leszczyński, *Stosowanie i wykładnia prawa administracyjnego*, op. cit., p. 44.

54 Among them, we can distinguish empirical notions, which become individualized in specific cases, value notions, which refer to other disciplines, or general clauses. I have pointed to this taxonomy in the article: M. Mincer, *Pojęcia niedookreślone w orzecznictwie Naczelnego Sądu Administracyjnego*, "Nowe Prawo" 1984, No. 7–8, p. 95 et seq.

and transfers duties to the law-applying entity[55]. At the same time, such clauses assume a normative dimension through such a reference[56].

However, in my opinion this does not mean the lack of possibility to give general clauses a certain universal meaning, or at least it is worth finding certain shared values or prerequisites referring to their particular groups. This could prove useful in the process of interpretation. In this way, the service role of doctrine can be fulfilled with regard to public administration and the judiciary. First attempts in this respect were taken with regard to the notion of societal interest[57], public interest[58], the common good[59] or public safety[60]. Still, the considerations regarding a series of vague notions are of a marginal nature and are made in the context of specific regulations, which is not conducive to their unification. This has already been stressed by Langrod, who indicated that "in administrative law there is the all-powerful, primitive method of using fragmented legislation, covering rules of all sorts of different content", which is difficult to correlate, which in turn causes referential difficulties[61]. Another typical thing is the lack of a more general overview from the point of view of the assumed legal axiology, the integrity of a legal

---

55 The process of objectification has not covered all these clauses, cf. J. Czarzasty, *Przyczynek do problematyki klauzul generalnych,*"Państwo i Prawo" 1978, No. 5, pp. 83–92. Cf. also M. Śliwka, "Znaczenie zwrotów niedookreślonych na tle orzecznictwa polskiego Trybunału Konstytucyjnego", *Studia Iuridica Lubinensia* 2010, No. 13, p. 262, or A. Choduń, A. Gomułowicz, A. Skoczylas, *Klauzule generalne i zwroty niedookreślone w prawie podatkowym i administracyjnym. Wybrane zagadnienia teoretyczne i orzecznicze,* Warszawa 2013, pp. 29–31.

56 P. Borszowski, "Określenia nieostre i klauzule generalne jako wyraz elastyczności prawa podatkowego-zarys problematyki", *Acta Universitatis Wratislaviensis*, Vol. 3508, Prawo CCCXV/1, Wrocław 2013, p. 48.

57 M. Wyrzykowski, *Pojęcie interesu społecznego w prawie administracyjnym*, Warszawa 1986, passim.

58 M. Jaśkowska, *Pojęcie interesu publicznego i jego funkcje w prawie administracyjnym*, [in:] J. Niczyporuk (ed.), *Teoria instytucji prawa administracyjnego. Księga pamiątkowa Profesora Jerzego Stefana Langroda*, Paris 2011, pp. 287–300., A. Borkowski, *Interes publiczny jako determinant działań władzy publicznej i klauzula generalna w publicznym prawie gospodarczym*, [in:] L. Kieres (ed.), *Nowe problemy badawcze w teorii publicznego prawa gospodarczego (z uwzględnieniem samorządu terytorialnego),* Wrocław 2010, p. 14.

59 M. Stahl, *Dobro wspólne w prawie administracyjnym* [in:] J. Boć, A. Chajbowicz (eds.), *Nowe problemy badawcze w teorii prawa administracyjnego*, Wrocław 2009, p. 47 et seq.

60 Ł. Kamiński, *Pojęcie bezpieczeństwa w prawie administracyjnym,* "Państwo i Prawo" 2013, Vol. 10, pp. 49–61.

61 J. S. Langrod, op. cit., pp. 375–376.

norm, the type of norms used in the shape of rules and regulations, etc. Additional problems are linked to the multicentricity of the legal system[62]. The norms of national law do not function in a legal vacuum, but against the backdrop of EU and international law, which also assume a high degree of discretionality. Moreover, EU law enjoys autonomy in the conceptual area[63]. This causes the need to include additional mechanisms that influence the degree of discretion of public administration, such as, for example, the imposition to apply a pro-EU interpretation. At the same time, the differences in the paradigm of legal interpretation between the national and Community legal order should be highlighted. By default, sequential system is binding in the national order, whereas in the Community order the binding system is connectionist, i.e. allowing the use of all interpretation tools equally[64]. Therefore, the multi-centric entanglement of the processes of using national law influences the way interpretations are made by administrative authorities, which should move away from the domination of linguistic interpretation in the direction of a wider use of both non-systemic axiology and the argumentative model, which includes, in the process of social communication, the protection and harmonisation of basic values[65].

4. The notion and scope of the administrative discretionary authority

One type of margin of decision is the administrative discretionary authority, which is available to an authority on the fourth level of applying law. It is, at the same time, some form of discretionary authority. This term, however, has been given a specific, narrow meaning. Not every manifestation of this authority, and not every margin of decision is therefore the same as discretionary authority.

---

62 Cf. E. Łętowska, *Multicentryczność współczesnego systemu prawa i jej konsekwencje*, "Państwo i Prawo", 2005, book 4, pp. 3–10.

63 M. Masternak-Kubiak, *Zasada autonomii prawa wspólnotowego i praktyka jej stosowania w Polsce,* [in:] M. Granat (ed.), *Stosowanie prawa międzynarodowego i wspólnotowego w wewnętrznym porządku prawnym Francji i Polski*, Warszawa 2007, p. 787 et seq.

64 This is also stressed by M. Romanowicz, *Dyskrecjonalność interpretacyjna i sędziego w czasach multicentryzmu,* [in:] *Dyskrecjonalność w prawie. Materiały*, op. cit., pp. 426–427 and 429.

65 Both L. Leszczyński and M. Zirk-Sadowski point to this; see L. Leszczyński, *Interpretacyjna rola kryteriów otwartych i innych decyzji stosowania prawa, rozdział VII* [in:] *System*, op. cit., vol.4, p. 323 and M. Zirk-Sadowski, *Pojęcie, koncepcje i przebieg wykładni prawa, rozdział III* [in:] *System*, op. cit., vol.4, pp. 174–175.

Discretionary authority is a conscious construct through which a legislator grants the discretion to select a legal consequence to a public administration body, which applies law externally, i.e. to organisationally non-subordinated entities[66].

I discuss the second element of the legal norm in the situation of formulating the legal consequence in the form of an alternative. I do not link to the norm's hypothesis. This is because a hypothesis refers to determining the actual situation, in relation to which a discretionary assessment of evidence can happen, which is, therefore, a different type of margin of decision[67]. At the same time, in order to allow for a more precise differentiation, the position of discretionary authority in the process of applying law is pointed to. Consequently, I bring the notion of discretionary authority to the final stage of applying law, namely determining legal consequences. This happens when the norm does not clearly determine these consequences, but explicitly leaves the choice to be made by an administrative authority[68]. Therefore, even if the interpretation of notions used can also refer to determining legal consequences, I do differentiate the hypothesis interpretation from discretionary authority, which provides for the choice of a resolution.

Discretionary authority is a construct assuming the broadest possible capability of discretionary power and the margin of decision. The authority, which has already made a validation and interpretation choice, had discretion in terms of subsuming a particular factual state to a specific legal provision, is additionally granted permission to choose a resolution. As Leszczyński rightly stresses, determining consequences can essentially encompass two types of activities: the choice of the type of consequence and its scale[69]. We are dealing with administrative discretionary authority in the first instance, when the choice of the consequence is clearly left to an administrative organ. The dimension of a consequence occurs in a situation in which consequences can be graded. The dimension can expand discretionary authority not only when an authority has the right to use a particular sanction, or not, but when it has the right to use it in a particular scale. There can also be a situation where the legislator does not give an authority any choice of the consequence, but instead enables an authority to grade it, which is indeed present in the case of disciplinary responsibility, or administrative sanctions, which is a special type of criminal-law sanction. By only highlighting this issue, I would like

66 I already have presented this notion of discretionary authority in the following paper: M. Mincer, *Uznanie administracyjne*, Toruń, 1983, p. 41 et seq.

67 M. Jaśkowska, [in:] *System*, op. cit., vol. 1., 2nd Ed., p. 263.

68 Ibidem, p. 271.

69 L. Leszczyński, *Podstawa decyzji stosowania prawa administracyjnego*, rozdział II, [in:] *System*, op. cit. vol. 4, p. 47.

to stress that I do not consider this kind of choice equivalent to administrative discretionary authority for various reasons (e.g. the issue of guilt and its degree), even though the discretionality we are dealing with here can influence the scope of discretionary authority, or be an open criterion in the case of a constrained decision.

Administrative discretionary authority is based on statutory empowerment. Legal provisions formulate appropriate authorisations. The phrase most frequently used here is "may" (e.g. Article 98 (1) of the Code of Administrative Procedure). The legislator may also formulate such authorisation through indicating the duty to use one of two equivalent solutions, which are also of equal legal weight (e.g. Article 9 (2) of Building Law Act)[70]. In this way, one assumes the use of open criteria, clearly leaving the law-applying entity with the choice, which is perfectly deliberate and takes into account the circumstances of an individual case. This individualisation can be reliant upon a number of different factors, which the legislator has clearly determined, be it by pointing to the aims of legal regulations in the introduction to a legal act, or by determining the consequence selection directives within the legal norm. As stressed by Leszczyński, when determining the consequences, an authority cannot stray from the criteria indicated in the legal provisions. There is therefore no possibility to base these consequences and their scope only on non-legal criteria[71].

Such a notion of discretionary authority is currently endorsed in the case law of Polish administrative courts. Therefore, special attention should be given to the fact that administrative discretionary authority signifies giving permission to a law-applying authority to choose a resolution[72]. It is treated as a possibility to choose legal consequences in the last phase of applying law[73]. As the Supreme Administrative Court highlighted in its judgement of 3 September 2010, "Making a resolution based on administrative discretionary authority is using the authority's permission to shape, in a particular case and in a particular factual state, legal

70 Building Law Act of 7 July 1994, consolidated text in the Journal of Laws of 2013, item 1409, as amended.

71 L. Leszczyński, *Interpretacyjna rola kryteriów otwartych i innych decyzji stosowania prawa*, [in:] *System*, op. cit., vol. 4, p. 337.

72 Supreme Administrative Court Judgement of 30 June 1987, IV SA 129/87, ONSA 1987, No. 1, item 43.

73 Cf. Supreme Administrative Court Judgement of 27 February 2007, case no. I OSK 579/06, LEX no. 341251, and Supreme Administrative Court Judgement of 14 February 2013, I OSK 2613/12, LEX, no. 1317987.

consequences within a degree of discretion set out by a provision of substantive law, or within binding procedural rules"[74].

Discretionary authority is therefore a conscious legal construct used by the legislator in order to leave the choice of a resolution to administrative bodies. This option must be included when reviewing decisions made by administrative bodies within such discretion. On the one hand, the legislators' choice should be respected, and in the case of judicial reviews, the principle of division of powers should also be taken into account. This issue is therefore connected with limiting judicial review to the question of the legality of an act, without any interference with the sphere of purposefulness[75]. On the other hand, in a rule of law there is no unlimited discretionary authority, which is excluded from both internal review and a review before an independent external authority. Including these reasons causes the striving to refine the notion of discretionary authority, and to clearly set the scope of its review. This is achieved by means of legislation, either through referring to the criterion of legality, as in Polish law[76], or in Austrian law[77], or through introducing the notion of discretionary authority mistakes into the provisions, in the form of exceeding or misusing discretionary authority (when the purpose of the authorisation did not match the purpose to which it was actually used)[78]. Against this backdrop we see the scholarly arguments around the notion of discretionary authority, and mistakes and limits of discretion[79].

The issue of limiting the review of discretionary authority is also emphasized in the Polish legal scholarship and case law. It is indicated that using this construct does not release an administrative court from investigating factual and legal circumstances of a case. This review is made possible thanks to a properly drawn up justification, among other things. Consequently, if discretionary authority is

74 Supreme Administrative Court Judgement of 3 September 2010, II GSK 745/09, LEX, no. 746123.

75 B. Wojciechowski, *Model zakresu swobody interpretacyjnej prawa administracyjnego, rozdział X* [in:] *System*, op. cit., vol. 4, p. 474.

76 Art. 1(2) of Act on the Organisation of Administrative Courts of 25 July 2002, consolidated text in the Journal of Laws of 2014, item 1647, as amended.

77 Art. 130 of the Austrian Constitution, Bundes-Verfassungsgesetz, BGBL 1930 No. 1, as amended.

78 § 114 Verwaltungsgerichtsordnung of 21 January 1960, BGBL I S. 17, consolidated text of 19 March 1991, BGBL I S. 686.

79 Such an argument is presented by M. Jaśkowska, *Uznanie administracyjne a inne formy władzy dyskrecjonalnej administracji publicznej, rozdział IV* [in:] *System*, op. cit. vol.1, p. 287 et seq.

used, the reasons for using it by an authority must be pointed to especially[80]. At the same time, the reviewing entity, despite a broad review of the legality of resolution, including the existence and accuracy of an act's legal basis, competence of an authority and accuracy of the procedure used, and obeying choice directives included in legal provisions, cannot refer to non-legal criteria of purposefulness[81]. An administrative court may not disregard the legislator's will and whom the legislator has authorised to make a choice.

5. Closing remarks

Differentiating between the notions of discretionality, the margin of decision and administrative discretionary authority, as I have indicated above, I believe to be useful for both reasons of doctrine and for practical reasons. They cover the various kinds of discretionality of public authorities, which, despite their similarities, have different scopes. Such an approach indicates, on the one hand, open criteria in terms of introducing, applying or exercising law by public authorities, and, on the other, issues that have so far escaped theoretical analysis. Such terminological differentiation enables us to simultaneously indicate common traits of the various forms of discretionality of public authorities, without blurring the differences between them. It can therefore serve as a bridge between the achievements of legal theory and philosophy, and the science of administrative law. At the same time, this differentiation talks about the origins of these notions, including both the broadly understood discretionality in European law, and a narrow perspective on discretionary authority in the continental legal system.

On the other hand, such an approach enables us to differentiate between authorisation granted clearly to administrative bodies from other forms of discretion these bodies have at their disposal. This can be significant for the assessment of activities undertaken by these bodies. For this reason, I declare the notion of the margin of decision to be useful. It accentuates the variety of public administration's activities in the course of applying law, and consequently in the sphere

80 Cf. Supreme Administrative Court Judgement of 23 September 1987, II SA 468/87, OSP 1988, no. 11–12, item 258, including W. Chróścielewski's commentary, Supreme Administrative Court Judgement of 19 January 2010, II GSK 1254/08, LEX, no. 595724. Supreme Administrative Court Judgement of 10 May 2012, II GSK 369/12, LEX, no. 1264785.

81 Cf. Supreme Administrative Court Judgement of 18 April 2007, II FSK 1708/06 LEX nr 341335, and Supreme Administrative Court Judgement of 26 July 2011, II FSK 426/10, LEX nr 1083134.

relating directly to the recipients of governing activities. Administrative bodies generally strive for the identification of the various forms of discretion granted to them. This is when the boundaries blur between the subject the choice applies to, and the directives according to which it should be made. The possibilities of choice, related to a particular subjectivity, accompany administration in its various activities and forms. By formulating legal provisions in many different ways, the legislator expects from an authority activities based on various criteria and values. Understanding their essence, subject and criteria is therefore significant for the correct performance of public duties.

This differentiation acquires an additional meaning in the science of administrative law, especially in relation to the duty to justify administrative decisions, and their review. The principle of binding public authorities by law, the principle of the division of power, and the principle of respecting competences should all influence the scope and boundaries of a review, which should be made possible by the appropriate motivation behind activities undertaken.

Mateusz Stępień
(*Associate Professor, Jagiellonian University, Poland*)

Administrative Discretion in the Light of Theory of Representative Bureaucracy

Abstract: The aim of the paper is to reconstruct and identify the role of administrative discretion in the theory of representative bureaucracy – to analyze administrative discretion considering its broader context.

Keywords: administrative discretion, representative bureaucracy, passive representation, active representation

1. Introduction

Discretion is one of the fundamental concepts in studies exploring decision-making processes and in general discussion on law, including especially the judicial application of law. However, it occupies a special place within studies of Public Administration. In the words of R. Cox, "seemingly no aspect of Public Administration engenders more discussion and controversy than the idea of discretion"[1]. Hence it is not surprising how much attention is paid to that issue – an understanding of the problem as well as range of methods involved in implementation and control of administrative discretion (further also referred to as AD) have, after all, colossal significance for civil rights. It strongly affects not only the status and functioning of public administration (further also as PA), but also the shape of the democratic order. Although the idea of administrative discretion has received a lot of attention, it has not yet been exhaustively developed. A fundamental weakness of existing approaches is that they examine AD without considering a broader context, which would include a comprehensive vision of PA.

This paper aims to reconstruct and identify the role of AD in the theory of representative bureaucracy (further also as RB). The theory of RB is one of the most important, dynamic and fastest growing thread in contemporary studies of PA. The term "thread" highlights a great diversity of research subjects within the theory of RB, which are based on similar principles and terminology and thereby enable to verify various claims regarding PA. In this sense, RB is, in general, a theoretical approach, which, among other things, provides a wider perspective on

1 R. Cox, *Creating a Decision Architecture*, "Global Virtue Ethics Review" 2000, 2(1), p. 20.

AD. In fact, the ideas developed within the theory of RB allow the introduction of normative guidance and enable implementation of reforms within PA, including AD. In that case, we can speak about prescriptive dimension of RB. Furthermore, RB is also a kind of ideology (or philosophy) of PA, which expresses a preference for certain values (eg. material equality) and occupies a particular place in political and ideological disputes. Thus, three levels of RB can be distinguished: descriptive-explanatory, prescriptive and ideological. This paper is by no means intended to reconstruct in details individual concepts developed within the theory of RB. It rather aims to develop a synthetic approach which would enable a comprehensive look at AD from the perspective of the assumptions underlying this theory[2].

2. Main Features of Representative Bureaucracy

To reconstruct the place and role of AD in the theory of RB a short description of the theory is required. We will focus on the most important features of the theory of RB that affect the understanding of AD, leaving aside its origins and development stages.

1. Recent studies of RB have focused on the idea of applying the category of "representation" also to PA. The crucial point here is that the concept of "representativeness" should not be limited only to the choice of representatives and their political activities on behalf of those they represent. According to the classical view it is the political sphere that relies on representation, while in the administrative sphere law should be instantiated by administrators who are neutral. In traditional approach PA is democratic, but only indirectly, because it is a part of the democratic system[3]. But at the root of the theory of RB lies the idea that it can be directly democratic (and to some extent, in some cases, it already is) through direct "representation" of citizens. In that sense, RB "concerns the ability of the

---

2 Within the theory of RB theoretical and empirical research directly concerning AD were conducted. See: K. J. Meier, J. Bohte, *Structure and Discretion: The Missing Links in Representative Bureaucracy*, "Journal of Public Administration Research and Theory" 2001, 11(4), pp. 455 470; J. E. Sowa, C. S. Selden, *Administrative Discretion and Active Representation: An Expansion of the Theory of Representative Bureaucracy*, "Public Administration Review" 2003, 63(3), pp. 700–710; J. D. Marvel, W. G. Resh, *Client Demographics, Bureaucratic Discretion, and Representative Bureaucracy*, "American Review of Public Administration" 2015, 45(3), pp. 281–310.

3 Already in the 1950s Norton Long, one of the first authors developing the theory of RB has noticed that "bureaucracy may be both more representative of the country and more democratic in composition than the Congress" (*Bureaucracy and Constitutionalism*, "American Political Science Review" 1952, 46(3), p. 812).

bureaucracy to represent the general public"[4]. At this point, it is important to emphasize that modern classical representation through political institutions is neither complete nor effective, which in turn creates space for innovations that are offered within RB. As a result, the public interest is protected in different ways and under conditions other than those assumed in a classical model of PA.

2. The theory of RB recognizes the necessity to reject the concept of narrowly understood individual rationality as the foundation of analysis of PA[5]. It draws particular attention to the social dimension of PA, which includes predominantly treating administrators as actors with specific beliefs, attitudes and values, often associated with belonging to various identity-based communities. In that sense, it takes the assertion that the administrators have strong and inalienable community identity that affects their (own) activity which is reflected in their actions, but also – not directly and in a symbolic way – affects the community they serve (eg. the client).

3. Against this background, it is necessary to distinguish so-called passive representation (in other approaches called formal, further also as PR) and active (real) representation (further as AR). The first one is that the employees of public organizations mirror in some aspects (such as "race", nationality, ethnicity, religion, sex, residence, class) the community they represent. But the very question of which properties are to be taken into consideration is widely discussed and differs in various approaches developed within the theory of RB. Nevertheless, regardless of characteristics involved, the problem of what kind of influence does PR have on implementing public tasks and on the overall quality of service, is central to this study. In turn, the AR occurs when the activity of "representatives" leads to real and expected consequences for society they represent. Thus, according to one of the hypothesis, appropriately selected staff of administrative organizations could have more efficacy if it reflects demographic background of the public it serves. Most authors agree that it serves to achieve more equitable outcomes for minorities and those who have been underrepresented[6]. Some consider consequences of

---

4 K. J. Meier, J. Copeus, *Representative Bureaucracy: Four Question*, [in:] *The SAGE Handbook of Public Administration*, eds. B. G. Peters, J. Pierre, London 2012.

5 Similarly: B. G. *Peters*, P. *Maravić, E.* Schröter, *Representative Bureaucracy: Concept, Driving Forces, Strategies*, [in:] *Representative Bureaucracy in Action*, eds. B. G. Peters, P. Maravić, E. Schröter, London 2013.

6 For instance, some authors suggest the following results of AR: "reflecting the interests and desires of these people"; "advancing the interests of groups with whom they share demographic origin" (S. C. Selden, *The Promise of Representative Bureaucracy: Diversity and Responsiveness in a Government Agency*, Armonk 1997, p. 5, 43); "to foster

"representativeness" more broadly, as an improvement in performing public tasks[7], a better representation of the "general public"[8], or simply as balancing administrative accountability and responsiveness[9].

4. It is acknowledged that the benefits of "representativeness" of public organizations result from the fact that the "representatives" more effectively recognize the preferences of those they represent – they are more focused on their needs and have better communication skills. On the other hand, the internal diversity of organization makes decision-making process more flexible and prone to different kinds of views and opinions. Moreover, also "those who are represented" better understand the limitations and dilemmas existing within public organizations, because it is easier for them to identify with "representatives"; frequently they are also more active. All these benefits should lead to the fact that public organizations will improve a decision making process and, ultimately, make it more efficient for the minority groups and the public.

5. A simple scheme organizing the study, which was described above, allows asking interesting questions, as well as to formulate and verify certain claims about RB. More specifically, a number of questions are raised to examine whether PR appears in particular conditions and what are its possible consequences (especially those symbolic ones); whether, how and under what conditions PR is transformed

improved equity for those who have been underrepresented in the implementation of public programs" (J. E. Sowa, C. S. Selden, *Administrative Discretion and Active Representation*, op. cit., p. 701); "decision making behavior on the part of a specific group of civil servants which tends to affect systematically the resource allocation of a specific group of citizens" (J. J. Hindera, *Representative Bureaucracy: Further Evidence of Active Representation in the EEOC District Offices*, "Journal of Public Administration Research and Theory" 1993, 3(4), p. 419).

7 For instance. J. K. Kenneth, R. D. Wrinkle, J. L. Polinard summing up their studies observed that: "far from finding that representative bureaucracy produces minority gains at the expense of nonminorities, this study finds both minority and nonminority students perform better in the presence of a representative bureaucracy. This finding suggests an alternative hypothesis to guide research, that representative bureaucracies are more effective than their nonrepresentative counterparts"; *Representative Bureaucracy and Distributional Equity: Addressing the Hard Question*, "The Journal of Politics" 1999, 61(4), p. 1035.

8 K. J. Meier, J. Copeus, op. cit., p. 420.

9 J. M. Gibran, *Exploring the Links Between Passive and Active Representation in Tennessee State Agencies*, "Public Administration Quarterly" 2013, 37(1), p. 37; see W. F. West, *Structuring Administrative Discretion: The Pursuit of Rationality and Responsiveness*, "American Journal of Political Science" 1984, 28(2), pp. 340–360.

into AR; namely, whether, how and under what conditions a public workforce that is demographically representative of the individuals it serves will have a positive impact on performing public tasks for clients with the similar background? Also, the question is raised, if, and to what extent public organizations maintain their own unique culture or ethos, which could possibly minimize the scale of transformation from passive into active representation? More broadly, what interferes with the process of transformation from PR into AR?

3. The Place of Administrative Discretion in Theory of RB

1. A distinctive feature of the theory of RB is that reflection on AD developed within it focuses mainly on what role does PA play in the political system. It should be emphasized that PA is of increasing importance to the system of liberal democracy. This is due to the fact that its relevance, the tasks associated with it and its actual impact on the formation of public policies are constantly increasing. Consequently, PA has a significant scope of discretion[10]. For advocates of RB, the presence of considerable AD, regardless of its numerous sources and varieties, is a matter of fact. As pointed out by J. E. Sowa and C. S. Selden, "the investment of discretionary power in administrative agencies is a fact of lfe"[11].

2. Despite the different approaches to RB, an increasing number of scholars agree that AD is, in general, a positive phenomenon[12]. Without considerable AD, the transition from PR to AR would not be possible. Obviously, although

10 B. G. Peters, P. Maravić, E. Schröter, *Representative Bureaucracy: Concept, Driving Forces, Strategies...*, op.cit., p. 6.

11 J. E. Sowa, C. S. Selden, op. cit., p. 700. As in his classic study D. Galligan put it: "[administrative] discretion must come to be accepted as the core of bureaucratic authority rather than the murky periphery" (*Discretionary Powers: A Legal Study of Official Discretion*, Oxford 1986, p. 1). M. Lipsky expressed a similar opinion on AD: "policy makers and economists might wish it were otherwise, but it seems clear that in the implementation of social welfare programs there remains an irreducible extent to which worker discretion cannot be eradicated"; "although hence characterized as a <relative concept>, discretion is <difficult, if not impossible> to reduce" (*Street-level Bureaucracy. Dilemmas of the Individual in Public Services,* New York 1980, p. 28, 15).

12 It does not mean that the negative aspects and dangers associated with AD are not taken into account. The authors are aware that the unelected administrators have real political power, which, in certain circumstances, may become a threat to democracy. As S. Kristov observed: "the greater the degree of discretion imputed on bureaucracy, the more vigorous its function, the stronger need for the accountability" *(Representative Bureaucracy*, New Yersey 1973, p. 21).

administrative discretion is a necessary condition for the existence of AR, the way it is exercised is far more important. With the appropriate demographically representative public workforce, AD will create space for "representativeness" of PA. Studies in the representative bureaucracy suggest that the link between passive and active representation becomes stronger as discretion increases[13]. It is commonly accepted that AD has great potential[14].

3. Such an approach does not mean that AD have to be considered as given, predetermined, stable or homogeneous. On the contrary, in the theory of RB it is investigated to what extent AD can be negotiable or "manipulable"[15]. Generally speaking, within this theory multidimensional determinants of the real scope of AD are being studied[16]. Thus, the real scale of AD is the result of the interactions between a number of factors (for instance, processes within the organization, personality traits of administrators, activities of "clients" of PA[17]). At this point, it is important to discuss the results of two recent studies on AD that appear to be crucial.

In the first study (conducted at The Farmers Home Administration implementing the project Rural Housing Loan Program) the empirical analysis was focused on the amount of AD administrators perceive themselves to have. AD was tested in two areas: (1) their relationships with clients and over outcomes, and (2) how does administrative organization work (agency operations)[18]. It has been proved empirically that the amount of AD administrators perceive themselves to have differs among individuals. Even administrators, who occupy the same position within public organization structure and are bound by the same regulations, perceive the

13 e.g.: K. J. Meier, J. Bohte, op. cit.; J. E. Sowa, C. S. Selden, op. cit.; Marvel, Resh op. cit.

14 K.C. Davis, referred to administrative discretion as "our principal source of creativeness in government and in law"; "discretion is a tool only when properly used: like an axe, it can be a weapon for mayhem or murder. In a government of men and of laws, the portion that is a government of men, like a malignant cancer, often tends to stifle the portion that is a government of laws. Perhaps nine-tenths of injustice in our legal system flows from discretion and perhaps only one-tenth from rules"; K. C. Davis, Discretionary *Justice*, Urbana 1971, p. 25.

15 J. D. Marvel, W. G. Resh, op. cit., p. 284.

16 Most authors are, in this respect, inspired by the work of P. G. Scott (*Assessing Determinants of Bureaucratic Discretion: An Experiment in Street-Level Decision Making*, "Journal of Public Administration Research & Theory" 1997, 7(1), pp. 1–22).

17 See G. S. Thielemann, J. Stewart, A Demand-Side *Perspective on the Importance of Representative Bureaucracy: AIDS, Ethnicity, Gender, and Sexual Orientation*, "Public Administration Review" 1996, 56(2), pp. 168–173.

18 J. E. Sowa, C. S. Selden, op. cit.

real discretion differently. Moreover, the more AD individual administrators perceive themselves to have, the more decisions are made that advance the interests of minorities. Consequently, the way administrators perceive themselves as having certain amount of AD, affects their activity and the scale of AR.

The second study (carried out on a group of public administrators randomly selected from nine Tennessee State Agencies) examined how organizational factors affect the amount of AD administrators perceive themselves to have[19]. Again, studies have shown that when the complexity of organization affects information flow, setting clear expectations by leaders about administrative responsiveness of their employees, has a clear impact on the amount of AD they perceive themselves to have. The study suggest that these factors are important for generating AR. This emphasizes the importance of "service oriented agency leadership, and clear role messages in setting a tone for organizational decision making and minimizing the potential for bureaucratic unresponsiveness which can be a consequence of organizational complexity". It is clearly stated how important it is for leaders to create and promote a culture oriented around "responsiveness to community needs, collaboration and mindfulness of the imperative to be accountable to their stakeholders", as it proved to support AD. Thus, clear and direct messages concerning mission, the objectives and the expectations set by leaders to promote activities that go beyond the narrow and mechanical norm implementation, are crucial for linking passive and active representation in complex program areas.

4. Most authors studying the ways in which AD is exercised agree that the vision of neutral, impersonally functioning PA is inadequate. As administrators have different personalities, identities and experiences/beliefs, they feel a connection with various "imagined communities". Their decisions are not neutral in the sense that they "mechanically" concretize law enacted by elected representatives. Their characteristics, which are not directly related to the positions they occupy as administrators, affect how law is applied in practice. Ultimately, the theory of RB tends to accept that although the administrators are not (or cannot be) neutral, at least in sense the dominant approach recognizes, such a state of affairs could be used to optimize the work of PA. Echoing American realists, such an approach could be called "realistic"[20]. That is, therefore, an empirical question and one which relates to how the administrators exercise AD? According to the theory of RB,

19 J. M. Gibran, op. cit.

20 See e.g.: J. Frank, *Are Judges Human?*, Parts I & II, "Univeristy of Pennsylvania Law Rewiev" 1931, 80(1)(2), pp. 17–53, 233–267.

introducing solutions "based" on such empirical knowledge can only be considered when that specific question has been answered.

5. What is commonly emphasized in such view is that values shared by the administrators are of fundamental importance for the exercise of AD. Also, it is at this stage of the process of applying law when axiological factors play the most significant role[21]. The administrators make decisions by using their freedom to operate in a manner "that reflects their own values"[22] and "attitudes"[23], and "seek to maximize the values that are silent to [them]"[24]. But what are the origins of those values? The authors founded their theory on a very simple sociological reasoning that both specific conditions and early socialization contribute to shaping a value system of administrators. Essentially, it is the demographic variables that set the boundaries of the socialization process. In consequence, through socialization processes individuals with the same sociodemographic background will share certain values. Thus, as a general rule, the discretion administrators have is exercised in accordance with their own axiological dispositions that are already developed as a result of socialization. Special attention is also paid to the factors disrupting the discretion of AD, namely those that impede the transition from PR to AR[25]. Placing values of the administrators at the core of their activities does not yet explain how they affect the exercise of AD. In this respect, two models are developed within RB.

6. In general, the first model ("responsiveness through similarity of values"), which is also the most prevalent in the theory of RB, maintains that values constantly, directly and automatically affect how AD is exercised (by administrators), thus leading to AR (PR → VALUES → AD → AR). Therefore, discretion is exercised based on individuals' axiological background, and it happens spontaneously.

---

21 H. Simon wrote about the role of "value premises" in the process of exercising AD (*Decision-Making and Administrative Organization*, "Public Administration Review" 1944, 4(1), p. 19).

22 K. J. Meier, J. Bohte, op. cit., p. 456. Similarly: J. L. Brudney F. T. Hebert, D. S. Wright, *From Organizational Values to Organizational Roles: Examining Representative Bureaucracy in State Administration*, "Journal of Public Administration Research and Theory" 2000, 10(3), p. 492.

23 J. E. Sowa, C. S. Selden, op. cit., p. *701;* J. D. Marvel, W. G. Resh, op. cit., p. 282.

24 K. J. Meier, T. S. M. Morton, *Representative Bureaucracy in the Cross-national Context: Politics, Identity, Structure and Discretion*, [in:] *The Politics of Representative Bureacracy*, op. cit., p. 99.

25 In this context red tape, organizational culture, strong organizational structure, organizational socialization, hierarchical character of PA, the scope of control, professionalization, routinization and formalization scale were analyzed.

Raised in different environments employees of public organizations, within the limits of their respective competences, use discretion "naturally" in accordance with their axiological preferences. A pluralistic workforce of a specific organization, in response to a variety of values, opinions and interests, somewhat automatically leads to appropriate (that is reflecting social values) decisions. This mechanism guarantees that outcomes expected from PA are achieved "naturally". In this case, AD is exercised in accordance with internal, but socially shaped personality traits of administrators. More importantly, exercising discretion requires adequate processes to occur within the organization, that would guarantee harmonizing the axiological preferences of administrators. In addition, if a bureaucracy is representative of the public it serves, the logic continues, then its decisions will more strongly reflect the values of that public.

7. The second approach ("active, deliberate advocacy"), which is by far significantly less popular, is based on the assumption that values shared by the administrators affect exercising AD in a more mediated, conscious, organized and planned (not ad hoc) manner. This comes about through developing specific organizational roles among administrators (PR → VALUES → AD → ROLES → AD → AR). Thus, axiological preferences of administrators should be developed into a mature organizational roles (described as e.g. "minority representative role"[26]) in order to generate AR. The process of developing such a role is both complex and multidimensional (and depends on the administrators' demographic backgrounds, organizational socialization, leadership, demand of minority groups[27]). Introducing the concept of organizational role to the theory of RB allows to question the adequacy of "demographic determinism" – with this approach an administrator who is not the part of a particular minority can adopt the role of its "representative". It should be emphasized that AD is essential for generating specific organizational roles and, subsequently, to make decisions based on them. However, recent studies on RB have shown that the process of creating new roles and the way they are performed by administrators influence AD, usually by increasing the amount

26 S. C. Selden, The Promise of Representative Bureaucracy, op. cit., s. 6; J. L. Brudney F. T. Hebert, D. S. Wright, *From Organizational Values to Organizational Roles*, op. cit.; S. C. Selden, J. L. Brudney, J. E. Kellough, *Bureaucracy as a Representative Institution: Toward a Reconciliation of Bureaucratic Government and Democratic Theory*, "American Journal of Political Science" 1998, 42(3), pp. 717–744.

27 See C. S. Rosenthal, L. C. Bell, *From Passive to Active Representation: The Case of Women Congressional Staff*, "Journal of Public Administration Research and Theory" 2003, 13(1), pp. 65–82.

of discretion administrators perceive themselves to have. We are therefore dealing with processes that are mutually dependent.

4. Some Polemic Thoughts on AD

In studying the theory of RB, a consistent (though incomplete) image of AD has emerged. However, even a preliminary evaluation of this approach requires some critical arguments to be considered[28]. Before we move forward, threads that seem interesting and worth consideration will be discussed.

1. The distinctive feature of the theory of RB is its "realistic" and heavily sociological way of looking at AD and decision-making processes within PA, which clearly differs from the approaches that are limited only to an analysis of case law on the control of AD or theoretical reflections (definitions, typologies) on this subject. Against this background, empirical studies examining how the real AD is created and exercised act as a breath of fresh air. At this point, it is important to emphasize the central role axiology of administrators plays when exercising AD (as a factor that directly or indirectly affect their decisions). Perhaps the most important benefit associated with the theory of RB comes from looking at AD from different perspective (of specific assumptions), which allows to consider more broadly the question of its admissibility, control tools, and its place in a broader political vision. Seen in such a context, AD appears to be a multidimensional phenomenon, and its functionality or non-functionality is dependent on many factors.

2. There is an innovative general approach concerning the control of AD developed within the theory of RB. In their classic study, H. K. Hibbeln and D. H. Shumavon proposed the typologies of control methods of AD that distinguish external, internal, formal and informal types[29]. The dominant approach within the theory of RB questioned the effectiveness of traditional tools, ie. the external and formalized (legal and political). Following the views expressed within RB, some new methods can be distinguished: the "constructivist" method, related to overcoming how administrators make decisions spontaneously, and "spontaneity-systemic" method, which rely on how, in fact, does the decision-making process work, in order to reach the goals of PA. RB follows the latter way, developing "soft" methods of how AD is exercised through appropriate structural changes (first, achieving PR, and then introducing conditions enabling the transition from PR

28 See P. S. Kim, *A Theoretical Overview of Representative Bureaucracy: Synthesis*, "International Review of Administrative Science" 1994, 60(3), pp. 385–397.

29 H. K. Hibbeln i D. H. Shumavon, *Methods for Structuring Administrative Discretion*, "State & Local Government Review" 1983, 15(3), p. 127.

to AR). The idea is to make changes that would result in an almost "automatic" control of AD through structural determinants of how it should be exercised. In this way, the strategy is developed, which can be described as "indirect control of AD", as it is not used for direct control of AD, but to create the conditions in which it will be spontaneously controlled. In many ways suggested reforms and improvements are an attempt to resolve the "organizational" dilemma, which lies in the fact that AD is both necessary and problematic (even if only due to the risk of abuse of power)[30]. So the main problem lies in introducing changes that will make AD not only necessary, but also unproblematic and fruitful.

3. It is worth noting that the theory of RB and the vision of AD associated with it, are of considerable importance for creating solutions favoring politics of recognition[31]. Although the theory of RB was developed in multicultural countries, its implications are much greater. It offers solutions that can be interpreted as tools of dealing with (cultural) pluralism by managing workforce composition of the organization and changing how they work. Potential effects are to be achieved through small, gradual changes. The point is in particular to: (1) provide a balanced workforce composition in order to accomplish benefits associated with the "responsiveness through similarity of values", or (2) to develop cultural competences in administrators to promote their sensitivity and empathy, and to create more inclusive ethos and a new model of leadership in order to create "active, deliberate advocacy". In this respect, the increase in AD simultaneously with the introduction of other changes can be considered as way of pursuing a policy of recognition.

4. To present some significant polemical, and even critical remarks concerning AD, one should start by pointing out the lack of proper development of theoretical foundations of the problem. The way AD is understood within the theory RB is not even fully investigated. Recent studies aim to provide a certain intuitive understanding of AD, or merely make references to other works (where AD is not precisely defined)[32]. However, no typology of AD has been proposed yet. This is particularly important, because there are different models of AD that should be taken into account when studying the subject. Thus, discretion associated with

30 See W. F. West, *Structuring Administrative Discretion: The Pursuit of Rationality and Responsiveness*, "American Journal of Political Science" 1984, 28(2), pp. 340–360.

31 See e.g.: Ch. Taylor, *The Politics of Recognition*, [in:] Multiculturalism: A Critical Reader, eds. D.T. Goldberg, Oxford 1994.

32 See P. Scott, *Assessing Determinants* of *Bureaucratic Discretion*: An *Experiment* in *Street-Level Decision Making*, "Journal of Public Administration Research and Theory", 7(1), p. 37.

exercising broad statutory delegations and resulting from faulty, too broad interpretation of law by public administrators should be treated differently[33].

5. It has been argued that scheme organizing the study of PA, which determines the role of AD, can be questioned. For instance, it is commonly accepted that values shared by administrators (which this approach recognizes as crucial for the exercise of AD) are shaped in the early processes of socialization. However, the coexistence of multiple identities may potentially devalue that vision[34]. The complexity and multidimensional character of socialization processes ultimately result in the existence of multidimensional identities of citizens, which in turn causes that common values shared by both administrators ("representatives") and citizens they represent become difficult to achieve. So it seems reasonable to conclude that it challenges especially the model of "responsiveness through the similarity of values". One can easily question the simple scheme on which the theory of RB is based by showing faulty assumptions about the relationship between social roots and values shared by administrators. If we accept not only that socialization is not always (or almost never) derived from a single source, but also that similar origins do not necessarily lead to the same experience or similar values, a scheme on which the dominant approach in theory of RB is based on needs to be questioned.

6. It has long been noticed that problems may arise from synchronizing AR with traditional goals of PA, such as meritocracy, professionalism, neutrality[35]. Leaving aside the problem of whether it is possible to link equality and "technocratic" values associated with the theory of PA, it is questionable that exercising AD is essentially based on actualizing axiological preferences (what model of "responsiveness through the similarity of values" implies) and that this should be used to control AD and to achieve goals targeted within PA. So it seems reasonable to conclude that in studying the exercise of AD among administrators a strong descriptive axiological determinism has not been proven. It is therefore a very strong assumption, and even a kind of an axiom, which, if challenged, would undermine entire theoretical

33 For instance, Ch. Koch distinguishes five types of AD, which enables him to assess the relationship between AD and judicial control over administration in a more nuanced way *(Judicial Review of Administrative Discretion*, "The George Washington Law Review" 1986, 54(4), p. 372). Similarly: M. Shapiro, *Administrative Discretion: The Next Stage*, "Yale Law Review", 92, pp. 1500–1519.

34 Similarly, e.g.: P. S. Kim, *A Theoretical Overview of Representative Bureaucracy…*, op cit., p. 390.

35 See e.g. V. Subramanian, *Representative Bureaucracy: A Reassessment*, "American Political Science Review", 1967, 61(4), pp. 1010–1019; H. Kranz, *Are Merit and Equity Compatible?*, "Public Administration Review" 1974, 34(5), pp. 434–440.

structure of the theory of RB. It's worth noting that the proposed description of the way in which AD is exercised is too simplistic and not entirely adequate. It does not mean that an argument about the impact that values shared by administrators have on exercising AD is entirely wrong, but rather suggests that its actual role as one of the factors should be investigated. Also, it is difficult to accept that when exercising AD administrators are driven by its own axiology (which is also a source of prejudices and stereotypes) as a starting point for programming the work of PA. According to the assumptions on which the theory of RB is based (according to the model of "responsiveness through the similarity of values"), administrative organizations operate properly, if axiological dispositions (including prejudices and stereotypes) of administrators are actualized first, and only then are balanced for the sake of a representative composition of the organization. In other words, a question may be raised whether we agree on a certain amount of bias involved in decision-making process, which can be used to achieve the organizational purposes?[36] A negative answer to this question can be regarded as criticism of RB.

5. Summary

A number of critical arguments can be raised against the theory of RB. Discussions on AD are in many respects unsatisfactory (being incomplete, unsystematic, exploring only some possibilities and not others). However, one cannot say that all reflections within the theory of RB are irrelevant. On the contrary, concepts developed within RB are extremely stimulating. What is perhaps the most "refreshing" is that they encourage us to think differently about the PA, including particularly the role and place of AD. From here it is not that far to seek new solutions and explore new ways to reform the public sphere (democracy).

At each level of the theory of RB highlighted in the Introduction a specific approach to AD is proposed, which can be regarded as innovative. Thus, at the descriptive-explanatory level, RB suggests the need to conduct empirical research on the role that personality and organizational factors, as well as those associated with the environment of administrative organizations, play in exercising AD. Based on these findings, at prescriptive level RB opens up a large space for management of AD in accordance to "spontaneity-systemic" method. Finally, by referring to ideological level, RB indicates the importance that fundamental preferences concerning the shape of the political community have for building realistic vision of how AD should be exercised.

---

36 Similarly: Hong-Hai Lim, *Representative Bureaucracy: Rethinking Substantive Effects and Active Representation*, "Public Administration Review" 2006, 66(2), pp. 193–204.

Barbara Adamiak
(Professor, Wroclaw University, Poland; The Supreme Administrative Court of Poland Judge)

Procedural discretion in public administration

Abstract: The article describes the procedural aspects of discretionary powers of public administration in the process of issuing an individual legal decision. The basis for this research is the Polish legal order, in particular, the applicable procedural provisions and the practice of their application by the administrative courts.

Keywords: administrative procedure, procedural discretion, facts of the case, judicial review of public administration

1. The position of public administration's procedural discretion in the fulfilment of the constitutional principle of democratic rule of law

Fundamental values derived from the constitutional principle of democratic rule of law include the individual's right to legal process. The basis for this is found in how a state ruled by law (*Rechtstaat*) is a state that is based on a system of legal guarantees of the rights of an individual subject to public authority. This system of legal guarantees in the right to legal process relies on subjecting to the regulation of procedural laws the path of procedural activities of a public administrative authority intended to resolve a case with an administrative decision. The question arises whether in a state ruled by law and founded upon subjection of the path of procedural activities to regulation by law there is any room for procedural discretion in public administration? This question is connected with examining whether discretion in public administration is to be associated exclusively with the norms of substantive law[1]. M. Jaśkowska stresses that:

> The specificity of application of administrative law applies also to the procedural norm of that branch of the law. [...]. In the application of that law there is therefore oftentimes

1 M. Jaśkowska, *Uznanie administracyjne a inne formy władzy dyskrecjonalnej administracji publicznej [Administrative discretion versus other forms of discretional power in public administration]* in: *System prawa administracyjnego, Instytucje prawa administracyjnego. [Administrative law: the system. Institutions of administrative law]*, Vol. 1, Warsaw: 2010, p. 249.

> a need to rely on analogy. The extent of permissible leeway is also significantly affected by the procedural model of inquiry adopted in the Code of Administrative Procedure. The latter is the product of the role of administrative law in protecting the public interest and the subservience of procedural law to substantive law. It is also for this reason that the authorities applying the law are allowed a large dose of freedom in that regard, for example with regard to their evaluation of the facts of the case. This relates to the broad scope of probative matter in such proceedings, very few restrictions on evidence, and the role of the authority as the host of the process.[2]

Procedural discretion of a public administrative authority may be examined in different scopes of regulation by administrative procedural law. The regulation of administrative procedural law leaves public administrative authorities with a wide sphere of freedom in undertaking procedural activities[3]. Such a margin of discretion is adopted by the regulation already with regard to the general principles and subsequently in the application of procedural institutions in the course of the proceedings. Therefore, provisions of procedural law leave public administrative authorities with freedom in giving legal shape to the course of administrative proceedings in a case. An example of procedural regulation that is up to the public administrative authority to fill with active content is Article 8 of the Code of Administrative Procedure, establishing the general principle of promoting confidence in the bodies of the state. According to Article 8: 'Public administrative authorities conduct the proceedings in a manner promoting the participants' confidence in public authority.' This solution is also found in Article 121.1 of the Tax Code: 'Tax proceedings should be conducted in a manner promoting confidence in tax authorities.' On the other hand, giving content to action consistent with conducting the proceedings in a manner promoting confidence in administrative authorities belongs to the relevant authority, and whether it corresponds with the standards that follow from the principle is up to the administrative court to judge. There is no doubt with regard to what the juridical nature of Article 8 CAP and Article 121.1 TC is. Article 8 CAP and Article 121.1 TC contain a legal norm binding public administrative authorities in their taking up of procedural actions. On the other hand, giving it specific content is left up to the public administrative authority. The scope of the content which it is given varies in jurisprudence. One example is the adoption of a wide concept of it that is not restricted to just the

2 *Ibidem*, p. 228.

3 B. Wojciechowski, *Model zakresu swobody interpretacyjnej prawa administracyjnego [Model of the scope of interpretive freedom in administrative law]* [in:] *System prawa administracyjnego, Wykładnia w prawie administracyjnym. [Administrative law: the system. Interpretation in administrative law]*, Vol. 4, Warsaw: 2012, p. 462.

one proceedings at hand. In its judgment of 25 June 2014 II FSK 2611/12 (LEX no. 1519010) the Supreme Administrative Court held:

> First of all, one must call attention to the necessity for the tax authority (as creditor) to respect the general rules of tax proceedings. In line with the one expressed in Article 121.1 TC, tax proceedings ought to be conducted in a manner promoting confidence in tax authorities. Violative of this principle must be found the conduct of a tax authority that initiates upon a party's application proceedings with regard to granting relief in the payment of tax arrears (Article 67a.1.2 TC) and prior to deciding the case also causes enforcement proceedings to be initiated (Articles 26.1 and 26.5.1 of the Act on Enforcement Proceedings in Administration).

In the judgment of 22 July 2015 II FSK 1572/13 (LEX no. 1783589) the SAC noted the substantive and the procedural aspect of the confidence principle by holding that:

> (...), truly from the point of view of giving effect to the principle of conducting proceedings in a manner promoting trust in tax authorities it is desirable that the authorities should decide similar cases uniformly; on the other hand, having made a specific decision in one case does not cause the tax authority to have an obligation to replicate such a decision in other proceedings, especially should it occur that the decision was fraught with defects. The core criterion in the evaluation of a decision is its legality and therefore consistency with the law, and in this context the principle of conducting the proceedings in a manner promoting confidence in tax authorities must in each specific case be perceived and evaluated also through the prism of other general principles of procedure, including especially the principle of lawfulness, viz. tax authorities operating on the basis of the provisions of the law.

A different aspect of compliance with this principle was noted by the SAC in its judgment of 29 January 2015 II GSK 2204/13 (LEX no. 1769747):

> (...) from the point of view of the time limit, not disputed in the case at bar, referred to in Article 2.22 of the Act on Payments in the Framework of Direct Support System, one must call in doubt the merits of the guidance given to the complaining party and demand for a motion to reinstate that time limit. This is because the motion was doomed to failure from the beginning. Hence, beguiling the complaining party with the possibility of reinstatement, when it was obvious that no such reinstatement was possible or permissible, must beyond all doubt me viewed as conduct violative of the standard the public administrative authority was obliged to upheld, which arises from Article 8 CAP in relation to Article 3.2.1 of the Act on Payments in the Framework of Direct Support System.

Especial significance must be attached to procedural discretion with regard to determining the facts of the case.

2. Procedural discretion in determining the facts of the case

The basic stage of application of the law includes determination of the facts. As part of the second stage J. Wróblewski classifies: 'the finding of a fact as proved on the basis of specific material and on the basis of the adopted theory of evidence and expression of such a fact in the language of the norm applied.'[4]

This is also the position held by L. Leszczyński[5], who distinguishes the determination of the facts within the decision-making process. Both in theory of the law and in the doctrine of administrative law a certain scope of discretionary power[6].

Distinguishing procedural discretion next to substantive discretion makes it possible to represent the entire sphere of discretionary power of public administrative authorities in issuing an administrative decision. One may risk the assertion that procedural discretion has a wider scope than substantive discretion. The scope of procedural discretion includes not only substantive discretion[7]. It cannot be limited solely to substantive discretion, but solutions adopted within procedural law give basis to distinguish it also within the area of those norms of substantive administrative law that — due to both the structure of the hypothesis and the legal consequence — exclude discretion in the public administrative authority. This is because the implementation of the legal consequence always remains in connection with the determination of the facts of the case. With regard to the application of substantive administrative law, the stage distinguished by J. Wróblewski — 'finding of a fact as proved on the basis of specific material and on the basis of the adopted theory of evidence and expression of such a fact in the language of the norm applied' — forces the subsumption of the fact found proved under the legal norm and binding determination of the legal consequence of the fact deemed proved under the legal norm applied.

Procedural discretion in determining the facts should be viewed in connection with the adopted solutions in administrative procedural law. Both in the CAP and in the Tax Code the standard for the determination of the facts is set already in

---

4 J. Wróblewski, *Sądowe stosowanie prawa [Judicial application of the law]*, Warsaw: 1972, p. 52.

5 L. Leszczyński, *Zagadnienia teorii stosowania prawa. Doktryna i tezy orzecznictwa [Problems in theory of application of the law. Doctrine and theses from jurisprudence]*, Cracow: 2004, pp. 62 *et seq.*

6 M. Jaśkowska, *ibidem*, p. 257, L. Leszczyński, *Stosowanie i wykładnia prawa administracyjnego [Application and interpretation of administrative law]*, in: *Wykładnia w prawie administracyjnym [Interpretation in administrative law]*, *op. cit.*, pp. 41, 42.

7 For the concept of discretion and modern concepts of administrative discretion see M. Jaśkowska, *op.cit.*, pp. 229 *et seq.*

the general rules, viz. above all directly in the general principle of objective truth, but it also follows from other principles and detailed regulation. The standard is thorough explanation of the facts. In accordance with the second norm of Article 7 CAP: 'In the course of the proceedings public administrative authorities (...), either on their own motion or on motion from the parties undertake any activities necessary to the thorough explanation of the facts (...);' and in the general principle of swiftness of proceedings (Article 12.1 CAP) the following was added: 'Public administration authorities should act swiftly and thoroughly in a case, employing the simplest means to handle it.'

In tax proceedings a general principle was given shape in Article 122 of the Tax Code, which mandates that: 'In the course of the proceedings tax authorities undertake all the necessary actions in order for thorough explanation of the facts (...), giving priority also within the principle of the swiftness of the proceedings to the tax authority's thorough and swift action, employing the simplest means to handle the case (Article 125.1 of the Tax Code). Is it possible from the general principle of objective truth to infer procedural discretion of a public administrative authority, or, in tax proceedings, a tax authority? Procedural discretion may be inferred whenever the provisions of procedural law do not subject the determination of the facts to a formalistic theory of evidence. From the principle of objective truth arises the obligation to take all the necessary actions for thorough explanation of the facts (Article 7 CAP, Article 122 of the Tac Code), while the actions themselves should be characterized by thoroughness (Article 12.1 CAP, Article 125.1 of the Tax Code). Taking all the necessary actions for thorough explanation of the facts does not define the legal nature of such actions, viz. are they they only procedural actions or also substantive actions, nor does it define their scope. Based on the regulation both in the CAP and the Tax Code, both classic procedural actions and substantive actions can be distinguished, for the determination of the facts. In introducing procedural discretion, discretion with regard to substantive actions must be excluded. The taking up of substantive activities in determining the facts of the case follows from the norms of substantive administrative law, which establish the collaboration of public administrative authorities in a case, and tax authorities in tax proceedings. According to Article 106.1 CAP: 'Where a provision of the law requires for a decision the taking of a position by a different authority (opinion or approval or some other for taking a position), such a decision is issued after the taking of a position by such an authority.' Such a solution was also adopted in Article 209.1 of the Tax Code: 'Where a provision of the law requires for a decision the taking of a position by a different authority, such as giving an opinion or approval or some other for taking a position, such a decision is issued after the taking of a position by such an authority.'

The obligation for public administrative authorities to collaborate is imposed by provisions of material law, which does not, however, make it element that is outside the determination of the facts of the case. Determining the facts with omission of the collaboration process makes it impossible to deem it to be a pattern consistent with the law. In consequence, it leads to a violation of the principle of objective truth, which is a ground for reconsideration of the case. Such a violation of the rule for determining the facts of the case is met with the sanction of mutability of the decision through reopening the proceedings (Article 145.1.6 CAP, Article 240.1 of the Tax Code). The making of a finding of the facts by the collaborating public administration authority, or, in tax proceedings, by a tax authority, is the result of a mandate arising from the provisions of substantive law, which means there can be no procedural discretion with regard to it.

Procedural discretion with regarding to determining the facts must be viewed in connection with classic procedural actions, which include actions in evidentiary proceedings. In imposing — on a public administration authority in general administrative proceedings and on a tax authority in tax proceedings — an obligation to take on the necessary actions for thorough explanation of the facts, both in Article 7 CAP and Article 122 of the Tax Code, no rules were indicated for the authorities to follow. Such rules may be inferred from the detailed regulation of provisions of procedural law with regard to evidence (Chapter 4 'Evidence' of Division II 'Procedure' of the CAP; Chapter 11 of Division IV of the Tax Code in tax proceedings). In setting the limits of procedural discretion in the determination of the fact, regard must be had to the regulation of determination of the facts in the relevant type of case as contained in substantive legislation.

In general administrative proceedings and in tax proceedings determination of the facts is based on the theory of an open system of evidence. According to Article 75.1 CAP:

> Everything must be admitted as evidence which may contribute to the explanation of the case and is not inconsistent with the law. In particular documents, witness testimony, expert opinions and visual inspection may be evidence.

In adopting an open system of evidence, provisions of the CAP do not associate findings of fact with a hierarchy of probative strength within the adopted open system of evidence. It is up to the public administrative authority to select such evidence as of which the conduct will lead to thorough, in-depth determination of the facts of the case. Being guided by the norm of substantive law, whether that is a creational norm or substantive non-discretion, the authority determines which facts are of significant relevance to the case, whether they require proof, and what evidence is necessary in order to prove such facts. Directives for the authority to follow in determining the evidence arise follow from the general directive of thorough, in-depth determination of the facts. There appears therefore to be complete discretion in the selection of evidence. The authority may base the determination of the facts on the evidence selected, relying on the open system of both evidence prescribed in the CAP and innominate evidence[8]. Such wide procedural discretion in the selection of evidence, however, is restricted by the provisions of the CAP and provisions contained in substantive legislation. The CAP requires certain evidence to be given a mandatory nature, thus depriving the public administrative authority of any possibility of determining the facts on the basis of other evidence instead. This is how any procedural discretion is to be excluded with regard to the expert opinion. While according to Article 84.1 CAP evidence from expert opinion includes some leeway of procedural discretion due to its being introduced with the following language: 'the public administrative authority may request an opinion from an expert or experts,' but this freedom must be excluded where special knowledge is required in the case. In cases with particularly intricate facts that are capable of explanation only through access to special knowledge, the public administrative authority has an obligation to choose this particular type of evidence. Provisions of substantive legislation may impose a direct exclusion of procedural discretion in the selection of this evidence. Such a solution is directly introduced in the Act of 21 August 1997 on Real-Property Management[9], mandating the appointment of an expert in those cases in which part of the determination of the facts is appraisal of real property. In accordance with Article 154 of that Act: 'The choice of the right approach and method and technique of property appraisal is made by the expert property appraiser (…).'

A limit of procedural discretion in the determination of the facts is drawn by equipping a certain type of evidence with an auxiliary nature. According to Article 86 CAP: 'Where upon exhaustion of evidence or due to a lack of evidence there remain unexplained facts relevant to the outcome of the case, the public administrative authority may, in order to explain such facts, interrogate a party (…).' The selection of this evidence is delimited by two cumulative prerequisites: – firstly, the exhaustion of other evidence or its absence altogether; interrogation of a party is therefore available, in the light of this particular ground, only where it

8 B. Adamiak in: B. Adamiak, J. Borkowski, *Kodeks postępowania administracyjnego. Komentarz [Code of Administrative Procedure. Commentary]*, Warsaw: 2014, p. 355.

9 Uniform text: Dz.U.2015.1774, as amended.

is impossible for the public administrative authority to determine the facts using other evidence, whether regulated by the provisions of the CAP or innominate evidence; – secondly, there remain unexplained facts significant to the outcome of the case; in accordance with this latter ground, interrogation of the parties is permissible where it is impossible for the public administrative authority to explain circumstances significant to the case without which the facts of the case cannot be established according to reality.

One other type of limit on procedural discretion can be found with regard to the selection of evidence from official documents. The freedom to select an official document as the basis for determination of the facts must be distinguished from the strength of the official document. The systematized order of the regulation of Article 75.1 CAP lists documents in the first place, which, however, does not imply restricting the selection of evidence to documents; this assessment is left up to the authority, unless the relevant provision excludes the freedom of selection by requiring the facts to be determined on the basis of an official document. An example of such a solution is found in Article 48.3.1 of the Act of 7 July 1994 — Construction Law[10], requiring the submission of a certificate from the head of a commune, mayor or president of a city stating that the construction is consistent with the determinations of either the binding local spatial-development master plan or decision concerning the conditions of land development and building, where there is no such local spatial-development master plan.

What is restricted is the freedom to assess the probative strength of an official document. According to Article 76.1 CAP: 'Official documents executed in the form prescribed by authorities state authorities competent to execute them, in the scope of the activities of such authorities, constitute evidence of what is officially attested in such documents.' A public administrative authority may not freely reject, without processing counter-evidence, the existence of a fact attested in an official document. Provisions of the CAP do not impose any limitations on the type of counter-evidence to impeach the existence of a fact attested in an official document.

Procedural discretion may be limited by the adoption of a specific division of competence in the determination of the facts, excluding evidentiary discretion. One example of such a solution can be found in the regulation of determining the facts in a case concerning the finding of an occupational disease. In accordance with § 8.1 of the Regulation of the Council of Ministers of 30 June 2009 in the

10 Uniform text: Dz.U.2016.290.

Matter of Occupational Diseases[11]: 'The decision confirming occupational disease or decision finding the lack of grounds to confirm occupational disease is issued on the basis of the evidence and in particular of data contained in a medical finding and the form for the assessment of the employee's or former employee's occupational exposure.'

With regard to the determination of the facts for the confirmation or non-confirmation of occupational diseases, the public administrative authority is restricted in the selection of evidence, through imposition of the requirement, in the Regulation, that this must be done in a medical finding issued by a medical practitioner, on the basis of the results of medical examinations and auxiliary examinations, the worker or former worker's medical documentation, documentation of employment, and assessment of occupational exposure. Exclusivity with regard to the diagnosis or non-diagnosis of occupational disease is reserved for a medical finding. Where the competent state health inspector deems that the evidence material contained in the medical finding is not sufficient to issue the decision, the inspector may require the medical practitioner who issued that medical finding to provide additional reasoning for such a finding, or apply to a second-tier unit for additional consultation or take other actions necessary to supplement the material. In its judgment of 14 February 2013 II OSK 2535/12 (LEX no. 1358516) the Supreme Administrative Court emphasized that the authority is bound:

> In the light of these provisions occupational disease is deemed to be a disease mentioned in the list of occupational diseases, if as a result of the evaluation of working conditions it may be held beyond dispute or with high probability that such a disease was caused by the operation of factors harmful to health existing in the working environment, or with the manner in which the work is performed, referred to as 'professional exposure'. An occupational disease may be diagnosed in an employee or former employee either during the latter's employment under occupational exposure or when no longer working under such exposure, on condition of documented symptoms of the disease occurring within the duration defined by the list of occupational diseases. As held in jurisprudence, the authority may not diagnose the disease without a medical finding — opinion, or contrary to it. This means that the determination of one of the important elements of classifying an illness as occupational disease is contingent upon the contents of a specialist medical finding. Such a view was set out in the resolution of a panel of 7 justices of the Supreme Administrative Court of 20 May 2002 and continues to the up-to-date (file ref. OPS 3/02, ONSA 2003/1/4). It was held, therefore, that the public administrative authority conducting the proceedings with regard to occupational disease has no right to make its own evaluation of the medical documentation leading to a different diagnosis, if no doubts

---

11 Uniform text: Dz.U.2013.1367.

> arise in the light of other evidence. Hence, the authority should evaluate the finding as evidence with the proceedings in compliance with the canons set by the provisions of the Code of Administrative Procedure.

From the solutions adopted in the Regulation it must be inferred that, with regard to determination of the facts for other activities necessary in order to supplement such material, only the evaluation of occupational exposure is left up to the authority. This follows from the solution adopted in § 6.2 of the Regulation of the Council of Ministers on Occupational Diseases, in connection with which occupational risk is evaluated, in the course of issuing a decision to confirm or not to confirm occupational disease, by the competent state health inspector.

An example of a limitation imposed on procedural discretion in the selection of evidence with which to determine the facts can be found in the regulation adopted in the Act of 12 March 2004 on Social Aid[12]. In accordance with Article 106.4 of that Act: 'The administrative decision granting or refusing to grant the benefit, except for a decision to refuse to grant a loan ticket or decisions with regard to foreigners such as are referred to in Article 5a, are issued after carrying out a family environmental inquiry.'

In tax proceedings procedural discretion also is delimited by the adopted theory of open system of evidence. According to Article 180.1 of the Tax Code: 'Everything must be admitted as evidence which may contribute to the explanation of the case and is not inconsistent with the law.' This regulation of open system of evidence is supplemented by the regulation adopted in Article 181 of the Tax Code, mandating that:

> Evidence in tax proceedings may be in particular tax books, declarations submitted by the parties, witness testimony, export opinions, material and information gathered as a result of visual inspection, tax information and other documents gathered during verification activities or tax audit, with the proviso of Articles 284a.3, 284.3 and 288.2, and material accumulated in the course of criminal proceedings or proceedings in cases of fiscal-criminal offences or fiscal infractions.

With the open-system theory, procedural discretion of the tax authority in the selection of evidence may be described as being complete. Such an assessment requires verification on the basis of the especial regulation of the position of the relevant type of evidence. With the enumeration in Article 181 of the Tax Code of a non-closed but still ordered system of evidence corresponds a limitation imposed on procedural discretion. Not without legal significance here is the listing of tax books in the first position. Doing so imposes a substantial restriction on

12 Uniform text: Dz.U.2015.163, as amended.

the tax authority with regard to the determination of the facts with substantive consequences connected with the assessment of tax basis. The Supreme Administrative Court emphasizes this limitation of evidentiary freedom in a number of judgments. And so in the judgment of 17 November 2011 II FSK 26/11 (LEX no. 1131418) the SAC held:

> One must subscribe (…) to the view of the Supreme Administrative Court expressed in the judgment of 12 May 2011, case ref. I FSK 837/10 (publ. by CBOS) that: 'On the one hand we do have an open system of evidence in tax proceedings. This because in accordance with Article 180.1 TX everything must be admitted as evidence which may contribute to the explanation of the case and is not inconsistent with the law. On other hand, Article 181 TC lists by way of example types of evidence that may be conducted in such proceedings. In the first place and not by accident the lawmaker listed tax books. This testifies to the importance of that evidence in tax proceedings. Hence Article 193.1 TX defines the probative strength of tax books. In accordance with the contents of that legal norm tax books kept in a conscientious and non-defective manner constitute evidence of what occurs from entries made in them. Thus the lawmaker has vested those books with especial probative strength. This is because this norm contains an evidentiary mandate binding in tax proceedings that imposes a restriction on the principle of substantive truth in favour of formal truth. Only where such books are kept in a non-conscientious or defective manner may the tax authority refuse to consider them evidence (Article 193.4 TC). To that end, however, Article 193.6 introduces an exceptional path enabling the omission of such books. According to the contents of that legal norm, where the tax authority finds the books to be kept in a non-conscientious or defective way, then in the minutes of examination of such books the authority defines for what period and in what part it does not consider the books to be evidence of what occurs from entries made in them. The tax authority serves a copy of such minutes on the party (§ 7). The party, within 14 days of the day the minutes are delivered, may submit reservations with regard to the determinations made there, providing simultaneously evidence enabling the tax authority to make a correct assessment of the tax basis (§ 8).'
>
> 5.4. In this case it is beyond dispute that the tax authorities had not impeached the binding force of the tax books under Article 193.6 TC. The Voivodeship Administrative Court accepted the position held by the appellate authority that the defect concerned did not have significant impact on the outcome of the case, as the minutes of the audit recorded defects and described irregularities. Such an assessment may not be upheld. This because rightly did the author of the appeal-in-cassation note that that the minutes of tax audit attested to irregularities, determined the sales structure according to assigned VAT rates arising from purchase documents, and inventories as at the end of 2004 and 2005, which means that an assessment of VAT basis occurred. She was also right in pointing out that the complaining party had not been advised what method, according to either Article 23.3 or 23.4 of the Tax Code, the authority assessed the tax basis. In consequence, the minutes of the audit assessed VAT rates, which is inextricably linked with assessing the tax basis without compliance with procedures provided for in the Tax Code, in

particular with omission of norms concerning the impeachment of the probative strength of records for VAT purposes.

Circumstances being as they are, it is necessary to repeat that for the lawmaker to introduce a special procedure for the impeachment of the probative strength of tax books means that omission of such regulation by tax authorities may not be deemed every time to be a procedural irregularity insignificant to the outcome of the case.

5.5. In these proceedings the amount of the tax liability was assessed at a different amount from the one arising from the records, in spite of the clear prohibition in that regard contained in Article 193.1 TC. It must be stressed that the minutes of examination of the books are an administrative act of sorts, of which either the execution or the impeachment ought to proceed in accordance with the procedure described in Article 193.(6–8) of the Tax Code. It is only the exhaustion of that procedural path which can produce grounds for successful impeachment of the books in the specified scope in the further course of the tax proceedings (compare the judgment of the Supreme Administrative Court of 23 September 2008, file ref. II FSK 878/07, publ.: http://orzeczenia.nsa.gov.pl). For the lawmaker to introduce a special procedure for the impeachment of the probative strength of tax books means that omission of such regulation by tax authorities may not be deemed every time to be a procedural irregularity insignificant to the outcome of the case.

An example of limitation of procedural discretion can be found in the binding force on the tax authority of an official document. A different aspect of compliance with this principle was noted by the SAC in its judgment of 9 July 2015 II GSK 1457/13 (LEX no. 1774175):

At the starting point, it is necessary to resolve the problem issue, significant to this case, which is the scope in which the tax authority is bound by data contained in the official register of lands and buildings, and, more strictly speaking, whether the information found in that register concerning the owner (co-owners) of the property is absolutely binding.

The disputed issue as laid out above requires assessment of the scope of the binding force of entries contained in the register of lands and buildings. In accordance with Article 21.1 of the Act — Surveying and Cartographic Law (SCL), the basis for economic planning, spatial planning, calculation of taxes and benefits, designation of properties in land-and-mortgage books, public statistics, property-management documents and registers of farms constitute data contained in the register of lands and buildings. In the opinion of the Supreme Administrative Court, the expression 'calculation of tax' as used in Article 21.1 SCL ought to be construed as determination (definition) of tax liability with regard being had to elements referring both to the persons and the matter as contained in the register of lands and buildings. It is a commonly held view in the jurisprudence of administrative courts, shared also by the judicial panel hearing the case at hand, that, pursuant to the regulation cited, the tax authority may not on its own classify the intended use of the functions of the property but should refer to the appropriate records of the register of lands and buildings (compare in.al. the resolution of 7 judgments of the SAC of 27 Apeil 2009, case ref. II FPS 1/09, available at www.orzeczenia.nsa.gov.pl). This means that, in principle, the manner of classification of the land (building) for taxation purposes with regard to property tax, is decided not as much by the actual use of the property as by its functions (intended use) disclosed in the register of lands and buildings. This reasoning is also subscribed to by the view of the Supreme Administrative Court expressed in the judgment of 21 December 2012, case ref. II FSK 986/11 (available at www.orzeczenia.nsa.gov.pl), in which emphasis was laid on how, in the light of 21.1 SCL, the basis for the calculation of tax is not the actual state of things but the state disclosed (recorded) in the register of lands and buildings, and that, in this context, it is impossible to speak of being formally bound by the register, which controls the calculation of the tax regardless whatever the nature of the lands concerned may be at any specific time. On the other hand, as the Supreme Administrative Court also noted in.al. in the resolution of a panel of seven justices of 18 November 2013, case ref. II FPS 2/13 (available: www.orzeczenia.nsa.gov.pl), the aforementioned rule of absolute binding force of register data may in some — extraordinary, as it were — cases be impeached within tax proceedings, even without need for prior change to the register itself. In the opinion of the SAC panel hearing the case at bar, deviation from the absolute binding force of entries contained in the register of land and buildings may take place when information contained in the register conflicts with the data disclosed in other public registers of which the precedence (before register data) arises from imperative provisions governing their maintenance, or where reliance on register data would need to entail omission of provisions contained in the tax statute with impact on the calculation of the tax (available register symbols do not provide for the designation of certain taxable objects expressly mentioned in the tax statute). In such a case the tax authority will have the obligation to omit information contained in the register of lands and buildings that conflicts with the binding data from a different public register or such register data as exclude the application of regulations contained in the tax code with impact on the calculation of the tax.

With the above discussion in mind, it is necessary to conclude that the land register may not decide the ownership of property (or perpetual usufruct), which translates into the identification of the subject of property taxation. In that respect, consistently with the public faith of land-and-mortgage books (Article 5 of the Act on Land-and-Mortgage Books and Mortgage), it is necessary to heed first the entries disclosed in the second division of the land-and-mortgage book (concerning ownership and perpetual usufruct). Such public faith, on the other hand, is excluded with regard to information contained in the first division of the book, viz. the one concerning the description of the property. Land-and-mortgage register books, similarly, besides, to the register of lands and buildings, constitute a public register, provided that entries concerning the owner (perpetual usufructuary) of the property as contained in the register may not undermine the presumption of veracity of the data contained in the second division of the land-and-mortgage book, which contains entries concerning the ownership and perpetual usufruct (Article 25.1.2 of the Act on Land-and-Mortgage Books and Mortgage). As the Supreme Court indicated in its judgment of 9 October 2013, case ref. V CSK 450/12 (LEX no. 1415129), an action to reconcile the legal status of a property as disclosed in a land-and-mortgage book with its actual legal status, based on Article 10 of the Act on Land-and-Mortgage Books and Mortgage, is, in principle, the only way to impeach the legal presumption of Article 3 of that Act, according to which the disclosed right from the land-and-mortgage book is entered consistently with the actual legal state of things.

Thus, where the taxpayer demonstrates in tax proceedings, pursuant to Article 194.3 TC, that, contrary to owner data concerning the owner (perpetual usufructuary) as disclosed in the land register, the actual ownership status (or perpetual usufruct) is regulated differently by the second division of the relevant land-and-mortgage book, the tax authorities must verify such a circumstance in order to arrive at a decision that refers to the actual owner (perpetual usufructuary) of the property, i.e. the one disclosed in the land-and-mortgage book, being the taxpayer in the understanding of the Act on Local Taxes and Fees. Such a possibility of impeaching register records under Article 194.3 TC must be regarded as an exceptional situation, one determined by the necessity to abide by other imperative regulation.

In determining the limits of procedural discretion in the selection of evidence for the determination of the facts regard must be had to that regulation in substantive legislation which contains evidentiary mandates. And thus, for example, Article 6.4 of the Act of 9 September 2000 on Civil Law Transaction Tax[13]:

If the taxpayer, despite notice referred to in subsection 3, has not specified the value or has provided a value not corresponding to the market value, the tax authority will assess such a value with recourse to an expert's opinion or an expert appraisal submitted by the taxpayer. Where the tax authority appoints an expert and the value determined in reliance on such an expert's opinion differs from the value stated by the taxpayer by more than 33%, the costs of the opinion are borne by the taxpayer.

3. Procedural discretion and free valuation of evidence

In the doctrine of administrative law a distinction is made between administrative discretion and free valuation. In making this distinction, J. Starościak explained the goal of it in a practical way, asserting:

The goal of discretion is the option for the administrative authority itself to determine its own conduct with regard to already determined facts. On the other hand, free valuation is the legal grant to the administrative authority of the competence to determine the facts. Nature protection according to the provisions of the law applies to venerable trees, beautiful landscape, animal species going extinct. However, in order to apply such protection to any specific object, one must previously determine what animal species are going extinct, whether the relevant landscape is beautiful etc. In making such determinations the administrative authority may rely on documents, expert studies and opinions etc. The valuation of the weight and business-like manner, completeness and usefulness of such opinions and studies and even the authority's own observations is the matter of

13 Uniform text: Dz.U.2015.626, as amended.

> free valuation of administrative authorities. The free valuation, therefore, concerns not the authority's conduct with regard to the facts determined, but to the initial determination of what factual circumstances we are dealing with.[14]

M. Jaśkowska notes that:

> Decision-making leeway at the stage of free valuation of proof may not, however, be identified with discretion (...). There is thus here a clear qualitative demarcation, given as free valuation refers to something that is and discretion refers to something that should be, i.e. the selection of the legal consequence. The scope of freedom granted to the authority on the second stage of application of the law, however, refers only to the acquisition of material about the facts and, for this reason, notwithstanding the existence of evaluative elements within it, it cannot be identified with discretion.[15]

While sharing in the view that discretion is a separate institution from free valuation of evidence, M. Jaśkowska does not preclude free valuation of evidence from classification under procedural discretion in determining the facts of the case. Another aspect is relevant to the formulation of procedural discretion. L. Leszczyński distinguishes in cognitive processes: '[...] two paramount aspects of evaluations (evaluative locutions) in the determination of facts in the application of the law. The one relates to the manner of normative naming of certain facts, the other to free valuation of evidence as a competence attributed to decision-makers.'[16]

In L. Leszczyński's opinion: 'The other type of intervention of valuation in the cognitive process of determining the facts is the so called free valuation of proof, which leads to the decision-maker's pronouncement of what facts will be deemed credible, sufficiently proved etc., and therefore — in short — what facts will be deemed the facts of the case. It should not, however, be confused with the classification of facts, which takes place during the decision-making stage of the process.'[17] This view merits complete agreement.

Procedural discretion of public administrative authorities in general administrative proceedings, and tax authorities in tax proceedings, finds expression in the free valuation of evidence as a principle adopted in those proceedings. According to Article 80 CAP: 'The public administrative authority evaluates on the basis of the totality of evidence material whether the relevant circumstance has been proved.' This is also what Article 191 of the Tax Code provides: 'The tax

14 J. Starościak, Prawne formy i metody działania administracji [Legal forms and methods of administration], in: *System prawa administracyjnego.* [Administrative law: the system] Vol. 3, Warsaw: 1978, p. 76.

15 M. Jaśkowska, *ibidem*, pp. 258, 259.

16 L. Leszczyński, *ibidem*, pp. 41, 42.

17 *Ibidem*, p. 42.

authority evaluates on the basis of the entire evidence material gathered whether the relevant circumstance has been proved.'

The limit of free valuation of evidence, set both in Article 80 CAP and Article 191 of the Tax Code, is the exclusion of fragmented valuation of the evidence material gathered, while no criteria have been adopted in the provisions of procedural law to qualify the valuation of the evidence material, e.g. from the perspective of the need to protect the public interest or the individual interests of a party (e.g. in-depth legal and business rationale). Such a view is held uniformly in the jurisprudence of administrative courts. And thus in the judgment of 3 April 2015 II FSK 2822/13 (LEX no. 1774314) the SAC noted that it was not possible to adopt a valuation of evidence through the prism of the complaining party's interests showing in an 'in-depth legal and business rationale'. Such valuation of evidence is not permissible. The SAC emphasized that:

> Principal significance here is acquired by — notwithstanding those already listed — the provision of Article 191 of the Tax Code as formulating one of the core principles of evidentiary proceedings — the principle of free valuation of evidence. In accordance with this provision, the tax authority evaluates on the basis of the evidence material gathered in the case whether the relevant circumstance has been proved. This means that the administrative authority, in evaluating the evidence material, is not constricted by any evidentiary rules, and it makes its findings of fact according to its own conviction, on the basis of the evidence material comprehensively examined. In theory of law, it is stressed that free valuation of evidence, so that it may not transform into arbitrariness, must be made with adherence to the norms of procedural law and the rules of such valuation. These rules consist in the following: relied on must be the material gathered in the course of the proceedings; that material must undergo comprehensive valuation; the valuation should refer to the individual proofs along with their importance to the case. The reasoning in consequence of which the authority determines the existence of factual circumstances should be consistent with the rules of logic and life experience (thus: B. Adamiak, J. Borkowski — *Kodeks postępowania administracyjnego. Komentarz. [Code of Administrative Proceedings. Commentary]* C. H. Beck, Warsaw: 1996, pp. 376 *et seq.*, the theses of which remain valid, in the opinion of the adjudicating panel, also within the framework of the procedural provisions currently in force). As long as the limits of free valuation of evidence are not exceeded by the decision-making authority, the Court, therefore, has no grounds on which to undermine findings thus made. Translating these general remarks onto the plane of the case at bar, it ought to be noted that the evidentiary proceedings carried out in this case led to gathering evidence material that bears the marks of completeness. Completeness of the evidence material is an utterly fundamental, in a way principal condition of finding that, firstly — the principle of objective truth has been satisfied, and, secondly, that the valuation of evidence made by the tax authorities is a valuation protected by Article 191 of the Tax Code.

In its judgment of 7 May 2015 I FSK 605/14 (LEX no. 1772871) the SAC emphasized:

> Attention must be called first of all to how it follows from the provisions of Article 122 and Article 187.1 TC that evidentiary proceedings are to be conducted according to the officiality principle. The tax authority must conduct *ex officio* the evidence that serves to determine the facts of the case. On the other hand, the principle of free valuation of evidence as adopted in Article 191 TC assumes that the tax authority in its valuation of evidence is not constricted with formal criteria; the authority is to evaluate the credibility and probative strength of the individual proofs on which it has based its decision. In order not to cross the boundaries of arbitrariness in such free valuation, the tax authority should be guided in its valuation of evidence gathered in the case in.al. by the rules of logic, consistency with the laws of science and life experience, regarding the proofs gathered as objective phaenomena, evaluating the evidence solely from the point of view of its significance and importance to the case at hand, the comprehensive nature of the valuation.

It belongs to the public administrative authorities, and in tax proceedings — to tax authorities, to evaluate the strength of a proof in the context of the entirety of the evidence for the determination of the facts of the case. Even in those cases where procedural discretion as to the selection of the evidence with which to determine the facts through imposition of evidentiary mandates indicating the type of required evidence, the valuation of the probative strength is left up to the authority within the limits drawn by provisions of the law. The jurisprudence of administrative courts presents a unified front in this regard. Among others, one could cite examples from the established line of jurisprudence with regard to the valuation of the probative strength of property appraisals. In its judgment of 5 March 2015 II FSK 1521/14 (LEX no. 1773537) the Supreme Administrative Court held:

> A property appraisal is exclusive evidence of an increase in the value of property in consequence of a completed split of such property. This follows from Article 149, Article 150.5 and Article 156 of the Act of 21 August 1997 on Real-Property Management (uniform text: Dz.U.2010.102.651, as amended) (hereinafter the "Act on Real-Property Management"). However, this does not mean it is entirely exempt from valuation by the administrative authority conducting those proceedings in which it is to provide the basis for findings of fact. As with any other evidence, the valuation of the appraisal is subject to Article 80 CAP, which commands the administrative authority to evaluate whether the relevant circumstance has been proved on the basis of the entirety of evidence material; Article 7 CAP, which mandates that any and all steps must be taken in order for a thorough determination of the facts; and Article 77.1 CAP, which imposes on the administrative authority the obligation of exhaustive collection and examination of the entire evidence material. From these provisions it follows that the administrative authority should exhaustively evaluate the appraisal, and should there be any doubt as to

its correctness, the authority should take action to remove such doubts. The only limitation imposed by the lawmaker on the choice of such action is the prohibition against replacing the appraisal as proof with some other proof with regard to determination of the value of real property. [...]

It is beyond a doubt, at the same time, that the execution of an opinion concerning the value of real property requires special knowledge in the understanding of Article 84.1 CAP, hence, in accordance with Article 7 of the Act on Real-Property Management, the preparation of such an opinion — in the form of the appraisal — belongs to the expert appraiser. For this reason, the appraisal may be subjected to valuation by the decision-making authority only with regard to probative value according to Article 80 CAP. Therefore, if a party to administrative proceedings is disputing the assumptions, findings and evaluations contained in the appraisal, the decision-making authority has the obligation, firstly, to determine which of such allegations may be evaluated under Article 80 CAP and which ones require special knowledge, so as to obtain — in consequence of such a finding — appropriate explanation from the author of the expert appraisal. This is because an expert appraiser appearing in administrative proceedings in the capacity of an expert has an obligation not only to draw up an opinion as to the value of the property but also to explain to the authority conducting the proceedings all of the issues and doubts raised in the proceedings with regard to such an opinion, such as which the authority requests the expert appraiser to explain.

If the decision-making authority deems the expert appraiser's explanation to be sufficient under Article 80 CAP, it is only then that the authority may expect the party to the proceedings disputing the opinion on the value of property to support its allegations with additional evidence, e.g. evaluation of the correctness of the preparation of the appraisal made by a professional organization of expert property appraisers pursuant to Articles 171.1 and 171.1a of the Act on Real-Property Management. The decision-making authority may not, on the other hand, require a party to the proceedings to support issues raised with an appraisal with additional qualified evidence (e.g. evaluation by a professional organization of expert property appraisers) without having previously exhausted on its own the options for valuation of the probative value of the appraisal under Article 7 and Article 80 CAP.'

Denial of probative value may come with a limitation. Thus, a public administrative authority may deny an official document its probative strength only if it has impeached its strength through counter-evidence, unless doing so is excluded by adopted legislative solutions. And so in the judgment of 21 May 2014 II OSK 3076/12[18] the SAC noted such type of limitations:

---

18 *Orzecznictwo Naczelnego Sądu Administracyjnego i Wojewódzkich Sądów Administracyjnych* [Jurisprudence of the Supreme Administrative Court and Voivodeship Administrative Courts 2015/3/60].

Vesting vital records, through Article 4 of the Law on Vital Records, with the character of exclusive evidence of events attested in them bars the data contained in a vital record from being proved by a public administrative authority with the use of other evidence (…). Determination of data concerning vital records on the basis of vital records means that the fact of birth or having been born in wedlock ought to be proved with an appropriate copy extracted from the vital record. Failing that, the authority may not determine the above circumstances on the basis of the so called totality of evidence material (Article 80 CAP). The lack may be supplemented in proceedings of a preliminary nature relative to the pending proceedings in the administrative case. The Law on Vital Records makes it possible, upon motion from an interested party, to determine the contents of a vital record where no such record (of birth or marriage) was made (Articles 32–33). When significant time has passed since the birth of the child, determination of the contents of the certificate of birth will be possible only to a court of law in non-contentious proceedings (judgment of the SAC of 19 July 2013, case ref. II OSK 650/12). If the circumstanced prescribed for doing so are met, vital records can also be recreated upon motion from an interested party or state body or authority, if the book of vital records is missing or has been destroyed (Article 34). The indicated provisions on vital records have a systemic nature, which necessitates the conclusion that their scope of application should be accounted for *ex officio* by authorities conducting administrative proceedings whenever doubts occur concerning events which vital records are the sole evidence to confirm.

4. Conclusions

The adopted legislative solutions with regard to determination of the facts, both in the CAP and in the Tax Code, permit demonstration that there is procedural discretion in public administrative authorities. Rejection of formalistic legal theory leaves the authorities with a large margin of freedom in the selection of evidence to conduct in order to determine the facts. This freedom is accompanied by freedom in the valuation of probative strength of the evidence conducted.

A significant preventive guarantee against arbitrariness in procedural discretion is found in the requirement of mandatory inclusion in the decision of a factual rationale, which should contain, in particular, the indication of what facts the authority deemed to have been proved, what evidence the authority relied on, and reasons for which it denied other evidence credibility and probative strength (Article 107.3 CAP, Article 210.4 of the Tax Code)[19].

The set limits of the procedural discretion available to a public administrative authority, and tax authority in tax proceedings, are subject to verification within the appellate chain and by the administrative court.

---

19 Concerning the rationale see L. Leszczyński, *ibidem*, pp. 48 *et seq.*

Evaluation of the correctness of the use of the available procedural discretion strongly marks its presence in the determination of the facts in the grounds of granting a complaint by the administrative court against a decision. According to Article 145.1.1.c of the Act of 30 August 2002 — Law on Proceedings Before Administrative Courts[20]: 'The court, in granting a complaint against a decision or order: reverses the decision or order in whole or in part upon having found: other violations of procedural provisions, where such may have had significant impact on the outcome of the case.'

Exceeding the limits of procedural discretion with regard to determination of the facts is classified as a violation of procedural provisions with significant impact on the outcome of the case.

The solutions adopted in the CAP and in the Tax Code provide the basis upon which to distinguish procedural discretion of which the scope is wider than that of substantive discretion. The significance of determination of the facts of the case encompasses the entire sphere of application of the provisions of substantive administrative law in the form of administrative decision.

20 Uniform text: Dz.U.2012.270, as amended.

Zbigniew Kmieciak
(Professor University of Lodz, Poland; The Supreme Administrative Court of Poland Judge)

Joanna Wegner-Kowalska
(Ph.D., University of Lodz, Poland)

Abuse of Administrative Discretion

Abstract: The article advocates for the clear definition of formal and material boundaries of administrative discretion and clear definition of ongoing relations between them. It also emphasizes the need to develop a methodologically correct catalogue of discretion errors.

Keywords: administrative discretion, abuse of discretion, judicial review

1. The concept of administrative discretion

The concept of discretionary power of in public administration (administrative discretion) is used in science, legal texts and case law of different legal systems with several meanings. It is determined by tradition, the goals of theoretical discourse, the existing legal regulations and practical findings. The concepts created in different circumstances have been integrated and developed under the EU law. In the above-mentioned legal order, the margin of decision marked with such phrases as "discretion", "*pouvoir d'appréciation*", "*pouvoir discrétionnaire*" or "der *Beurteilungsspielraum*", is usually identified with all margin types of findings, assessments and settlements, not just with the freedom to choose one from several legally authorized options of action.

It should be reminded that K.C. Davies, in his classic work, described the exercise of discretionary power as the choice between behaviour X, Y and Z. It "Discretion" is therefore the margin which a decision-maker has in determining the legal consequences of finding the facts.[1] This is in contrast to the EU legal order in which there is basically no difference between the freedom of interpreting ambiguous (not precisely defined) legal terms and the margin of choice of decision option. As emphasised by A. Nałęcz – "it has never been accepted"[2]. The concept

1 K.C. Davis, *Discretionary Justice*, Baton Rouge 1969, p. 4, similarly – M.E. Dimock, *Law and Dynamic Administration*, Praeger 1980, p. 129 and following.
2 A. Nałęcz, *Uznanie administracyjne a reglamentacja działalności gospodarczej*, Warszawa 2010, p. 65, polemically – Z. Kmieciak in the review of this book, "Państwo i Prawo" 2011, No. 5, p. 107.

of discretion is used in other contexts, for example while choosing an option of an administration action form (*Optionenermessen*)[3]. The broad understanding of the discretionary power generally complies with D.J. Galligan's concept. According to it, the margin of an administrative action defined by Galligan is the peculiar "complex value" that is a result of findings and assessments at all stages of the decision-making process. The author identified three key components of the process: 1) finding the facts; 2) setting the standards; and 3) applying the standards to the facts. The decision-maker's freedom, tantamount to fulfilling discretionary power, applies to each of them[4]. Under this formula, reconstructing some premises, and especially specifying content of a vague concept used by the statute, is necessary to make a final decision. In opinion of D.J. Galligan, determining the meaning of this concept is also a "discretionary element". He does not conceal the fact "that there are no clear or precise lines between one sense of discretion and another"[5].

Another example of the broad understanding of discretion is the Dutch legal concept concerning "free competences as opposed to *competencies liées*". Two forms of discretion are distinguished in this legal system: 1) discretion in policy (*beleidsvrijheid*), which implies that the legislator does not prescribe the nature of decision to be taken by an administrative authority when legal conditions for exercise of powers are fulfilled; and 2) discretion in assessment (*beoordelingsvrijheid*), which means that an administrative authority itself determines whether the legal requirements for the exercise of powers have been met in the case at hand[6].

The division into "free competences and fettering competences of administration" is derived from tradition of the French law (*le pouvoir discrétionnaire – la competénce liée*)[7]. The first of these concepts refers to the sphere marked as *liberté de l'Administration*. As indicated by D. Truchet, determining the margin of this freedom is up to a judge, controlling a decision in its various aspects. So it is not the law, but a judge who is the most important link in the process of the establishment of this control[8]. In France, the scope of the administrative courts'

---

3 E. Schmidt-Aßmann, *Verwaltungsrechtliche Dogmatik*, Tübingen 2013, p. 85.
4 D.J. Galligan, *Discretionary Powers*, Oxford 1986, p. 9.
5 *Ibidem*, p. 10.
6 O.F. Essens, M.J.M. Verhoeven, *Traditional Variations in the Dutch Administrative Judicial System*, in: *Traditions and Change in European Administrative Law*, eds. R. Caranta, A. Gerbrandy, Groningen 2011, p. 170.
7 In the context of the legality principle C. Debbasch, F. Colin, *Droit administratif*, Paris 2014, p. 107–108.
8 D. Truchet, *Droit administratif*, Paris 2011, p. 218 and following.

jurisdiction is derived from the administration margin defined by the statute. Practically speaking, there are degrees of control exercised by a judge (*les degres du contrôle*). It may be normal control (*le contrôle normal*) or minimum control, also referred to as limited (*le contrôle minimum or restreint*)[9]. The latter is applied as a result of exercising an appeal in the form of *recours pour excés de pouvoir*[10].

In this paper, we use the term "administrative discretion" in the narrow sense, that is in conformity with views already well-established in Polish jurisprudence, including the deeply justified statement of M. Mincer[11]. It is worth mentioning that this point of view corresponds fully to the content of Recommendation No. R (80) 2 Concerning the Exercise of Discretionary Powers by Administrative Authorities, adopted by the Committee of Ministers of the Council of Europe on 11 March 1980. Under point 1 of the appendix to the Recommendation, "the term discretionary power means a power which leaves an administrative authority some degree of latitude as regards the decision to be taken, enabling it to choose from among several legally admissible decisions the one which it finds to be the most appropriate". Point 12 of the explanatory memorandum observes that the Recommendation does not apply to administrative decisions in those cases in which the legislator uses so-called "undetermined legal concept" (*un concept juridique dit indetermine, unbestimmter Rechtsbegriff*). Legal concepts within this category are not defined in detail by the legislator himself but nevertheless can have "an objective meaning which the administrative authority should identify in individual cases"[12].

Administrative discretion is always limited by law[13]. The degree of the margin associated with administrative discretion is of course varied, and depends on the legislator. This led F. Houle and L. Sossin to identify two types of decision-making which may be undertaken by the Canadian administrative authorities (tribunals): administrative and adjudicative ones. Administrative bodies which perform administrative decision-making functions are legislatively granted the power to

9 C. Debbasch, F. Colin, *op. cit.*, p. 688–690, D. Truchet, *op. cit.*, p. 219–220, and F. Colin, *Droit public*, Gualino éditeur 2014, p. 347–348.

10 F. Colin, *op. cit.*, p. 342 and following; more about this measure F. Brisson, *La recours pour excés de pouvoir: tendances récentes du contentieux administratif*, Elipses 2004.

11 M. Mincer, *Uznanie administracyjne*, Toruń 1983, especially p. 63 and following.

12 See also M. Wyrzykowski, *Pojęcie interesu społecznego w prawie administracyjnym*, Warszawa 1986, p. 49 and following, and Z. Kmieciak, Ogólne zasady prawa i postępowania administracyjnego, Warszawa 2000, p. 101–104.

13 W. Wade, C. Forsyth, *Administrative Law*, Oxford 2009, p. 286 and following.

exercise broad discretion. Adjudicative decision-making, however, is based on stricter criteria. This kind of activity is the closer to the idea of a court of justice[14].

2. The errors of administrative discretion

There are many typologies of discretion errors/illegality presented in the literature. These classifications result from the description of legal structures, formed in the course of judicial review of public administration and – to some extent – the solutions adopted in the positive law[15]. Generally speaking, two areas of discretion illegality can be identified in the European legal systems: 1) the failure to exercise discretion; and 2) the abuse of discretionary power[16]. Apart from these forms of illegality (*Ermessensunterschreitung* or *Ermessensnichtgebrauch,* and *Ermessensmissbrauch or Ermessensfehlgebrauch*), theories developed in the German legal culture additionally distinguish errors described as the excess of discretionary power (*Ermessensüberschreitung*)[17]. This occurs when authority goes beyond the statutorily determined legal consequences of the facts findings[18]. The internal and external bounds of discretion can be distinguished. The former (*"inneren" Ermessensgrenzen*) are reconstructed as a result of testing the compliance of administrative action with discretion purposes (*Ermessenseinräumung*). The external bounds of discretion (*"äußeren" Ermessensgrenzen*) are determined by the content of a statute. Their violation occurs when an authority sets non-statutory legal

---

14 F. Houle, L. Sossin, *Tribunals and Guidelines: Exploring the Relationship Between Fairness and Legitimacy in Administrative Decision-Making,* "Canadian Public Administration" 2006, vol. 49, No. 3, p. 296–297.

15 More about this see M. Mincer, *op. cit.*, p. 117–138 and M. Künnecke, *Tradition and Change in Administrative Law. An Anglo-German Comparison*, Berlin–Heidelberg 2007, p. 73 and following.

16 See for instance M. Künnecke, *op. cit.*, p. 83 and following, H. Maurer, *Ogólne prawo administracyjne/Allgemeines Verwalungsrecht*, Wrocław 2003, p. 94–96, W. Wade, C. Forsyth, *op. cit.*, p. 259 and following, and A. Carroll, *Constitutional and Administrative Law*, Harlow 2009, p. 322.

17 M. Künnecke, *op. cit.*, p. 89, T. von Danwitz, unter Mitarbeit von K. Ritgen, *Europäisches Verwaltungsrecht,* Berlin–Heidelberg, p. 368–370, F. von Alemann, *Die Handlungsform der interinstitutionellen Vereinbarung Eine Untersuchung des Interorganverhältnisses der europäischen Verfassung*, Berlin–Heidelberg–New York 2006, p. 305, and M. Jaśkowska, *Uznanie administracyjne a inne formy władzy dyskrecjonalnej administracji publicznej*, in: *System prawa administracyjnego*, t. 1 – *Instytucje prawa administracyjnego*, eds. R. Hauser, Z. Niewiadomski, A. Wróbel, Warszawa 2010, p. 277–279.

18 M. Jestaedt, *Maßstäbe des Verwaltunghandelns*, in: *Allgemeines Verwaltungsrecht*, hrsg. H.-U. Erichsen, D. Ehlers, Berlin–New York 2010, p. 375.

consequences of facts findings, or when it mistakenly assumes that it is entitled to rule based upon the discretionary power[19].

The concept which is mostly used in the French legal order is *excés de pouvoir*, distinguishing, however, variations of this illegality of an administrative activity. In accordance with the views grounded in case law, the substantial bounds of the administrative discretion, taken under consideration by courts in the course of judicial review, is the concept of the manifest error of appreciation (*l'erreur manifeste d'appréciation*). The limited scope of this control (*contrôle restreint*)[20] could be presented as follows:

> control of administrative discretion = normal control (*contrôle normal*) – legal classification of facts or events (*la qualification juridique des faits*) + the manifest error of appreciation (*l'erreur manifeste d'appréciation*)

The concept of abuse of power (*l'eccesso di potere*) adopted in Italy is the reflection of the findings of the French Council of State. The violations of law defined with this term include errors of a formal or material nature, such as internal inconsistency of a legal text, discrepancy of action's line (*disparità di trattamento*), defects in the instructional proceedings (*difetto d'instruttoria*), in findings of facts, or in justification of decision, blatant and obvious injustice (*ingiustizia grave e manifesta*), an obvious illogicality and breach of the proportionality principle[21].

A broad catalog of administrative discretion errors, well reflecting the ideas and structures developed in common law countries, was constructed by A. Carroll. A failure to exercise discretion occurs when an administrative authority: 1) delegates its power to decide to a subordinate without statutory body to do so (unlawful delegation); 2) allows its power to decide to be exercised by another and unauthorised body (surrender or abdication of discretion); 3) limits its freedom of action by rigid rules of policy (fettering discretion by policy); 4) restricts its power to decide by contractual obligations or other undertakings (fettering of discretion by contracts); or, 5) decides under the dictation of another authority or as a result of improper pressure[22]. Administrative authority abuses its discretion

---

19 *Ibidem*, p. 374–375.

20 See D. Truchet, *op. cit.*, p. 221.

21 R. Chieppa, R. Giovagnoli, *Manuale di diritto amministrativo*, Milano 2011, p. 353 and following, and E. Casetta, *Manuale di diritto amministrativo*, Milano 2011, p. 549 and following; as to the concept of discretional activity of administration see G. Rossi, *Principi di diritto amministrativo*, Torino 2010, p. 268 and following.

22 A. Carroll, *op. cit.*, p. 322–323; this kind of errors is also defined as "retention of discretion" – see W. Wade, C. Forsyth, *op. cit.*, p. 259.

(i.e. uses it unlawfully) if it: 1) takes into account wholly irrelevant or extraneous considerations or, conversely, fails to take into account that which was relevant (irrelevancy); or 2) uses its power to achieve a purpose or an objective which is not that for which the power was given (improper purpose). All these cases are treated by the author as *ultra vires* administration action.

However, the a subtle difference of opinion has appeared in the doctrine regarding the abovementioned qualification. As J. Adler states, an action presents the characteristics of *ultra vires* if a decision "is outside the language of the statute". In the light of case law of courts and administrative tribunals, "the terms «lack» or «excess» of jurisdiction mean the same as *ultra vires*, although a distinction is sometimes made between lacking jurisdiction at the outset and straying outsider jurisdiction by some subsequent defect"[23]. Considering the matter in this context, the author distinguishes "narrow" and "wide" *ultra vires*. He links the latter to errors described as improper purposes and irrelevant considerations and reminds at the same time that even though a decision maker (administrative body) "keeps within the express language of the statute, its motive may be improper or it may be influenced by irrelevant factors or it may overlook relevant factors". At the end of his argumentation he comes to the following conclusion: "This applies even where the statute appears to give the decision maker an unrestricted subjective discretion using such expressions as «if the minister thinks fit», since even the widest discretionary power is in principle reviewable"[24]. For the purpose of further considerations, it seems important to quote the classification of the grounds of judicial review in administrative cases.

In the opinion of J. Adler, this basis is formed by: 1) illegality – errors of law, and (in certain cases) errors of fact, fettering discretion, "narrow" *ultra vires*, and "wide" *ultra vires* in the sense of acting for an ulterior purpose, taking irrelevant factors into account or failing to take relevant factors into account; 2) irrationality in the sense of unreasonableness ("Wednesbury" test), and lack of proportionality; and,3) procedural impropriety – violating important statutory procedures, bias, lack of a fair hearing, and a failure to give reasons for a decision[25]. It is worth mentioning that errors classified as abuse of discretionary power create the grounds of

---

23 J. Adler, *General Principles of Constitutional and Administrative Law*, Palgrave Macmillan 2002, p. 369.

24 *Ibidem*, p. 374.

25 *Ibidem*, p. 368, similarly – D.J. Galligan, *op. cit.*, p. 266 and following, A.W. Bradley, K.D. Ewing, *Constitutional and Administrative Law*, Harlow 2007, p. 727 and following, and H. Barnett, *Constitutional and Administrative Law*, London–New York 2013, p. 594 and following.

review relating to the substance or content of the official decision (action) that is under review[26]. According to the research conducted by M. Künnecke, this basis largely overlaps with the criteria for adjudication by the German courts in cases of administrative discretion. They differentiate between two main types of errors, the first occurring within the decision-making process and the second – regarding the result of a decision in its substance[27].

In Poland, terms like "exceeding the bounds", or "exceeding the legal bounds of administrative discretion" are used regularly[28]. They traditionally refer to every error/ illegality of discretion, usually without making abuse of discretion a separate legal category. Austrian discourse formulated at the turn of the 19th and 20th century had a decisive influence on formation of the concept of discretion, its bounds and rules of control in the Polish legal system[29]. To some extent, they have been enriched with new, original components. Legislation and legal practice changes, which were made after the legal and political system transformation had started in Poland in 1989, show the tendency to reproduce very anachronistic schemes, conceived earlier.

3. Exceeding the bounds of administrative discretion in the Polish system of law

After Poland regained independence in 1918, administrative discretion was excluded from judicial review. The Article 3 point b of the Act of 3 August 1922 of the Supreme Administrative Tribunal stipulated that the jurisdiction of the Court established with that Act did not cover cases "in which administrative authorities are entitled to adjudicate based on free discretion, within the bounds provided for this discretion"[30]. The Act did not provide any definition of administrative discretion or its bounds. In the view of the authors of the bill, the decisions made within the free administrative discretion were excluded from the scope of the jurisdiction of the Tribunal due to the inability to combine "full" judicial review

26 See especially A.W. Bradley, K.D. Ewing, *op. cit.*, p. 727 and 729.

27 M. Künnecke, *op. cit.*, p. 89–92 and 110, B. Raschauer, *Allgemeines Verwaltungsrecht*, Wien–New York 2009, p. 214, and J. Bast, *Grundbegriffe der Handlungsformen der ED entwickelt am Beschluss als praxisgenerierter Handlungsform des Unions- und Gemeinschaftsrechts*, Berlin–Heidelberg–New York 2006, p. 64–65.

28 See for instance A. Habuda, *Granice uznania administracyjnego*, Opole 2004, *passim*.

29 D. Malec, *Najwyższy Trybunał Administracyjny 1922–1939 w świetle własnego orzecznictwa*, Warszawa- Kraków 1999, p. 84.

30 Journal of Laws of 1926, No. 68, item 400, as amended, consolidated text.

with the principle of government and ministers' responsibility for their actions. At that time it was feared, too, that such control would have been equivalent to the Tribunal (appointed to examine lawfulness of decisions) invading issues of expediency. Limiting the range of the judicial review of administrative decisions was also justified with practical considerations, namely the desire to prevent the Tribunal from the excessive burden of adjudication tasks[31].

When the Supreme Administrative Tribunal Act went into effect, it was accused of "sticking too much to Austrian patterns"[32]. The Czechoslovak Act of 2 November 1918, which was indicated as the pattern to be followed, did not exclude exercising administrative discretion from the scope of judicial review. At that time, the modification of the judicial review rules by granting an individual the right to bring claims corresponding to the French construction *recours pour excés de pouvoir* had already occurred[33]. The basic principles of examining whether the bounds of administrative discretion are exceeded were established when the Supreme Administrative Tribunal Act was in force. They are respected even now, in spite of two fundamental changes to the legal and political system, which took place in Poland after the Second World War and the transformation of administrative courts, including the reform of 2002. It should be remembered that the restriction of the Tribunal's jurisdiction was drawn by the words: "within the bounds left for this discretion".

The Tribunal therefore had the jurisdiction to examine whether administrative body using administrative discretion, had been entitled to do so by the statute, and whether it had not gone beyond the scope of the provided authority. Irrespective of that, the Tribunal had the right to make judgments whether the competent administrative body had breached the provisions of the administrative proceedings. In the event of finding the facts of the case had been established contrary to the documentation of the files, or had been incomplete, or that the administrative body had infringed the forms of administrative proceedings, the Tribunal was able

31 D. Malec, *op. cit.*, p. 83–87.

32 *Ibidem*, p. 86.

33 See for instance W.L. Jaworski, *Nauka prawa administracyjnego. Zagadnienia ogólne*, Warszawa 1924, p. 34, K.W. Kumaniecki, *Ustrój państwowych władz administracyjnych na ziemiach polskich*, Kraków 1921, p. 140, J.S. Langrod, *Zarys sądownictwa administracyjnego. Ze szczególnym uwzględnieniem sądownictwa administracyjnego w Polsce*, Warszawa 1925, p. 264–266, *idem*, *Kontrola administracji*, Warszawa-Kraków 1929, p. 149. The drafts of regulations on the administrative justice prepared by J.S. Langrod were placed in the latter paper; the clause of free discretion was excluded there.

to quash the decision even without public hearing[34]. This means that every decision issued within the administrative discretion could have become a subject of control from the standpoint of the procedure. Thus, the bounds of this discretion were also determined by procedural rules[35].

The criterion of the discretion correctness examination, defined as "arbitrariness of decision", has been hardly clear from the beginning. This negative feature is clearly different from the margin of an authority action which is allowed by the law and essence of discretion. The Supreme Administrative Tribunal first expressed its opinion on this matter in its judgment of 17 November 1922, L. Reg. 62/22. The following thesis was formulated: "if it was to be said that the supervisory authority had exceeded its free discretion or had gone so far that its decision had obvious features of total arbitrariness, the interference of Supreme Administrative Tribunal would be permissible"[36]. There was drawn the conclusion that usage of administrative discretion had to be consistent with the general principles of law, expressed in the Constitution and other laws.

Contemporary commentators of this judgment and the case law of administrative courts too often ignore the fact that there is clear distinction between two situations: exceeding the bounds of administrative discretion and the total arbitrariness of a decision. Keeping strictly to the reasoning presented by the Tribunal, we come to the conclusion that the second of these errors is a qualitatively different law violation than exceeding the bounds of discretion in any of the previously discussed forms. It is certainly something close to the French structure *l'erreur manifeste d'appréciation*, or illegality, defined in the legal order of the German language area or in the common law systems as abuse of discretion. Unfortunately, the analysis of case law of the Polish administrative courts does not indicate that in Poland this concept has been developed in as creative and thoughtful way as it has been in other countries. A natural way for the doctrine and the case law to follow would be to define clearly the grounds of review relating to the substance or content of an administrative decision. It seems to lack the creativity and persistence in searching for solutions that might improve the effectiveness of judicial protection by various forms of administrative discretion control. As a

34 See the Article 19 of the Act of the Supreme Administrative Tribunal, and the Article 84 of the ordonance of the President of the Republic of Poland of 27 October 1932 of the Supreme Administrative Tribunal (Journal of Laws of 1932, No. 94, item 806).

35 D. Malec, *op. cit.*, p. 86–87 and 92.

36 The sentence cited after D. Malec, *op. cit.*, p. 89.

consequence, this peculiarity with all the nuances of the substantive and procedural margin bounds of administrative action has not been examined in detail[37].

The problem is that after the reactivation of Polish administrative justice in 1980 under the provisions that do not explicitly exclude from judicial review the decisions taken within administrative discretion, we continue to move within the former and inevitably quite simplified scheme. The only limitation that must be taken into account by the administrative courts controlling activity of public administration is the very broad criterion of legality[38]. This criterion is used in the Article 1 § 2 of the Act of 25 July 2002 Law on the System of Administrative Courts. This provision stipulates: "the review […] shall be performed from the point of view of conformity with law, unless otherwise provided by statute". Article 145a § 1 of the Act of 30 August 2002 Law on Proceedings Before Administrative Courts[39], defining the jurisdiction competences in the scope of merits review, limited them as follows: "In the case referred to in the Article 145 § 1 point 1(a) or point 2, where the circumstances of the case so justify, the court shall oblige the authority to render a decision or order within a specified time limit, indicating the manner in which the case should be handled or determined, unless the determination was left to the discretion of the authority". Meanwhile Article 184 *ab initio* of the Constitution of the Republic of Poland states, that the Supreme Administrative Court and other administrative courts shall exercise control over the performance of public administration, to the extent specified by statute. This provision does not use the words "conformity with law", and refers to rules of control laid down in ordinary legislation.

Thus, both the Constitution and the statutes leave a wide margin of exercising the judicial control of discretion to administrative courts. The courts, however, are not provided with a pattern of control that would be powerful enough and methodologically correct. It is worth mentioning that the tendency to limit the legal forms of discretion control in the administrative procedure did appear in matters within the jurisdiction of independent adjudicating bodies (the local-government appeal boards)[40].

---

37 The justification for judicial review on substantive grounds in cases of abuse of discretion were presented by W. Wade, C. Forsyth, *op. cit.*, p. 287 and following, and A.W. Bradley, K.D. Ewing, *op. cit.*, p. 729.

38 As to the difficulties in differentiation between the judicial review of legality and expediency of administrative activity – see Z. Kmieciak, *Postępowanie administracyjne i sądowoadministracyjne a prawo europejskie*, Warszawa 2010, p. 120–122.

39 Journal of Laws of 2012, item 270, as amended, consolidated text.

40 See the Article 138 § 3 of the Act of 14 June 1960 – the Code of Administrative Procedure (Journal of Laws of 2016, item 23, consolidated text) binding in 1999–2003

4. Survey of the contemporary case law

A classic example of the understanding of the judicial review of decisions issued under the provisions constituting the discretionary power of an authority are the findings and assessments made in the judgment of the Supreme Administrative Court of 21 January 2016, II FSK 2978/13. In the case in which the judgment was formulated, the tax authorities stated that the condition of tax arrears deduction was fulfilled in the form of "vital interest of the taxpayer". Refusing to apply the tax relief, however, they relied on the margin associated with determination of the legal consequences of proven facts. Such a conclusion stemmed from the statutory provision using the following words: "the tax authority […] can". Examining the legality of the decision ending case, the administrative court of first instance probably considered the taxpayer's serious health condition and difficult financial situation. Quashing the contested decision, however, the court pointed out only procedural errors committed by the tax authorities – not substantive law errors, or an infringement corresponding to the structures of other legal systems, like "*l'erreur manifeste d'appréciation*", abuse of discretion/ *Ermessensmissbrauch* or *Ermessensüberschreitung*. The court obliged relevant authorities to reconsider, whether due to fulfilling the condition of "important interests of the taxpayer" (his difficult life situation), there are grounds to grant the requested relief. The Supreme Administrative Court considered the arguments of the administrative court of the first instance and dismissed the cassation appeal raised against the judgment. It underlined, however, that in the present case the judicial review was limited to "the analysis of the procedural aspects of the decision" due to "the discretionary nature of the controlled decision". This statement seems to suggest that administrative courts avoid testing the substantive bounds of administrative discretion and focus on procedural issues in situations similar to the one described above.

The Supreme Administrative Court aligned itself with a point of view presented above, in its judgment of 16 October 2008, II GSK 380/08. It stated that the "administrative discretion does not mean arbitrariness". Based on that statement, it drew the conclusion that due to the "achievements of the previous case law and the doctrine, the judicial review of the discretionary decisions is limited to compliance with the procedural rules in making them". The court justification cannot be regarded as consistent, as further on it contains the following observation: "Only correctly identified legal basis for the administrative action allows the

binding in 1999–2003, and still binding the Article 233 § 3 of the Act of 29 August 1997 – Tax Ordinance (Journal of Laws of 2016, item 613, as amended, consolidated text).

authority to consider all the relevant circumstances of the case, and this in turn determines taking the discretionary decision in accordance with the law". This consideration was supplemented with a statement that incorrectly determined legal basis of a decision results in the incorrect application of the provisions governing the authorization to occupy a road lane and the omission of a positive premise. Meanwhile, "only examining all the statutory conditions of granting a permit allows the authority to individualize the assessment and make a discretionary decision within the bounds of the law, with proper balancing of the public interest (protection of the lane and the road safety) and the interest of the party (special circumstances for granting a permit)". The court ultimately came to the conclusion that "basing the decision only on the procedural provision, which allows the authority to issue the decision and consider selectively the statutory premises for granting a permit to occupy a roadway, justifies raising the complaint of arbitrariness against the decision".

The conservative view expressed in the judgment of the Supreme Administrative Court of 25 February 2014, II FSK 666/12 fits the same trend of jurisprudence. It pointed out directly: "The discretionary nature of the tax authority's decision determines also the manner and scope of the legality control of such a decision by the administrative court". In the court's opinion, this control includes in fact the examination "whether during the proceedings the entire evidence material was collected, whether the relevant facts were explained and whether after the comprehensive and careful consideration of the collected material the premises conditioning the application of the [...] provision were assessed correctly". As it was highlighted, the judicial review of discretionary decision refers to "the procedure prior to its release, but not the decision itself, which is a result of making a specific choice".

Another, much more comprehensive, rational and coherent argumentation was presented in the judgment of the Supreme Administrative Court of 14 January 2011, I OSK 1496/10. It noted that "making decisions based on discretion cannot mean voluntarism or arbitrariness". Next, it reminded that the scope of discretionary power "is always determined by the law; and discretion framework is defined by the competence provisions, the proceeding rules and the substantive law". The Court also added that, by making a discretionary decision, "the authority is bound not only with the provision, but also with the purpose of the provision and established ethical standards". Administrative discretion does not permit an authority's "arbitrariness in dealing with the case, but at the same time does not oblige it to satisfy every demand of a citizen". Taking into account the conditions of an axiological nature, the Supreme Administrative Court finally came to the conclusion that the examined allegations of "the exceeding of discretion, abuse of discretion, or acting contrary to the purpose of discretion are groundless".

The more profound statement of the Supreme Administrative Court made in its judgment of 15 November 1999, V SA 820/99 deserves an equally positive assessment. It was pointed out that the authorities presented the "mistaken" view on administrative discretion. As it was noted by the court, both administrative instances accepted that discretion "means the inadmissibility of a decision made in favour of the party until the authority does not possess an internal belief about the purposefulness of such a decision". The subjective part of administration beliefs – as it was remarked – is the unknowable sphere both for the court, and for the applicant. Administrative discretion is, however, a sphere within which an official is entitled to interpret a statute in the name and on behalf of the state with increased personal responsibility. Recalling the judgment of the Supreme Administrative Court of 11 June 1981, SA 820/81[41], it was noted that "if in matters left by the statutory provisions to the administrative discretion, the public interest does not preclude it and it is possible for the administration, that authority is obliged to settle matter in favor of the party". In this way, the Article 7 of the Code of Administrative Procedure creates the "presumption of positive outcome, unless there is no real possibility (positive outcome is impossible for factual reasons) or a positive outcome is against the public interest". Referring clearly to the structures developed in the foreign legal orders, the court judged that "administrative discretion is sometimes understood incorrectly". In its opinion, occasionally, discretion is used improperly; common mistakes while using discretion include: 1) exceeding the discretion bounds set by a statute; 2) failure to recognize the bounds of discretion occurring, among others, when an administrative body does not make use of the granted authority or does not cover it entirely; 3) abuse of discretion, which occurs when the decision is within the law, but the authority uses discretion in a different purpose or in a different way than it is provided by the law; 4) limiting use of discretion by "narrowing" its field, or as a result of occurrence of certain events, for example threat of serious damage; or, 5) violation of an individual's constitutional rights or the fundamental principles of the law. In case in which the complaint was lodged, the court discovered the "abuse of administrative discretion", involving the absence of indication what kind of general considerations (threat to general good) and which specific circumstances justified a refusal of permission to settle

---

41 "Orzecznictwo Sądów Polskich i Komisji Arbitrażowych" 1982, No. 1–2, item 22, with gloss of J. Łętowski.

for an immigrant. Referring to the arbitrariness of the decision was then classified as defective in the light of the statutory premises of the adjudication.

Without investigating the question of methodological correctness of the classification of administrative discretion errors presented by the Supreme Administrative Court, it should be indicated that even when the concept of discretion abuse is used, the definition of the premises justifying this assessment causes many difficulties. The Polish courts usually stop at recalling generally described substantial aspects of discretion, without specifying them in the reasons for a decision. The role of control criterion of administrative discretion is performed therefore by general clauses, such as the principle formulated in the Article 7 of the Code of Administrative Procedure, or constitutional norms. This tendency is presented in the statement put in the judgment of the Supreme Administrative Court of 4 November 1999, III SA 7860/98[42]. The court did not agree with the tax authorities' point of view that the provisions which form the basis for making discretionary decisions, after fulfilling their conditions (examining the premises of important interest of taxpayer and the public interest), "allow the authorities in any such case to make any decision they consider as suitable". This practice was classified as the example of abuse of administrative discretion. The court also explained that the discretion is "is not of the same free nature, as it used to be under the legislation of the interwar period". The cases in which authorities were entitled to adjudicate in accordance with so understood discretion were excluded from the jurisdiction of the Supreme Administrative Tribunal. The court pointed to the fact that public authorities acting within discretion are primarily obliged to respect the legal order resulting from the Constitution and cannot be restricted to the application of the statutory provisions, directly relating to the case in question. In its opinion, there may be "cases in which in the binding legal order, the instructions limiting the margin of decision result from the norms included in the acts having priority over the statute (that is in the Constitution or international agreements ratified upon prior consent granted by the statute)".

The Supreme Administrative Court made the equally radical and widely justified statement in the judgment of 2 March 2016, II FSK 2474/15[43]. It stated that avoidance by the administrative court of the first instance of the merits of administrative discretion and confining itself to assessment of the formal aspect of case (whether a decision of the tax authorities complies with the procedural

42 LEX No. 40672.

43 http://orzeczenia.nsa.gov.pl//cbo/query.

rules) violates the Article 77 section 2 of the Constitution of Republic of Poland by barring the recourse by any person to the courts[44].

5. Exceeding the bounds of administrative discretion or abuse of discretion?

The abovementioned examples confirm the correctness of the thesis about the inadequacy, not to say the disability, of the scheme of administrative discretion control, adopted by the Polish courts. As far as this problem is concerned, little has changed since discretion was excluded from the judicial review. The role of a court was then, and is now, to examine whether the legal bounds of administrative discretion have been exceeded. Our research shows that judgments, in which the courts directly indicate an infringement of those bounds as a result of abuse of discretion, or committing a differently defined error of a material nature are rare. We believe, that it is necessary to go beyond this scheme which has been fixed for a long time, and to introduce – like other countries do – more sophisticated forms exercising the discretionary power control. Realization of this requirement does not mean the rejection of the concept of exceeding the legal bounds of administrative discretion.

The meaning of the presented suggestion boils down rather to a clear distinction between the formal and substantive bounds of administrative discretion and a precise definition of the relations between them. This operation would "call things by their names" and provide the administrative courts with a more effective and useful means of protection. Currently, these courts too often use a kind of camouflage, qualifying an insult of an obviously different nature (substantial errors) as an infringement of procedural law. As a result of this, many judgments are inconsistent with regard to indicating the criteria (basis) of judicial review and reconstructing their significance. This practice can to some extent be explained by the technical defects (deficiency of the methodology of judge-made adjudication). Of course, it does not undermine the overall conclusion about the general assessment of the judicial review of administrative discretion in Poland.

Particularly promising perspectives for Polish administrative justice are created by constructing abuse of discretion in two versions: "irrelevancy" and "improper purpose". Adopting it, thus adapting the concept of judicial review on substantive

44 According to the Article 77 section 2 of this Act, "Statutes shall not bar the recourse by any person to the courts in pursuit of claims alleging infringement of freedoms or rights", see also L. Garlicki, *Komentarz do art. 77 Konstytucji,* in: *Konstytucja Rzeczypospolitej Polskiej. Komentarz,* ed. L. Garlicki, Warszawa 2007, p. 23–31.

grounds with different cultural background, would closely correspond – contrary to appearances – to the findings of the native doctrine regarding the "external bounds of administrative discretion". Contrary to occasional fears, the postulate elaborated in this study is not inconsistent with the essence of judicial review. In Poland, the traditional point of reference for it is the conformity with law as regards public administration engaging in or refraining from activity. We are not sure if we have fully exploited the potential interpretation of this concept, which is too often understood in the simplest – which does not always mean correct – way. It appears to be true, what A.W. Bradley and K.D. Ewing said: "judicial review is no substitute for administrative or political control of the merits, expediency or efficiency of decisions". That said, the authors believe that the courts are able to ensure that decisions made by administrative authorities conform to the substantial law and the standards of the fair procedure are observed[45]. There is no reason not to apply this rule in the sphere of administrative discretion. The only question which arises is: how to reconcile the abovementioned, Constitution-based rule with the requirements of efficiency, flexibility, economy and effectiveness of administration? The source of inspiration for forming appropriate legal solutions – both by the legislature and case law – should be both our own tradition and the experience of other countries more advanced in the development of the Rule of Law.

45 A. W. Bradley, K. D. Ewing, *op. cit.*, p. 725.

Part II

Adam Szot
(Ph. D., Maria Curie-Sklodowska University in Lublin, Poland)

Discretionary powers of the public administration in law application processes and its judicial control[1]

Abstract: The objective of this work is to demonstrate the expressions of the discretionary powers of the public administration in the process of the issuing of binding individual legal decisions and the scope in which the judicial control of the administration can verify the correctness of activities of the administration within the limits of its margin of decision.

Keywords: Discretionary power, judicial control of the administration, law application, law interpretation

1. Introductory remarks

Having in mind the need to create opportunities for public administration agencies to adapt their actions to individual situations and needs in the dynamically changing social reality, the legislator grants them a specific scope of decision-making margins, i.e. discretionary powers. At the same time, there are also other sources of such powers in the law application process, emerging irrespectively of the legislature's intention.

The objective of this publication is to show the expressions of the actual discretionary powers of the public administration in law application processes, i.e. the processes of the issuing of binding legal decisions shaping, in a dominant manner, the rights and obligations of an individual as well as the degree to which they are or can be subjected to the control of an independent court. This approach differs from the one presented in the literature so far for two principal reasons: (1) it refers to the search for sources of the actual scope of the margin of decision and

1 This paper emerged in connection with the realisation of a research project financed from the funds of the National Centre of Science granted pursuant to the decision number DEC-2013/11/N/HS5/04212. entitled: "The influence of judicial decisions on the discretionary power of public administration in the law application processes" ["Wpływ orzeczeń sądowych na dyskrecjonalną władzę administracji publicznej w procesach stosowania prawa"]. Deliberations contained in this publication were described more extensively in the monograph: A. Szot, *Swoboda decyzyjna w stosowaniu prawa przez administrację publiczną*, Lublin 2016.

not only that part of it that results from the contents of legal norms, and (2) it is analysed in an comprehensive manner with regard to particular phases of the law's application process while most of the research conducted so far concentrated on some of them only. The continental legal culture is at the background of the analysis and, for the sake of the greater clarity of the discussion, references are made to solutions existing in the Polish legal order.

The descriptive model of the law application process in its administrative type does not principally differ from the court model of law application. From the decision-making perspective[2], it covers lines of reasoning of an entity applying the law, each of them ending with the making of a fragmentary decision, pursued to issue the final decision with the specified content. The process consists of two main phases, i.e. preparatory phase during which the decision maker ascertains the facts and the legal status of the case and the principal phase directly leading to the formulation of the final decision, covering the qualification of facts from the perspective of the reconstructed normative basis for a decision and the determination of consequences of such a qualification. In the case of the administrative type of law application, one more stage that chronologically precedes all the lines of reasoning mentioned above has to be included in the said model. It is the pre-decision phase, when a decision is made to commence the law application process, i.e. its existence is determined.

The discretionary power of a public administration body in the process of law application can be understood as an actual possibility for the administering entity to select one of the alternative, legally permissible, contents of fragmentary decisions being a part of that process that, in the agency's opinion, are supposed to lead to the issue of the final decision most comprehensively attaining the assumed goal in line with the adopted administrative policy, within the limits determined by the law in force.

2. Discretionary powers of the administration – different perspectives

The discretionary powers of the administration can be analysed from two different perspectives, i.e. from a dynamic perspective (related to the decision-making process i.e. ordered sequence of actions) or a static perspective (covering the

2 See A. Korybski, L. Leszczyński, *Decision making approach in a study of the enactment and application of law: A pragmatic context of legal theory*, [in:] *Legal Theory and Philosophy of Law: Toward Contemporary Challenges*, eds. A. Bator, Z. Pulka, Warszawa 2013, p. 156–181.

analysis of sources of discretionary power from the point of view of the scope and type of discretion available to the decision maker).[3]

The static perspective refers to the search for sources of the discretionary power at different stages of the law's application process and, in particular, focuses (from the perspective of jurisprudence) on the study of binding legal norms. However, it should be noted that, in addition to freedoms resulting from the conscious decision of the legislature, other sources can also exist in the decision-making processes. The Polish theory of law makes a distinction between "explicit freedoms" and "hidden freedoms". The first group of freedoms is linked to the legislature's deliberate use in the law-making processes of constructions granting a certain range of margin of decision to entities applying the law (e.g. general clauses). The second group of freedoms is a consequence of specific processes of creation and application of the law and the editing of legal provisions and their interpretation. Freedoms deliberately created by the legislature are part of a specific concept of the law making policy implemented with the use of appropriate technical and legal means.[4] L. Leszczyński mentions the following legislative measures modelling the conscious scope of the margin of decision: the way in which legal provisions are formulated and normative acts are constructed (e.g. the use of vague concepts, avoidance of legal definitions, constructing framework legal acts), creation of extra-legal references via which the legal system opens to extra-legal criteria and the use of the administrative discretionary authority concept in the administrative law.[5] The author distinguishes the following sources of decision-making freedoms independent of the legislature's will: the social context of the law (expressed as a possibility for a decision-making entity to extend the application of a legal norm to include situations not foreseen by the legislature and in the use of social values), characteristics of the legal language and characteristics of the law application process (resulting from reductionist reasoning taken up in the course of the process or free evaluation of evidence).[6] Therefore, an in-depth analysis of this issue requires the grasping of the complexity of the reasoning at each stage of that process, considering both those sources of freedom that were generated deliberately and those sources that are modelled independently from the legislature's intention.

3 M. Król, *Pojęcie luzu normatywnego stosowania prawa*, "Państwo i Prawo" 1979, No. 6, p. 62.
4 L. Leszczyński, *Zagadnienia teorii stosowania prawa. Doktryna i tezy orzecznictwa*, Zakamycze 2001, p. 43.
5 Ibid., p. 43–45.
6 Ibid., p. 41–43.

The scope of the decision-making discretion available to the entity applying the law is determined by the contents of legal norms; it also results from the specificity and complexity of decision-making processes and the social reality in which such processes take place and in which the administering entities operate. This fact authorises an important thesis: that there are no decision-making processes in which the entity applying the law would have not even the minimum degree of freedom (scope of discretion).

In turn, the dynamic perspective on decision-making freedoms assumes that the final decision is reached via the gradual elimination and ruling out of abstractly defined alternative choices.[7] The elimination of individual potential choices takes place in stages as the facts of the case are learned and as their complete establishment approaches.

The understanding of the discretionary power mentioned at the beginning as an actual possibility of choice (irrespectively of its source) as one of the alternatives for the applying entity corresponds with the concept of the discretionary power used in the Anglo-Saxon literature when referring to the public administration.[8]

Two approaches to the discretionary power can be observed in European law: the narrower one (in principle, identifying that power with the possibility to choose the settlement method) and the wider one (including decision-making freedoms accompanying different stages of law application). However, the wide definition of the discretionary power that means: "all ways in which the law grants the flexibility right to an agency applying the law, leaves a certain degree of the decision-making power to it, both intentionally and unintentionally" prevails in this law and in the judgements of the Court of Justice of the European Union and the European Court of Human Rights.[9]

---

7 Ibid. p. 63.

8 See, among other things, D. J. Galligan, *Discretionary powers – a Legal Study of Official Discretion,* Oxford 1986, passim; Ch. C. Eriksen, *The European Constitution, Welfare State and Democracy. The four freedoms vs. national administrative discretionary authority,* Routledge 2011, passim; Ch. C. Eriksen, *The Expansion of International Law and the Use of National Administrative discretionary authority: The Impact on Administrative Battlefields,* New York 2013, passim; G. E. Treves, *Administrative discretionary authority and judicial control,* "The Modern Law Review" 1947, vol. 10, p. 276–291.

9 More in: M. Jaśkowska, *Uznanie administracyjne a inne formy władzy dyskrecjonalnej administracji publicznej,* [in:] *System prawa administracyjnego,* vol. 1: *Instytucje prawa administracyjnego,* eds. R. Hauser, Z. Niewiadomski, A. Wróbel, Warszawa 2010, p. 292–298 and the case law cited there.

One example of a narrow approach to the discretionary power is the Recommendation of the Committee of Ministers of the Council of Europe of 11.03.1980 concerning the exercise of discretionary power by administrative authorities[10] that defines discretionary power as a power which leaves an administrative authority some degree of latitude as regards to the decision to be taken, enabling it to choose, from among several legally admissible decisions, the one which it finds to be the most appropriate.

The above-mentioned definition can be interpreted as referring to the reasoning of the entity applying the law at the last stage of the process, i.e. the margin of decision formulation. Therefore, it will be identical with the concept of the "administrative discretionary authority approval" – the possibility of choice from among two or more legally admissible and legally equivalent contents of the final decision in the law application process. It also seems that a different understanding is possible.

If we adopt the decision-making perspective of the law application as the starting point we will observe that the process consists of a range of lines of reasoning, each of them ending with the issue of a decision: a fragmentary decision. Therefore, the definition of the discretionary power introduced in the above-mentioned Recommendation can be applied to each expression of freedom at all stages of the process and is equivalent to the concept of the decision-making freedom proposed above. There is no doubt that the adoption of this reasoning has one advantage: it expands the scope of provisions of the Recommendation to include all lines of reasoning pursued by administering agencies in the law application process.

Irrespectively of whether the decision-making latitude is intentional or not, the agency applying the law cannot choose a fragmentary decision going beyond the legal framework of its operation. Therefore, there is no unbounded margin of decision or "discretion"[11].

Discretionary power is an actual freedom, i.e. it covers both freedom in the legal sense and unintentional discretionary powers. The legal existence of the margin of decision is implied, in particular, by the legislature's purpose principles and technical legal barriers resulting from the imperfection of the legislative technique.[12]

10 Recommendation No R (80) 2 of the Committee of Ministers concerning the exercise of discretionary powers by administrative authorities.

11 The concept of "discretion" was used in the 1980ies. More in: Z. Duniewska, *Istota i granice dyskrecjonalnej władzy administraċyjnej w świetle standardów europejskich*, "Studia Prawno-Ekonomiczne" 1999, R. LIX, p. 12.

12 Ibid., p. 13.

3. Discretionary powers of the administration in the law application process

The margin of decision refers to all lines of reasoning pursued by the entity applying the law. At the same time, it should be analysed for each of them separately due to their complexity in individual phases of the process. Therefore, we can talk about the margin of decision as regards the making of a decision to initiate the law application process, freedom related to the determination of facts and interpretation of the law and, finally, freedom as regards the qualification of facts in any particular case, determination of consequences of such a qualification and justification of the decision.

(a) Initiation of the law application process

The decision to initiate the process aimed at the issue of an individual and authoritative resolution by an administrative agency with regard to an entity is first on the list of fragmentary decisions on which the entire procedure depends. Discretionary power as a part of the pre-decision phase depends on whether the legislature, in the laws in force, links the appearance of a specific fact (e.g. the submission of an application for an administrative decision within the limits of the entity's legal interest) to the obligation to examine the case, or rather leaves it to the discretion of the entity applying the law.

Such a situation of co-existence of a legal norm and a fact can be defined as a decision-making situation, i.e. the moment when the problem to be solved by the agency arises. Its occurrence causes the preliminary reflection of the decision-maker regarding the subject of the case, the decision-makers' potential competence as regards dealing with the case and the initial determination of the procedure and possible resolutions. It can also result in the making of a decision to initiate the law application process and pass to the complete determination of facts of the case and the reconstruction of the normative basis for the decision and, after that, the issue of a final decision. However, the administering agency deals with a potential administrative case up to that point.

In addition to cases of the explicit undertaking of an agency to take action, situations worth noting are those in which further proceedings will depend on that agency's decision (made within the limits of its discretionary power). The administering entity will be free to make a decision to commence the decision-making process, among others, when the legislature entrusts specific tasks to it but does not indicate the method of their execution. In such a situation, the agency is obliged to choose the action that attains the determined goal as fully as possible considering the complex conditions in which it operates and means it has at its disposal. Such actions can include the issue of a decision to apply the law (one or more decisions) subject to the fact that it is a legally admissible action, i.e. there is a competence norm in the legal system that authorises the agency to act in this manner.

(b) Determination of facts of the case

The determination of facts of the case takes place in conjunction with the validation and interpretation reasoning, which allows the entity to specify the range of facts to be proven in the case. The rules of the substantive law in force specify the catalogue of facts of the case that have to be determined prior to the issue of a decision regarding a specific case. The margin of any decision of administrative agencies regarding the determination of facts related to the case depends on how strongly that process is determined by the legal norms. They can indicate facts that have to be determined in a more or less detailed manner, or they can impose an obligation on the agency to carry out specific evidence (e.g. site visit, the hearing of a party).

The more casuistic the legal regulation, the narrower the scope of discretionary power of the administration, which has to act in line with the pattern of behaviour contained in the legal norm. Of course, it does not mean that a more general legal norm entails greater freedom for the agency, as the facts determined at least to a degree that is "sufficient" to make a decision is the basis for each law application process and there is always a legal norm or a legal principle putting the decision-maker under the obligation to determine the facts as comprehensively as possible (for example, art.7 of the Polish Code of Administrative Procedures at the same time being a legal principle provides that ["in the course of] the procedure, public administration agencies [...]take all action *ex officio* or at the request of parties as necessary to determine the facts accurately [...]").

However, irrespectively of the scope of determination with the contents of legal norms, it is worth noting that certain facts that the administrative agency will strive to determine are specified in the evaluative form in the law in force, while individual facts and the entire evidence material is subject to the decision-makers' evaluation. The first of these issues is a consequence of the necessity to determine the facts expressed by the legislature in a manner that requires certain evaluations, which entails the need for more complex efforts (than in the case of facts expressed descriptively) in order to ascertain their existence; it will entail the establishment of the occurrence of a certain fact and, after that, its evaluation.[13]

13 More in: J. Wróblewski, *Sądowe stosowanie prawa*, Warszawa 1988, p. 190–192. More extensively about assessment expressions in the interpretation and application of the

The latter of the said issues, i.e. the evaluation of facts and of the entire evidence material refers to the evaluation of the reliability and sufficiency of evidence in order to demonstrate a specific circumstance and, after that (at the stage of the final qualification of facts), to evaluate the sufficiency of determined facts (collected evidence) in order to issue a law application decision.

(c) Determination of the legal basis of the decision

The margin of decision being a part of the determination of the legal status of the case refers to two lines of reasoning in this phase of the law application process, i.e. validation reasoning and derivative reasoning. The former is related to the determination of the source of a legal norm while the latter is related to the reconstruction of legal content from that source. When analysing these issues, one has to find out to what degree the decision-makers are obliged to consider specific sources in the law application process, and to what degree it has freedom in this area; whether it can refuse to apply a source whose validity it ascertained and, finally, how it should carry out the normative reconstruction process and what it can or should do in the event of an ambiguity of meaning, establishment of the existence of a conflict or a loophole in the law. Due to drafting constraints of this publication, it shall be limited to just a few most important issues here.

At the stage of the validation reasoning, the margin of decision depends on the "characteristics of the validity criteria and on the adopted law validity concept".[14] As regards the legal regulations being the basic source of the law in the continental legal culture, it is the reference to their thetic justification. In turn, the use of other law application decisions (precedents) or non-legal criteria as validation arguments in the interpretation process requires the use of arguments whose nature is functional and axiological. The scope of the discretionary power of the administration at the validation stage also depends on the type of the reconstructed legal norm (competence, procedural or material norms).

The margin of decision of the administering entity at the stage of the reconstruction of a norm from legal regulations has to be viewed from two perspectives,

---

administrative law: L. Leszczyński, *Interpretacyjna rola kryteriów otwartych i innych decyzji stosowania prawa*, [in:] *System prawa administracyjnego*, vol. 4: *Wykładnia w prawie administracyjnym*, eds. R. Hauser, Z. Niewiadomski, A. Wróbel, Warszawa 2012, p. 340–345. See also the SAC judgement of 10.07.2012, II OSK 694/11, CBOSA; SAC judgement of 14.06.2011, II OSK 1092/10, CBOSA.

14 J. Wróblewski, *Decyzja sądowa a koncepcja systemu prawa*, "Acta Universitatis Lodziensis, Zeszyty Naukowe UŁ Nauki Humanistyczno-Społeczne" 1978, issue 28.

i.e. the freedom of choice of interpretation rules and the method of its execution as well as the freedom to depart from the literal content of a regulation. The former is linked directly to the reconstruction of the normative basis for a decision and refers to each law application process. The entity applying the law will encounter the latter after the end of the reconstruction process if interpretation results obtained with the use of different interpretation rules diverge.

(d) Qualification of facts and determination of legal consequences

The issue of a final decision and the end of the law application process is preceded by the qualification of all the collected facts from the perspective of the interpreted normative basis for a decision. The qualification involves "checking" whether both factual backgrounds, i.e. the factual background of the case and an abstract background covered in the norm overlap with each other.

Therefore, the statement that components of the determined factual background fill the scope of legal norm requires a "comparison" of the actual fact with a fact stated abstractly, which can frequently entail significant difficulties.[15] For example, difficulties can result from the method of creation of legal regulations and edition of the legal text when the legislature departs from the creation of legal definitions or uses general clauses. An imprecise specification of concepts related to facts of the case in a legal norm, frequently expressed in an assessing manner, entails the granting of a certain discretionary power to the agency applying the law in connection with their qualification.[16]

The end of the fact qualification process from the perspective of the qualification norm leads to the stage of formulation of the final decision. Referring to the concept of J. Wróblewski, we can distinguish – with certain remarks – two types of situations involving the legal determination of the content of such a decision in the law application process by legal norms. On the one hand, these are cases in which the ascertainment of specific facts of the case, by the agency, results in the issue of a single-content decision. On the other hand, there are situations in which the legislature leaves a certain margin of decision in the form of the possibility to choose alternative contents of the final decision.[17]

15 See L. Leszczyński, *Zagadnienia teorii stosowania prawa…*, p. 73.

16 See B. Wojciechowski, *Model zakresu swobody interpretacyjnej prawa administracyjnego*, [in:] *System prawa administracyjnego*, vol. 4: *Wykładnia w prawie administracyjnym*, op. cit., p. 452.

17 More in: J. Wróblewski, *Sądowe stosowanie prawa*, op. cit., p. 240–242.

The former situation arises if consequences of the occurrence of facts of the case are determined in an unambiguous, categorical and unconditional manner. In such a situation, the decision-maker has no possibility of evaluation of the grounds for the issue of a decision with the defined content. In such a situation, if the legal norm unambiguously determines legal consequences of a fact, the resolution of the case is fully determined by that norm.[18] In the Polish doctrine, such situations are called "constrained decisions" in contrast to decisions with regard to which the agency has a certain degree of discretion.

The latter situation occurs if the legal norm grants some discretion to the decision-makers, involving the opportunity to choose from among various consequences. As J. Wróblewski stressed, that latitude is subsequently constrained by consequence choice directives[19] that constrain, in a varied manner, the freedom that the legislature initially granted to the decision-maker in the norm granting the right to issue such a decision. The Polish doctrine of the administrative law uses the concept of the "administrative discretionary authority" to describe such cases, indicating that the difference between decisions based on discretion and constrained decisions, is of a different method of formation of the substantive legal basis.[20]

(e) Justification of the final decision

The justification of the law application decision in the physical and procedural sense appears chronologically after its issue; however, it is essentially "constructed" by the administering entity throughout the entire process.[21]

The margin of decision related to the justification of decisions has to be viewed from two perspectives, i.e. determination of whether an agency is obliged to issue the justification in a formal sense or whether it belongs to its discretionary power and, secondly, the specification of the content of the justification itself or the freedom to choose arguments.

---

18 See ibid., p. 215.

19 Ibid., p. 241–242.

20 M. Mincer, *Uznanie administracyjne*, Toruń 1983, p. 152.

21 More in: L. Leszczyński, *Zagadnienia teorii stosowania prawa...*, p. 77. A similar approach to the process of "generation" of the statement of reasons is presented by J. Zimmermann (*Polska jurysdykcja administracyjna*, Warszawa 1996, p. 133) who writes that the justification of a decision "should not be an action that, in the course of jurisdiction activities, occupies a separate, closed section of time after the formulation of the administrative settlement. The justification cannot be «made» as an addition to the finished settlement [...]".

The legislature determines the range of freedom of the administering agency deciding to "express" the statement of reasons for the final decision. The binding art.107 of the Polish Code of Administrative Procedures explicitly indicates cases in which this obligation is imposed on the entity applying the law and when the entity can abstain from it.[22]

In turn, the entity has more margin of decision at the stage of the determination of the justification's content, i.e. the choice of arguments to be included in it. However, this freedom is not unlimited. The administering entity is bound by legal norms and the axiology expressed in legal principles.

4. Judicial control of the administration vs. its discretionary power

The control exercised by the courts over the administration is mostly the control of its activities in compliance with the law. The verification of the way in which the agency uses its margin of decision at this stage of the decision to commence the law application process entails two key problems: whether the agency took action in a situation in which it was obliged to do so and whether it exceeded the limits of its authority (whether it acted within the legally determined limits).

In cases initiated *ex officio* in connection with the reaction to the factual background, the scope of the verification will mostly depend on the degree to which the agency is bound with the occurrence of specific facts. If the legislature links the occurrence of such a fact with the consequence in the form of the obligatory initiation of the formal administrative procedure, the control will involve checking whether the agency correctly "reacts" to the occurrence. In that case, the evaluation of compliance with the law of the action taken by the administering agency will be of primary importance. If the legal norms impose the obligation on the agency to behave in a specific manner at the moment of learning about the occurrence of a relevant fact, the failure to comply with this obligation shall equal the violation of the legal norms. The inactivity of the public administration agency can constitute the grounds for a complaint to an administrative court in the Polish legal system.

22 "Art. 107. (...)§ 4. It is possible to depart from the justification of a decision if it fully accepts the claim of a party; however, this possibility does not apply to decisions disposing of disputable interests of parties and decisions issued as a result of an appeal. § 5. An agency can also abstain from the justification of a decision if the existing statutory regulations provide for the possibility to abstain from or limit the justification in the context of the interest of the State security or public order."

At the same time, situations in which the initiation of the law application process depends only on the agency's decision and, as such, is not subjected to the verification from the perspective of the legality criterion remain beyond the scope of the evaluation by the court and thereby also outside the scope of the possibility of a complaint to a court for the agency's failure to act. However, a situation seems possible in which a citizen invokes the proportionality principle and submits a court complaint against the decision made against that citizen if the agency had a different (non-authoritative) opportunity to resolve the case (attain the assumed goal).

Verification of the reasoning of the administration agency leading to the cognition of facts of the case refers to checking how the agency ascertained these facts, and whether the collected material is complete and was correctly evaluated. Finally, the way in which facts are "highlighted" in the justification of a decision is subjected to an evaluation. Therefore, it is checked as to whether the administering agency determined the factual background with the use of legally permissible measures, in line with the procedure in force, including the instigation of all measures of inquiry required under the law and determined all facts of the case, in particular, the facts that it was obliged to determine under the legal norms and, finally, whether its evaluation of individual facts and the entire material collected was correct and whether it stated the reasons for its decision in line with code requirements.

The legal status of an administrative case and the method of its determination by the administering agency, in particular, the final result in the form of a normative base for a decision and the compliance of the agency's actions with it is the key concern of the court verifying the activities of the public administration. The related reasoning will be reduced to the confrontation of results of the agency's interpretation with a specific norm, i.e. results of the interpretation received by the court. Such confrontation leads to a conclusion regarding the compliance or divergence of these two components and the conclusion involves the evaluation of the correctness of the validation and derivation reasoning.

According to the said art.107 of the Polish Code of Administrative Procedures, the content of an administrative decision should contain, among other things, an indication of the legal basis for an action and the statement of legal reasons. It entails the need to refer to the content of legal regulations in a decision and "explain their meaning" to the addressee. Of course, a separate issue is whether the agency in its justification of the decision demonstrates all validation and derivation arguments that actually influenced the final normative decision, or whether all the arguments it refers to reflect its actual reasoning or some of them are mentioned as a "decoration" only.

The verification of the reasoning aimed at the determination of the legal background of the case consists of the verification of the interpretation reasoning with regard to the determination of the authority of the agency to resolve the case, procedural actions to be taken in the course of the process, as well as the material aspects of the process and the final decision. The court shall verify both the selection of appropriate sources of the law and the determination of their validity and applicability[23] as well as the correctness of the determination of the contents of the legal norms. It means that the reconstruction process and its final effect in the form of a norm to be applied will be examined.

As regards the final decision formulation stage, the judicial control over the activities of the administration being a part of the administrative discretionary authority is particularly interesting. The fact that a decision is based on a norm authorising the administrative discretionary authority, does not rule out such control; however, it entails the limitation of its scope. If such a norm grants the possibility to choose legal consequences to the entity then each choice within the limits of its discretion is legal and cannot be undermined by the court. The court examines the decision's compliance with the law but does not examine its fairness or efficacy.[24] Therefore, the control over such decisions does not involve the examination of the content of the resolution itself but rather of the way in which the agency reached a specific resolution and whether that resolution is "within the limits" defined by the law.

This control is reduced to the verification of whether the issue of a decision was preceded by a correctly executed procedure, in particular, whether all necessary steps were taken to accurately clarify the factual background and whether the legal background of the case was correctly determined. When doing that, the court cannot limit itself to the acknowledgement of the existence of the legal basis for the issue of a decision based on discretion only; it also has to check whether the agency considered all regulations (legal norms) potentially applicable to the case.[25]

The justification is a component of the decision based on administrative discretionary authority that should be analysed in depth by the administrative court. A correctly constructed statement of reasons makes it possible to check whether the administrative agency executed the procedure correctly (correctly determined

---

23 Among other things, see SAC judgement of 13.12.2007, I FSK 114/07, CBOSA.

24 See the SAC judgement of 10.07.2009, I OSK 1293/08, CBOSA.

25 See the judgement issued by the SAC in Warsaw on 26.05.1981, SA 810/81, CBOSA; SAC in Warsaw judgement of 11.02.1981, SA 233/81, CBOSA.

the factual and legal background). However, its control should not be limited to checking whether the justification contains all the components specified in the regulations "surface structure"; it should also verify whether the justification follows the principle of persuasion and the principle of promotion of the citizens' confidence in the agencies "deep structure". In particular, a negative resolution should be justified persuasively and clearly when it comes to facts and the law, so that there is no doubt that all circumstances of the case were deeply considered and evaluated and that the final resolution is their logical consequence[26].

As mentioned above, the judicial review also includes checking whether the application of the administrative discretionary authority was admissible in a specific case. If the answer to this question is positive, the court shall focus (considering matters discussed above) on checking whether the administrative agency exceeded the limits of discretion. The court should examine whether the decision (or, specifically, its resolution) is within the limits specified in the law. If the legislature leaves freedom for the agency issuing a decision to choose consequences only a particularly material (glaring) violation of the said framework of such discretion will constitute a violation of the law.[27]

5. Conclusions

Summing up, it is worthwhile to repeat the thesis formulated at the beginning: that there are no law application processes where a public administration agency has not at least a minimum degree of discretionary power. This situation also results from the occurrence of such expressions of the margin of decision – in addition to deliberately created sources of decision-making latitude – that are not captured by the will and knowledge of the legislature. In connection with this fact, one can ask whether a certain scope of activity of the public administration fails to be captured by legal regulations and whether this situation can lead (in extreme cases) to their arbitrariness to the detriment of an individual.

It seems that such a situation should not occur in a system with effective mechanisms of verification of decisions made by the administration, applied by independent courts (those not involved with the activities of the administration). The judicial review of the administration directs (more or less directly) the reasoning of the public administration agency being a part of its discretionary power and, in civil law culture countries, court awards even become a factor influencing the way in which such power is exercised.

26 See the Kielce VAC judgement of 19.03.2009, I SA/Ke 57/09, CBOSA.
27 See the SAC judgement of 7.11.2008, II GSK 455/08, CBOSA.

At the same time, the judicial review is not unlimited. Compliance with the law (legality) is its basic and, in principle, the only criterion. In general, a court will check whether an agency acts in line with the law in the course of the law application process and whether it exceeds the limits defined by the law. Therefore, the issue of the judicial review of administrative decisions taking place on the basis of some different criteria is still current. For example, the advisability or rationality of a decision could be the basis for such a review. Additionally, it is worthwhile to note the "legality of purpose" structure existing in the Polish legal regime, which assumes that the action of an agency has to be not only compliant with the literal wording of a regulation but also with the purpose for which it was established.[28] In this sense, the incompatibility of a decision with such a purpose can be considered the taking of action in violation of legal norms.

28 More in: W. Jakimowicz, *Zewnętrzne granice uznania administracyjnego*, "Państwo i Prawo" 2010, issue 5, p. 52.

Zbigniew R. Kmiecik
(Associate Professor, Maria Curie-Sklodowska University in Lublin, Poland)

Eliza Komierzyńska-Orlińska
(Ph. D., Maria Curie-Sklodowska University in Lublin, Poland)

The Manifestations of Public Administration's Discretionary Power in the Control of Administrative Decisions[1]

Abstract: The aim of the article is to show that the character of the control of administrative decisions performed by public administration authorities determines the scope of their discretionary power in this field.

Keywords: administrative decision, appellate proceedings, extraordinary controlling proceedings, expediency reasons

1. Public administration control is fundamental to the functioning of the State as it plays a leading role in its organization and activity. "Since the time when King Darius of Ancient Persia sent out his trusted officials to oversee the activity of his provincial deputies; since the time when Aristotle created the foundations of the theory of the State; till the present day – the issue of control still remains the basic element of every organizational system, whatever the place and whoever is served"[2]. In this way, control has become one of the main structural elements of an effective and functioning organization, and its role has increased with the increase

1 The paper had been prepared as a result of cooperation in the process of realization of the research grant DEC-2013/11/N/HS5/04212, entitled: "The influence of judicial decisions on the discretionary power of public administration in the law application processes" financed by the National Science Center (Narodowe Centrum Nauki).

2 J. Łętowski, *Prawo administracyjne. Zagadnienia podstawowe,* Warszawa 1990, p. 281. J. Szreniawski states that trusted officials of the Persian ruler Darius the Great, who were considered to be "the eyes and the ears of the King", are a common example of the usual ancient supervisory activities (see *idem, Prawo administracyjne. Część ogólna,* Lublin 1994, p. 145). W.L. Jaworski holds that "law which is not grounded in the absolute [morality], hangs in the air and the last sanction is a physical force [...]". He then asked, giving the answer in the same time: "What can happen in the world where relativism prevails, where the absolute in human souls does not exist? Mankind then seeks for the

of the meaning of the organization[3]. It, thus, could be said to be a process that is elemental to every sphere of human life[4]. As evidenced in the aforementioned examples, one can see that control has accompanied public administration for a long time, indeed, since the start of the notion of administration, and it evolves with the development of administrative practices. J. Jagielski underlines the notion that "the indissoluble relationship of administration and control results from their notably objective premises"[5], because – as it was already shown – control is an inseparable element of every organized activity, independent of whatever this activity is, and, hence, it must be addressed in the processes of administering. Public administration cannot dispense with control, as control allows for oversight and valuation of its activity, thus, in the end, it is effective in in assuring the correctness and efficiency of this activity. It can be said, then, that control is a factor in stimulating the continuous and uninterrupted improvement of the entire administrative apparatus. A lack, therefore, of this control pushes the public administration towards deterioration of its function, and makes it impossible to maintain the intended activity[6]. However, E. Ochendowski rightly notes that "the role of control in the administration can be described as secondary. It is as original as the immediate activity of the public administration body itself. The task of control is to prevent mistakes in administrative activity. This task must affect the scope of the construct of the system of control, as control has to be proportional to the extent of administration's activity. Hence, the secondary role of control must be adjusted to the original activity of the public administrative body"[7].

J. Jagielski notes other reasons for the close connection between public administration and control[8]. These are:

a) the held responsibility of public administration for executing different, vast and often complicated public tasks and functions which have enormous meaning for the effective functioning of the State and the society. Thus, it has to be under control;

---

palliative and in our domain, i.e. in law, finds it in the means of control" (*idem, Nauka prawa administracyjnego. Zagadnienia ogólne,* Warszawa 1924, pp. 193, 195).

3 As put forward by S. Jędrzejewski, *Kontrola administracji,* Poznań 2000, p. 9.

4 J. Boć [in:] J. Boć, T. Kuta, *Prawo administracyjne. Zagadnienia podstawowe,* Warszawa 1984, p. 180.

5 J. Jagielski, *Kontrola administracji publicznej,* Warszawa 2007, p. 7.

6 *Ibidem,* p. 8.

7 E. Ochendowski, *Prawo administracyjne. Część ogólna,* Toruń 2009, p. 420.

8 J. Jagielski, *op. cit.,* p. 8.

b) public administration, being a form of executive power, is overseen by legislators with considerable administrative power. Moreover, it holds the possibility acting for both good and ill. Hence, necessity arises of it being placed under control (most of all, because of the necessity of securing the rights and freedom of the individual);
c) control of public administration is indispensable for the continuous stimulation of this administration towards the goal of making it more effective and efficient in its actions;
d) such determinants of public administration activity as lawfulness and legality, as well as postulates of "sound administration" and "right to sound administration" are determinants of an increase of meaning regarding the necessity of control being placed over public administration.

The Author accurately comes to the conclusion that "[…] certainly, today, there is no question as to the need to control the administration, while at the same time, there is a problem in how to control it […]"[9].

Control, as M. Zirk Sadowski emphasizes, is a praxeological category. This means it is a fact-finding study that generates a comparison of the existing situation to that of the desirable state[10]. This notion, in ordinary language, is a form of publicism seen in treatises, in administrative and judicial adjudication[11].

The common designation "control of the administration" does not have a specific, particular meaning within the Polish doctrine of administrative law. "It is a given or a larger scope of activity which comprises the whole set of different inspections aimed at the activity of public administration authorities, or, in the traditional model, the control of public administration is considered to be the judicial control of administrative acts which is recognized as being the most significant in the outer relationships of administration"[12]. In addition, with regard to the notion: "control of the administration", this can be used in a stricter sense as being a means of overseeing the activity of public administration authorities, or in larger sense (in a broader sense) as a form of control of the other activities

9 *Ibidem*, pp. 8–9.
10 M. Zirk-Sadowski, *Kontrola administracji publicznej*, [in:] *Administracja publiczna*, ed. J. Hausner, Warszawa 2011, p. 259.
11 J. Jagielski, *op. cit.*, p. 11.
12 S. Jędrzejewski [in:] S. Jędrzejewski, H. Nowicki, *Kontrola administracji publicznej. Kontrola a nadzór. Struktura systemu. Instytucje*, Toruń 1995, p. 4.

executed by these authorities[13]. J. Boć draws attention[14] towards the observation that, on the one hand, therefore, public administration can be the controlled entity, and, on the other hand, public administration can be the controlling entity, and some other times, it can be simultaneously controlled and controlling (both under internal control and exerting control).

In the Polish science of administrative law, the notion of control is not the subject of much controversy, although it is formulated in different ways[15]. As E. Olejniczak-Szałowska states, "A commonly accepted definition is that formulated by W. Dawidowicz. Accordingly, control is an activity, the point of which is that it is:

a) a fact-finding study;
b) a means of comparing the fact-finding study to the ideal, to that which should be, i.e., what is expected by the model of behaviour or norms of conduct, and, hence, a means of formulating an appropriate opinion on this basis;
c) a way of, in the existence of a divergence between the extant state and the desirable state, ascertaining the reasons of this divergence;

---

13 E. Olejniczak-Szałowska, *Kontrola administracji,* [in:] Z. Duniewska, B. Jaworska-Dębska, R. Michalska-Badziak, E. Olejniczak-Szałowska, M. Stahl, *Prawo administracyjne. Pojęcia, instytucje, zasady w teorii i orzecznictwie,* Warszawa 2013, p. 498.

14 J. Boć [in:] *Prawo administracyjne,* ed. J. Boć, Wrocław 2007, p. 376.

15 Among others, see: J. Starościak [in:] J. Starościak, E. Iserzon, *Prawo administracyjne,* Warszawa 1963, p. 266; J. Starościak, *Prawo administracyjne,* Warszawa 1969, pp. 357–358; J. Homplewicz, *Kontrola administracji (problematyka teoretyczna),* Kraków 1976, pp. 13–17; J. Służewski, *Zarys nauki administracji,* Warszawa 1979, p. 126; Z. Rybicki [in:] Z. Rybicki, S. Piątek, *Zarys prawa administracyjnego i nauki o administracji,* Warszawa 1984, pp. 261–262; J. Boć [in:] J. Boć, T. Kuta, *op. cit.*, p. 180; J. Szreniawski, *op. cit.*, p. 146; S. Jędrzejewski [in:] S. Jędrzejewski, H. Nowicki, *op. cit.*, pp. 6–8; E. Ura, E. Ura, *Prawo administracyjne,* Warszawa 1999, p. 201; S. Jędrzejewski, *Kontrola…*, pp. 18–19; *idem, Zakres pojęcia "nadzór" w doktrynie prawa administracyjnego (kolejna próba zbliżenia poglądów),* [in:] *Administracja publiczna u progu XXI wieku. Prace dedykowane Prof. zw. dr. hab. Janowi Szreniawskiemu z okazji jubileuszu 45-lecia pracy naukowej,* Przemyśl 2000, pp. 280–282; J. Boć [in:] *Prawo…*, ed. J. Boć, p. 376; G. Szpor [in:] *Prawo administracyjne,* ed. Z. Niewiadomski, Z. Cieślak, I. Lipowicz, G. Szpor, Warszawa 2007, pp. 304–305; J. Jagielski, *op. cit.*, p. 11–15; R. Lewicka, *Kontrola prawotwórstwa administracji o charakterze powszechnie obowiązującym,* Warszawa 2008, p. 115–117; E. Ura, E. Ura, *Prawo administracyjne,* Warszawa 2010, p. 58–59.

d) a way of formulating of recommendations aimed at generating a course of action aimed at the expulsion of undesirable occurrences and at preventing potential divergences"[16].

Therefore, the essence of control is the observation of unacceptable practices, and, subsequently, analysing their character, and, finally, describing inferences and proposing remedial activities to the superior authority over the audited entity[17]. As E. Ura rightly notices, "The control authority usually does not have the possibility of directly influencing the activity of the inspected bodies, it is able only to give recommendations. The results of the control action and the inferences generated by the control activity are introduced to the higher-level authority holding dominion over the inspected body. The possibility of authoritative direct intervention in the controlled sphere or in the issuing of remedial administrative acts as a result of control are possible only when the control authority has a specific, explicit statutory authorization. Without such an authorization, the control authority is only able to investigate, judge the action, couch and submit the report. The control is of an authoritative character only in this meaning that the controlled entity cannot decline to be audited, while application of the authoritative measures to address the stated incorrectnesses does not rest with the control authority. This function can only be fulfilled by the supervisory authority alone. If control is exercised by the higher authority in the administrative hierarchy over the controlled entity, and, therefore, the being the entity responsible for its activities, and if this higher authority in the administrative hierarchy is able to use the authoritative measures in relation to subordinated entity in the structure of being a controlled entity, the control adopts a qualified form of supervision"[18].

The aim of control is, therefore, to bring about improvement in public administration activity through eliminating stated transgressions and preventing the coming about of similar unfavourable occurrences. In this manner, the approximation of the activity of controlled entities to the defined standard is to take place and the improvement of the very standard is going to happen. The essential is that, basically, control of the audited entity is a common, routine activity, not just an unusual event coming about in the last stage of any project undertaken by the entity[19]. In addition, one cannot forget that the methods of control ought to be

---

16 E. Olejniczak-Szałowska [in:] Z. Duniewska, B. Jaworska-Dębska, R. Michalska-Badziak, E. Olejniczak-Szałowska, M. Stahl, *op. cit.*, p. 498.

17 E. Ura, E. Ura, *op. cit.*, p. 201.

18 *Ibidem*, p. 58–59.

19 E. Olejniczak-Szałowska [in:] Z. Duniewska, B. Jaworska-Dębska, R. Michalska-Badziak, E. Olejniczak-Szałowska, M. Stahl, *op. cit.*, p. 499.

appropriate. An inappropriate range of interests or the search for what is wrong alone, and not recognition of what is right, are defects in the common activity of the controlling entities[20].

The Polish doctrine of administrative law indicates the features of correct control practices. The most common indicated features are[21]:

1) Formality. As S. Jędrzejewski underlines, in ordinary language, official control is an audit undertaken by virtue of the office (ex officio)[22]. Formality means "Controlling activity in the State must be led by the explicit authorized controlling entities which act according to the procedure envisaged by a statute"[23]. Formality of the control means that the procedure of a control is defined, although – as A. Sylwestrzak states – "it should be built upon such incommensurable social practices as politeness, kindness or ability to create an atmosphere of co-operation in the course of control. Therefore, the formality of control is related to many unofficial activities which altogether have a significant civil influence on the very style of its execution within the modern State"[24]. In contrast to official control, unofficial control is undertaken on an outside demand, usually on the request of a complaint with regard to public administration activity. Official control is, most of all, aimed at protecting public interests, although in the sphere of legality, it is in charge of ensuring that the controlled entity is in observance of law in general, including that it holds a general respect for individual rights. Unofficial control is aimed at, most of all, if not only, upholding the protection of the interests of the individual. This form of control activity consists of settling disputes between individuals and administrative bodies. Unofficial control is undertaken on demand, it is a form of reaction to cases of the incorrect activity or inappropriate behaviour which can come into being as a result of public administration activity. Traditionally, institutions of unofficial control are: judicial control of public administration and instance control[25];
2) Activity. By its very nature, official control should be characterized by activity. The control held by the virtue of the office, on the controlling entity's initiatives (which can be both planned audit and ad hoc audit) should lead

20 J. Szreniawski, *op. cit.*, p. 147.
21 E. Olejniczak-Szałowska [in:] Z. Duniewska, B. Jaworska-Dębska, R. Michalska-Badziak, E. Olejniczak-Szałowska, M. Stahl, *op. cit.*, p. 500.
22 S. Jędrzejewski [in:] S. Jędrzejewski, H. Nowicki, *op. cit.*, p. 29.
23 A. Sylwestrzak, *Kontrola administracji publicznej w III Rzeczypospolitej Polskiej,* Gdańsk 2004, p. 14.
24 *Ibidem.*
25 S. Jędrzejewski [in:] S. Jędrzejewski, H. Nowicki, *op. cit.*, p. 29.

to the disclosure of all detectable incorrectnesses in the controlled entity's activity. It should hold such characteristic features as clear-sightedness and straightforwardness of assessment. Moreover, it is fundamental that it should react not only due to the instigation of superior entities or upon the request of qualified administrative bodies (qualified to initiate the control), but also it should react to signals resulting from the complaints or criticisms raised by ordinary citizens, the media or other sources. The activity undertaken by the controlling body should also be appropriate to the job at hand – to discover incorrectnesses and the consequences of this incorrectness, and to undertake measures to prevent its rising in the future. By the way, one should note that activity is not only a feature of official control. It is also a feature of unofficial control. However, in this case, this activity is secured in a particular manner, e.g. by establishing binding cut-off dates for the handling of complaints or for the application of other legal measures[26];

3) Impartiality. The assessment of controlled activity should be objective. Impartiality of control is only secured when the controlling entity is not tied to the controlled entity through the relationship of direct supervision; when the controlling entity is not responsible for the activity of the controlled entity. "Only when the external control authority, is, most of all, an independent control body, is it able [...] to ascertain incorrectness and make recommendations of appropriate corrective measures. It is, therefore, clear that for securing the feature of impartiality of control, there should be routine independent inspections [...]"[27]. Unfortunately, there is a risk that public administration, acting lawfully in a formal sense, will cause injustice. Thus, when public administration undertakes authorized actions, to achieve public acceptance of its decisions, it should always be guided by public interest and just the interest of influential individuals[28]. J.S. Langrod wrote: "Judicial control of administration has become, essentially, a safety valve of lawfulness (Aucoc's designation), and, at the same time, a precursor of all forms of impartial control of the administration in general"[29]. Hence, in order that public administration does not

26 S. Jędrzejewski, *Kontrola...*, p. 49.

27 *Ibidem*, p. 50.

28 K. Chochowski, *Aktualność myśli Profesora Jerzego Stefana Langroda w przedmiocie zasadności bezstronnej kontroli nad administracją publiczną*, [in:] *Teoria instytucji prawa administracyjnego. Księga pamiątkowa Profesora Jerzego Stefana Langroda*, ed. J. Niczyporuk, Paris 2011, p. 76.

29 J. S. Langrod, *Instytucje prawa administracyjnego. Zarys części ogólnej*, reprint, Kraków 2003, pp. 314–315.

undergo degeneration, and to prevent pathological occurrences coming about within public administration, impartial, judicial control of administration is necessary[30];

4) Proportionality. The whole activity of public administration should be under control; Indeed, the whole set of activities of the controlled entity is to be under control, "not only the last element of this set, although in reality, this very element (e.g. administrative decision) is most often the reason for the start of the control practice"[31]. Still, the apparatus of control should not be overextended, at least for the reason that it generates negative economic results; control excess is an undesirable occurrence as it results in disorganization in the normal routine activity of organizational entities of public administration when it is over the limit of real needs. It is essential that the frequency of control be reasonable, be dependent on real needs[32], and be adequate;
5) Expertness. Control of the administration should be performed by entities which, at least, are equal to the controlled entity in their held scope of knowledge and experience. In addition, the control entities should act efficiently and straightforwardly in their inquiries. Expertness, as well as professionalism are also easily seen when the measures of control are well-chosen, and when the inferences after the control are adequate[33]. S. Jędrzejewski ascertains: "An auditing bodies' lack of expertness is particularly damaging – it threatens not only the authority of the organ which is represented by the auditor, but also it makes the control worthless. Furthermore, it can even be harmful[34];
6) Efficiency. It is important to select legal measures and institutions which are able to correctly and efficiently reveal transgressions[35]. Generally speaking, efficiency of control means effectiveness of control. With regard to public administration, this consists of the following elements: a) proper selection of the topic of control; b) a suitable choice of professional and knowledgeable auditors; c) coordination of the different kinds of control: ensuring non-conflict in the activity of diverse controlling entities, and the different instances in which

30 K. Chochowski, *op. cit.*, p. 77.

31 J. Boć [in:] J. Boć, T. Kuta, *op. cit.*, p. 182.

32 E. Olejniczak-Szałowska [in:] Z. Duniewska, B. Jaworska-Dębska, R. Michalska-Badziak, E. Olejniczak-Szałowska, M. Stahl, *op. cit.*, p. 500; S. Jędrzejewski, *Kontrola…*, p. 51.

33 J. Zimmermann, *Prawo administracyjne,* Kraków 2006, p. 412.

34 S. Jędrzejewski [in:] S. Jędrzejewski, H. Nowicki, *op. cit.*, p. 32.

35 So states E. Olejniczak-Szałowska [in:] Z. Duniewska, B. Jaworska-Dębska, R. Michalska-Badziak, E. Olejniczak-Szałowska, M. Stahl, *op. cit.*, p. 500.

> control is initiated and comes about – both in the phase of planning and in the phase of realization; d) the ability of the controlling entities to react in a broad sense to initiatives originating within the general public (complaints and motions, the activity of trade unions, political parties or formal associations)[36].

To all these aspects of control, one can add others which are complementary. These include: legality, the intent at ascertaining the truth[37], independence of control, political neutrality, diligence (straightforwardness), operativity, rapidity, efficacy, cheapness (economy), simplicity of setting the procedure of control in motion, and terminality.

The distinguished Professor of Administrative Law, W.L. Jaworski, emphasized the meaning of control with regard to public administration: "Control, and once again, control – is fundamental to the maintenance of the health of the state. But control cannot cross its own bounds and it cannot become the government itself"[38]. Contemporary public administration has to act on this basis and be within the bounds of law. Therefore, it should be pleased that it holds public trust. Indeed, there is a lot of rightness in the statement that control is the foundation for trust.

2. The administrative proceedings are one of the three principal legal proceedings (apart from the civil and criminal proceedings) in which decisions that regulate the legal situation of individuals are taken in particular cases. At the same time the administrative proceedings are the only one of the three types, in which an entirely correct decision without any, even insignificant defect, can be challenged. The decision (ruling) that ends the administrative proceedings is an administrative decision. It is in this decision that the public administration authority gives a ruling on the rights and obligations of an individual addressee, defining or determining his position under the law. The determination of a person's legal position through an administrative decision may consist in granting, refusal to grant or withdrawal of a right or in the imposition or cancellation of an obligation. The binding establishment of a person's position under the law by an administrative decision may consist in authoritatively declaring the inception or extinction of a right or obligation by operation of law (*ipso iure*). The definition of the addressee's legal position (by determining or establishing it in binding terms) is the contents of decisions issued in the primary proceedings, i.e. the ordinary

---

36 A. Sylwestrzak, *op. cit.*, p. 13–14.

37 *Ibidem*, p. 12–13.

38 W. L. Jaworski, *Notatki*, Kraków 1929, p. 32–33, quoted after: M. Maciołek, *Przyczynek do zagadnienia kontroli gestii administracyjnej*, "Państwo i Prawo" 1995, no. 10–11, p. 135.

first-instance proceedings. The content of the decisions ending the secondary or supervisory proceedings is obviously different.

Internal control (i.e. exercised by the administration) of administrative decisions issued in the first instance takes on diverse forms. The remedies that make up this system of control may aim:

a) only to verify a decision (regarding its legality or binding force);
b) only to challenge a decision (by quashing or amending it);
c) to verify (from the standpoint of legality and expediency, or legality only) and challenge a decision (by quashing, amending or declaring it invalid).

Verification of a decision in respect of its legality is to declare that it has been issued with contravention to the law (in Polish law – Art. 151. 2, the Code of Administrative Proceedings[39], Art. 158.2, CAdPr). The controlling authority issues this kind of a decision when, despite finding it fundamentally defective, it cannot deprive it of its binding force, for example because the period of time limitation of quashing or declaring the decision invalid has elapsed, the decision with the defect of invalidity has already produced irreversible legal consequences, or a defect of the proceedings did not influence the content of the decision issued.

Verification of a decision in respect of its binding force is to declare the decision expired (in Polish law – Art. 162.1, CAdPr). The authority which issued a decision shall declare the decision expired if it became groundless. A decision may be groundless because, for example, the party exercised a right to perform a single action, which was permitted by the decision (i.e. the right which was the subject of the decision ceased to exist), the party lost qualifications necessary to exercise its rights[40], the party which had personal rights died[41], the party renounced a right[42], the object to which a right related ceased to exist[43], the period for which a decision was issued has elapsed (time limit of validity of a decision). To oversimplify it, one can say that the groundlessness of a decision stems from such circumstances

---

39 Henceforward CAdPr.

40 J. Borkowski [in:] J. Borkowski, J. Jendrośka, R. Orzechowski, A. Zieliński, *Kodeks postępowania administracyjnego. Komentarz*, Warszawa 1989, p. 269.

41 L. Żukowski [in:] K. Chorąży, A. Wróbel, L. Żukowski, Postępowanie administracyjne, postępowanie przez NSA oraz postępowanie egzekucyjne w administracji, Lublin–Rzeszów 1992, p. 95.

42 See Z. Janowicz, Postępowanie administracyjne i postępowanie przed sądem administracyjnym, Warszawa–Poznań 1997, pp. 242–243.

43 See the judgment of the Supreme Administrative Court (NSA) of 11 October 1985, SA/Wr 556/85, ONSA 1985, no. 2, item 21.

(factual or legal), which, if they occurred before the issuance of the decision, i.e. in the course of the proceedings, would be the grounds for discontinuance of the proceedings (the objective of the issued decision ceased to exist or became impossible to achieve). The reason for expiry of a decision can also be a failure by a party to fulfill a specific condition subject to which the decision was issued.

To challenge a decision without its prior verification is to quash or amend the decision for reasons of expediency (in Polish law – under Art. 154, Art. 155, Art. 161 and Art. 162.2, CAdPr). In such cases, an authority does not verify a decision with regard to its compliance with the law because this fact is of no significance from the standpoint of admissibility to challenge the decision.

To challenge a decision preceded by its verification as to the legality and expediency is to quash or amend the decision as a result of the appellate proceedings (or the proceedings initiated by the submission of application to reconsider the matter when there is no higher-level authority over the authority which issued the decision in the first instance).

To challenge a decision preceded by its verification with regard to legality only is to quash or amend the decision as a result of the reopened proceedings (in Polish law – Art. 151.1.2 CAdPr) or to declare a decision invalid (in Polish law – Art. 156. 1 CAdPr).

The challenging of a decision may be accompanied by the ruling concerning the merits of the matter or not. The absence of a new ruling concerning the merits of the case may result from the lack of such a need (the proceedings were groundless from the beginning or became so) or the lack of powers to rule on the merits of the matter by the controlling authority (the proceedings to declare a decision invalid). The challenging of a decision combined with a simultaneous ruling anew regarding the essence of the matter is termed "amending".[44]

3. The appellate proceedings have two goals, the actualization (and the necessity to realize the second) depending on the result of the realization of the first objective. It can be therefore said that the first goal has to be realized by the authority in the course of the appellate proceedings whereas the second one is conditional. The unconditional goal of the appellate proceedings is to verify the decision of the first-instance authority or to confirm its correctness in the broad sense, i.e. from the standpoint of both its legality (compliance with the law) and expediency, rightness (compliance with social and individual interest). The other, conditional goal of the appellate proceedings is to again dispose of the matter as to the merits, i.e.

---

44 Z.R. Kmiecik, *Wszczęcie ogólnego postępowania administracyjnego*, Warszawa 2015, pp. 355–356.

to apply the norms of substantive administrative law once again to the addressee of a decision. The second goal is actualized when, as a result of the realization of the first goal, it turns out that the decision appealed against has a significant defect and at the same time there are no grounds for discontinuing the proceedings or declaring the decision invalid. The second goal will be implemented either by the appellate authority or by the first-instance authority, depending on whether the evidence gathered by the first instance authority allows ruling on the case as to its merits or whether the issuance of such a ruling requires the explanatory proceedings almost in whole or in larger part. Appeal can therefore be termed as a procedural institution by means of which the parties (or other authorized entities) may demand verification and – possibly – challenging (cassation or amending) of the decision of the first instance authority.

Cassation of a decision consists in quashing it without ruling again on the merits of the matter. The cassation quashing of a decision can be accompanied by the simultaneous discontinuation of the proceedings before the first instance authority or by remanding the matter for reconsideration. It should be the rule that upon finding a defect which provides grounds for reopening the proceedings the appellate authority quashes the decision appealed against and remands the case for reconsideration to the first instance authority. The appellate authority may also confine itself to merely quashing the decision appealed against. The amending of a decision consists in quashing the decision issued by the first instance organ and ruling again as to the merits of the matter which is the object of the decision appealed against.

In the appellate proceedings, the discretionary power of the second instance authority is only remedial. The appellate authority only examines whether the first instance authority did not abuse its power by issuing an illegal and/or ineffective (unjust) decision. Therefore, when examining the decision not only in respect of its compliance with law (legality) but also in respect of expediency (justness), the appellate authority in a way also utilizes its discretionary power. If it quashes the decision appealed against because, in its view, it is inexpedient (although legal), at the same time this authority will have to issue a new decision which will reflect its own idea of which ruling is right in light of specific factual and legal circumstances.

This conception of discretionary power of the appellate authority manifests itself not only at this stage of issuing a decision. It can be also reflected in the course of the proceedings, i.e. when a party will withdraw the appeal it has submitted. The authority is not bound by the party's withdrawal of the appeal and it will refuse to allow the appeal to be withdrawn if due to the withdrawal a decision infringing upon the law or contrary to the public interest would remain in force (Art. 137, sentence two, CAdPr). It follows from the foregoing that the second instance authority will accept a party's withdrawal of the appeal only when the decision appealed against (of the first instance authority) is correct with regard to legality and expediency as well as when, without infringing upon the law, it is unjust in light of the interest of the party. A decision must therefore be within the limits determined by the scope of discretion granted to the authority by the provisions of substantive law while its admissible defect (in the context of withdrawal of the appeal) may consist only in infringing upon the interest of a party.

The authority thus assesses the decision appealed against in the context of admissibility of withdrawal of the appeal but regarding its (decision's) legality and expediency, disregarding – out of the circumstances taken into account when ruling on the merits of the matter – only the question of the compliance of the decision with the interest of a party. The doctrine assumes that the conditions for the inadmissibility of withdrawal of an appeal should be interpreted narrowly by the appellate authority because they are an exception to the rule that a party has the right of appeal. This directive is of significant importance, especially when applied to the condition for the infringement upon the public interest, which in itself (the condition) is evaluative.

4. The aims of the extraordinary administrative proceedings are varied. In the case of the proceedings initiated for legal reasons the goal is to verify and possibly challenge (quash, amend or declare invalid) a decision issued under the ordinary procedure (although the proceedings may also result only in the declaration that a decision was issued in contravention to the law, when it is impossible to challenge the decision despite finding it defective). With the extraordinary proceedings initiated for expediency reasons the aim is only to challenge (quash or amend) or only to verify a decision issued under the ordinary procedure (from the standpoint of binding force). While in the proceedings initiated for legal reasons the administrative authorities may verify a decision only without challenging it, even if it is defective, in the case of the proceedings initiated for expediency reasons they only challenge a decision without verifying it, or they only verify it but not with regard to its legality but only to its binding force.

In the extraordinary supervision proceedings initiated for legal reasons there is no room for the discretionary power of administrative authorities. Both in the case of reopening of the proceedings and in the proceedings to declare a decision invalid, the competent administrative authority may deprive a decision of its binding force only when one of the enumeratively specified circumstances occurred, which comprise particularly serious legal defects.

In the cases justifying the reopening of the proceedings, it is the proceedings that have a defect in the first place. A defect may consist in the violation of procedural norms, usually the rules of the evidentiary proceedings, or in the occurrence (or disclosure) of circumstances in view of which the grounds on which the ruling was based are no longer valid. The defectiveness of the decision is here consequent upon the defectiveness of the proceedings, it is therefore secondary[45]. Consequently, if it turns out as a result of the reopened proceedings that the defect of the proceedings in no way influenced the content of a decision (for example the participation of an employee that should be disqualified), the decision is not quashed. The reopening of the proceedings may also be requested when the Constitutional Tribunal ruled that the normative act on the basis of which the decision was issued did not comply with a higher order act, i.e. the Constitution, an international agreement or a statute. In cases justifying the declaration that a decision was invalid the defect is inherent in the decision itself[46]. The declaration of decision's invalidity produces legal effects *ex tunc*, i.e. it abolishes (annuls) legal effects with retroactive force (if it is at all possible). This does not mean, however, that the decision declaring a decision invalid is declaratory (a decision with the defect of invalidity is not invalid by operation of law)[47]. Contrary to the wording used in Art. 156 et seq., CAdPr, the public administration authority does not in fact declare a decision invalid but only invalidates it with retroactive force.

The purpose of the proceedings to declare a decision invalid is to examine if the decision issued under the ordinary procedure has a qualified defect and, if such a defect is ascertained and negative premises are absent, to eliminate it from legal transactions with retroactive force. The purpose of reopening the proceedings is not only to examine whether a decision issued under the ordinary procedure has a qualified defect and possibly to eliminate it from legal transactions but also to rule again on the matter examined under the ordinary procedure. The declaration that a decision is invalid has therefore features of a supervision measure whereas

---

45 L. Żukowski, *Wznowienie postępowania administracyjnego w K.P.A.*, "Administracja", Zeszyty Naukowe Centrum Podyplomowego Kształcenia Pracowników Administracji Państwowej 1988, no. 3, p. 54.

46 L. Żukowski, Stwierdzenie nieważności decyzji na tle konstrukcji prawnych służących wzruszaniu decyzji ostatecznych w ogólnym postępowaniu administracyjnym, "Administracja", Zeszyty Naukowe Centrum Podyplomowego Kształcenia Pracowników Administracji Państwowej 1987, no. 1, p. 46.

47 See E. Iserzon, *Moc obowiązująca aktu administracyjnego i domniemanie jego ważności*, Ruch Prawniczy, Ekonomiczny i Socjologiczny 1965, no. 1, pp. 58, 62.

the administrative authority carries out self-supervision in the course and as a result of the reopened proceedings.

5. The discretionary power of the public administration is fully and directly manifested in the extraordinary controlling proceedings initiated for expediency reasons. The expediency reasons that justify the initiation of the extraordinary proceedings are varied. They can embrace: the interest of a party, the public interest, the need to eliminate the condition that threatens particularly protected goods, a discrepancy between the formal and actual enforceability of a decision, elimination of a decision from legal transactions if a party did not fulfill a condition or actions subject to the fulfillment of which the authority granted the party a right. This diversity translates into the diversity of the goal of this category of the extraordinary proceedings, which is either only to challenge a decision (which may take the form of quashing or amending), or only to verify it from the perspective of the binding force of the decision (as a result the authority may declare the decision expired).

Unlike the appellate proceedings, the authority does not examine here whether the first instance authority did not abuse its power by issuing an illegal and/or inexpedient (unjust) decision, it only examines whether the expediency reasons do not argue for the invalidation of the final decision, which may be both legal and expedient (just).

A characteristic feature of the extraordinary legal remedies initiated for expediency reasons is that, unlike the foregoing extraordinary remedies initiated for legal reasons, they also enable challenging entirely correct (non-defective) decisions. It should be also emphasized that, contrary to frequent opinions in the doctrine, these remedies apply also to correct decisions rather than exclusively to correct decisions. The argument, in support of a different thesis, that the remedies initiated for legal reasons (reopening of the proceedings and the proceedings to declare a decision invalid) apply to defective decisions is not acceptable because the grounds for challenging a decision under the procedure of using those last remedies do not contain the grounds for challenging a decision under the procedure applied to remedies initiated for expediency reasons. If therefore certain special circumstances and reasons (not provided for in other regulations) justify the possibility of challenging correct (non-defective) decisions, these apply the more so to defective decisions.

6. The basic conditions for challenging a decision for expediency reasons is justification by the public interest or just interest of the party (Art. 154 and Art. 155 CAdPr). The Polish Code of Administrative Proceedings treats these premises in an alternative (equivalent) way: the quashing or amending should be "the public interest or just interest of the party". Consequently, the concurrence of these circumstances is not required. Nevertheless, one cannot recognize that the expediency of challenging a decision because of one of the foregoing interests should be the sufficient grounds for challenging the decision regardless of the assessment of this challenge in light of the other protected interest. Although it is enough that one factor justifies the quashing or amending of the decision, the other should not, however, counter such challenging. This requirement directly stems from the general principle of the administrative proceedings (in Art. 7 *in fine* CAdPr), according to which, when disposing of the matter, the administrative authority should take into account the public interest and just interest of the citizens.

The reasons of the public interest or just interest of the party is a sufficient condition for challenging the final decision only when the party has not acquired a right by force of this decision. Otherwise, to challenge the decision will also require the consent of the party which acquired a right under the verified decision.

The acquisition of rights by an administrative decision, making the admissibility of challenging a decision conditional on the consent of the party which acquired the rights, is defined in a very broad sense: as any advantage gained by the party from the disposal of its case by this decision. An advantageous ruling for a party is therefore not only to grant it a specific right under the decision but also to declare in a binding way that the party has a given right by operation of law because only when such an act was issued, the party can, in contentious cases, effectively invoke its rights. The party also derives a legal advantage from the disposal of the matter, consisting in the abolishment of an obligation formerly imposed upon it (party) or in the declaration that it expired. Finally, an advantage to the party may involve a decision imposing an obligation upon it. The amendment to such a decision may impose an obligation to a greater extent or on less advantageous conditions (e.g. change of the time limit of the fulfillment of an obligation) and thereby worsen the legal situation of the party. The party can thus derive advantages both from constitutive and declaratory decisions[48], as well as both from decisions issued upon its application and *ex officio*.

---

48 The Supreme Administrative Court ruled against the admissibility of challenging declaratory decisions in this procedure (as decisions that do not create any rights and obligations) inter alia in judgments of: 14 March 1997, I SA 235/96, ONSA 1997, no. 4, item 186; 22 July 1998, I SA 154/98, LEX no. 45052; 29 October 1999, I SA 2088/98, LEX no. 48625. These judgments are based on the position once expressed by J. Borkowski (*Zmiana i uchylanie ostatecznych decyzji administracyjnych*, Warszawa 1967, p. 30), which he gave up, however, as the doctrine did not accept it (*Glosa do wyroku NSA z 31 sierpnia 1995 r., SA/Po 313–314/95*, Glosa 1996, no. 12, p. 16).

The consent of a party to quash or amend a final decision under the procedure in question is therefore not required only in the case of a negative decision (one dismissing the demand of the party), a decision withdrawing a formerly granted right in whole or declaring the right expired, and a decision imposing an obligation upon the party to the maximum extent[49]. Only such decisions do not benefit the party in any way, and when amended or quashed they do not worsen the party's legal situation. The foregoing decisions may not however be verified pursuant to Art. 154 CAdPr if the case involves parties with conflicting interests because one of the parties will then be able to infer its right from the decision[50].

7. In cases when the public or individual interest is especially threatened, a correct decision that grants a right to a party may be quashed or amended even without the consent of the party. This is the so-called "expropriation of a right". In the Polish legal order, the administrative authority may do so if challenging a decision is necessary in order to eliminate a threat to human life or health, or to prevent significant damage to the national economy or material interest of the State (Art. 161 CAdPr).

Literature and judicial decisions assume that the condition for the admissibility of quashing or amending a decision under Art. 161 CAdPr. should be to demonstrate that the public administration authority ineffectively tried to quash or amend a decision pursuant to other provisions of the Code (e.g. under Art. 154, 155 or 163), and that the authority failed to declare the decision invalid or quash it because the proceedings were reopened.[51] This view cannot be agreed with.

Art. 161 clearly stipulates that the competent authority may quash or amend any final decision unless – in any other manner (than by quashing or amending the decision) – it is impossible to eliminate or prevent the threats specified in the Article rather than if, in any other manner, it is impossible to challenge the decision whose existence (enforcement) causes or may cause such threats. As Z. Janowicz rightly observes, "the authority should (…) seek any possible solutions under these circumstances before it decides to apply the final, necessary

49 E. Iserzon [in:] E. Iserzon, J. Starościak, Kodeks postępowania administracyjnego. Komentarz, teksty, wzory, formularze, Warszawa 1970, p. 260.

50 See the Supreme Administrative Court judgment of 15 July 1999, I SA 1644/98, LEX no. 48558.

51 See for example P. Przybysz, *Kodeks postępowania administracyjnego. Komentarz*, Warszawa 2004, p. 348; W. Chróścielewski [in:] W. Chróścielewski, J.P. Tarno, *Postępowanie administracyjne. Zagadnienia podstawowe*, Warszawa 2002, p. 161.

possibility: to quash or amend the decision".[52] "Quashing or amending a decision" as such, regardless of what procedure should be applied, is therefore the final possibility rather than quashing or amending a decision pursuant to the procedure of "expropriation of a right" admitted by Art. 161 CAdPr. From the standpoint of the principle of durability of final administrative decisions the reason for challenging a final decision does not matter at all as long as the reason is clearly admissible in the provisions of the law in force. The principle of durability of final administrative decisions requires that prior to challenging a decision under the procedure of "expropriation of a right" (Art. 161 CAdPr.) the authority consider (and, possibly, should circumstances permit it, try) the possibilities (ways) of eliminating the state constituting the ground for applying it (the procedure) that do not involve challenging the issued decision.

As J. Zimmermann stresses, a special threat permitting the "expropriation of a right" (stipulated under Art. 161 CAdPr.), requires a speedy, often instant action, in which there is certainly not enough time and room for the extended jurisdiction proceedings. Amendment is therefore carried out here "under the intervention procedure", and the resultant administrative decision more resembles the so-called immediately effective administrative act than a typical decision that is the result of the jurisdiction proceedings and at the same an act of the application of substantive law. The effective prevention of threats defined as "the state of administrative necessity" most often requires not so much amending a decision but only quashing it, and after quashing, it requires acting by way of other forms available to the administrative authority. These can also be other decisions, not connected with the decision being quashed.[53]

---

52 Z. Janowicz, *Kodeks postępowania administracyjnego. Komentarz*, Warszawa 1999, p. 460. The problem is similarly treated by W. Dawidowicz, *Zarys procesu administracyjnego*, Warszawa 1989, p. 212.

53 J. Zimmermann, *Polska jurysdykcja administracyjna*, Warszawa 1996, p. 208.

Marcin Kamiński
(Associate Professor, Jagiellonian University, Poland)

Intensity of judicial control of discretionary administrative power. Theoretical remarks from a comparative law perspective

Abstract: The issues of scope and boundaries of judicial control of the exercise of administrative discretionary powers are an essential element of the various theoretical conceptions of administrative discretion. This study concerns the levels and the grades of intensity of the judicial verification of legality of the administrative discretion in the light of French, German and UK administrative law. Special attention has been devoted to the problems of formal and substantive limits of the judicial verification of discretionary administrative acts.

Keywords: discretionary administrative powers; judicial control of administrative discretion; formal (external) and material (internal) legality

1. General conceptual remarks on discretionary administrative power

In a theory of administrative law the concept of discretion in the most general sense is defined as the power to make a decision that cannot be determined to be correct (legal) or incorrect (illegal) in any objective way[1]. This kind of the public power involves a right of administrative authority to choose between more than one legally possible course or mode of action. It can be argued that there is a room for a reasonable and purposeful choice of administrative action in the sphere of exercising discretion. Therefore the discretionary power implies freedom of choice and the competent authority may decide whether to act or not to act and – if it is provided – how to act[2]. In other words, the discretion is based on the power of administrative body to choose between alternative courses or modes of action.

As argued by Denis Galligan, the discretion entails a power in the decision-maker to make policy choices, not just to deal with the individual case, but to develop a coherent and consistent set of guidelines which seek to achieve ends

1 See e.g. J. H. Grey, *Discretion in Administrative Law*, Osgoode Hall Law Journal 1979, Vol. 17, No. 1, p. 107.
2 S. de Smith, R. Brazier, *Constitutional and Administrative Law*, London 1994, pp. 583 ff.

and goals within the scope of powers. In his opinion "discretion" must include "discretion to make rules"[3]. This view can be associated with an assertion that the discretion is strictly combined with a deficiency of legal standards which must be complemented by administrative authorities. In such cases the competent authority may construct or concretise normative patterns, the contents of which are created by means of a reference to extralegal normative systems (e.g. system of moral norms). Nevertheless, complementation of a legal basis by means of policy values is connected with the freedom of choice within boundaries of legal system.

In a general theory of law the concept of administrative discretion is considered in various ways. Assuming some simplifications it may be stated that there are two dominant definitions of discretion in a legal literature[4].

The first of them is more general and universal, drawing attention to the room of permissibility of choosing (discretion as "the power to choose between two or more courses of action, each of which is thought as a permissible")[5]. The authority who possesses the discretionary power is allowed to make a choice irrespective of a basis of normative permission. This kind of the power may be based on a vagueness of legal norms, on an absence (or limitations) of control, or on a deficiency of legal standards.

The second definition is connected with the Dworkin's model of rules. According to Dworkin there are three different meanings of "discretion"[6]. In the broadest sense the discretion takes place "when someone is in general charged with making decisions subject to standards set by a particular authority". Dworkin argues in this context that discretion – "like a hole in a doughnut" – "does not exist except as an area left open by a surrounding belt of restriction". Therefore it is the relative concept. In turn, a weak sense of "discretion" can be considered dually. On the one hand we can say that "for some reason the standards an official must apply cannot be applied mechanically but demand the use of judgment". On the other hand we use this term to say merely "that some official has final authority to make

3 D. Galligan, *The Nature and Function of Policies within Discretionary Power*, Public Law 1976, p. 332.

4 See E.L. Rubin, *Discretion and its discontents*, Chicago-Kent Law Review 1997, Vol. 72, pp. 1300–1301.

5 H.M. Hart Jr., A.M. Sacks, *The Legal Process: Basics Problems in the Making and Application of Law*, New York 1994 (prepared for publication from the 1958 tentative edition by, and containing an introductory essay by, William N. Eskridge, Jr. and Philip P. Frickey), p. 144.

6 R. Dworkin, *Taking Rights Seriously*, Cambridge (Massachussets) 1977 (1978), pp. 31–32.

a decision and cannot be reviewed and reversed by any other official". One may finally distinguish a strong sense of "discretion". This sense consists in that on some issue an official is "simply not bound by standards set by authority in question". The quoted author aptly notes that in this "strong sense" the discretion is not concerned with an openness of legal norms (standards) or with a definitive power in applying them, but is structurally related to the lack of legal standards. Dworkin believes that there are no cases where the official (judge) is not bound by legal standards. In the light of Dworkin's theory of "principles, policies and other sorts of standards" a legal system is "gapless" (with a determinate and complete contents) and even in "hard cases" lawyers "make use of standards that do not function as rules"[7]. Therefore according to this approach the administrative or judicial authority is never empowered to fill legal gaps by the exercising limited law-creating discretion. This view has been subjected to criticism from H.L.A. Hart[8]. The latter author indicates that in many cases ("legally unprovided-for or unregulated") the judge (authority) – exercising the discretion – must simultaneously and in parallel apply the established law and make the new law. The law-making power of this authority is conferred and confined by the positive law. The Dworkin's theory of principles (non-conclusive norms) does not eliminate a moment for law-making activity, because even in the "hard cases" the competent authority is required to choose between different legal principles. The operations of making a choice or concretising of such legal standards are based on a delegated competence to create the law through a transfer of extralegal norms or values to the legal system. The law-applying authority must act in such cases "as a conscientious legislator".

Having regard to considerations conducted in a theory of American administrative law it is worth mentioning that the term "administrative discretion" can be used in five different meanings[9]. The first type use of discretion is the explicit conferred power to make individualizing decisions in a process of application of general rules to concrete facts (individualizing discretion). The second type of use is connected with the granting of discretionary power through the vague, ambiguous or incomplete legal norms. By means of this kind of "competence freedom" the administrative authority is empowered to fill gaps in order to realize assigned public tasks and functions (executing discretion). The third type of discretion concerns the power to make state policy (policymaking discretion). In this field of administrative powers the authority has a very broad scope of freedom

7 R. Dworkin, *Taking Rights...*, p. 22.
8 H.L.A. Hart, *The Concept of Law*, Oxford 1994, pp. 272–275.
9 See Ch.H. Koch Jr., *Judicial Review of Administrative Discretion*, The George Washington Law Review 1986, Vol. 54, pp. 471 ff.

because of the openness of competence norm. There are also two types of the administrative discretion which are uncontrollable. If no judicial or administrative control is permitted, the authority has "unreviewable discretion" (so-called "unbridled discretion" i.e. exercise of the power may not be reversed by a higher authority). If the decision of the authority cannot be reviewed by its nature, the authority is exercising "essential discretion" ("numinous discretion"). This type of discretion cannot be held to the explicit or implicit legal standards. Due to lack of normative standards in the legal system a decision is uncontrollable from the legal point of view.

2. Forms of discretionary administrative power

Discretionary administrative power manifests itself in many legal orders in forms which are not uniform. Depending on legal cultures and traditions the construction of administrative discretion may take a variety of forms which have differential scopes, contents and features.

In the United Kingdom administrative law one can be distinguished four categories of the discretionary administrative power[10]. The first form exists when a legislator has granted the administrative authority such power by an express statutory clause. In this case the statutory power is explicit and results from subjectively or objectively formulated provisions. "Subjective discretion" can be expressed by language phrases of the type: "if the minister thinks fit", "if the minister believes that", "if it appears to the tribunal that". "Objective discretion" is in turn connected with phrases of the type: "if the minister has reasonable ground to believe that", "if there is evidence that". The second form of discretionary power is a consequence of legal standards formulation. It is alleged that the law as well as the language are open-textured. Legal provisions which contain vague or ambiguous terms constitute a source of "imprecise statutory standards". In the continental legal theory such category of legal terms is called "undetermined (undefined) concepts" (e.g. "reasonably necessary", "public interest"). Administrative authorities are required to make choices between differential meanings of these open concepts. There is no conceptual difference between express and implied forms of discretionary powers[11]. Therefore the undetermined legal concepts establish as well the discretionary

---

10 P.P. Craig, *Discretionary power in modern administration – Landesbericht Großbritannien*, in: *M. Bullinger* (ed.), *Verwaltungsermessen im modernen Staat*, Baden-Baden 1986, pp. 79–83.

11 M. Künnecke, *Tradition and Change in Administrative Law. An Anglo-German Comparison*, Berlin – Heidelberg – New York 2007, p. 74.

power. The third form of discretionary power – which is typical for British legal order – is a royal prerogative. This category of power is described as "that special pre-eminance which the King has, over and above all other persons, and out of the ordinary course of the common law, in the right of his royal dignity"[12] (e.g. making of war or peace, appointment and dismissal of ministers, dissolution of Parliament, assent to bills). The fourth type of discretionary power is concerned with the regulatory activity of central government. The specific character of such governmental activity results from the unclear legal basis (e.g. discretion to grant or withhold contracts to achieve particular goals of governmental policy).

A broad approach to the meaning of administrative discretion is also characteristic for French administrative law. Irrespective of a "bound competence" (*la competence liée*) which is connected with a duty of action or inaction, there is the "discretionary power" (*le pouvoir discrétionnaire*) within legal boundaries of which an administrative authority is empowered to act freely. The authority is conferred with the competence which may be exercised in a not bound way in different stages of law-applying process. This means that the administrative official may be vested with the discretionary power in the fields of interpretation, legal qualification of facts and choosing of legal consequences. One may argued that the above-mentioned kind of power is manifested itself parallel in the interpretation of law, the subsumption of facts under legal norms and the establishing of legal consequences (effects). This approach leads to the identification of administrative discretion with a freedom of mutual connection between legally relevant facts and contents and goals of administrative acts which are concretisations of the law[13]. The discretionary power encompasses therefore not only the interpretation and the application of law but also a premise of purposefulness (*opportunité*) which determines choices in the field of legal permissible competence behaviours[14]. It may be observed that the French concept of discretion covers not merely classical competence to act freely (according to the criterion of purposefulness) but also various forms of legal assessment of relevant facts.

12 P.P. Craig, *Discretionary power...*, p. 81.

13 Cf.e.g. A. de Laubadère, J.-C. Venezia, Y. Gaudemet, *Traité de droit administratif, T. 1: L'organisation administrative, la juridiction administrative*, Paris 1990, p. 538.

14 B. Varadinek, *Ermessen und gerichtliche Nachprüfbarkeit im französischen und deutschen Verwaltungsrecht und im Recht der Europäischen Gemeinschaft*, Aachen 1995, p. 31; M. Geurts, *Verwaltungsgerichtliche Kontrolldichte. Ein Vergleich zwischen Deutschland und Frankreich unter besonderer Berücksichtigung des technischen Sicherheitsrechts*, Frankfurt am Main – Berlin – Bern – New York – Paris – Wien 1999, p. 57.

In comparison with the British and the French conceptions a theory of German administrative law represents a completely different approach to the discretion[15]. Traditionally in the German administrative law the concept of discretion is confined to the sphere of choice of legal consequences. It may be argued that on the one hand in the Germany prevails the narrow sense of discretion (*Ermessen in einem engeren Sinne,* discretion in the strict sense) and on the other hand in the UK and in France dominates the broad sense of this concept (*Ermessen in einem weiteren Sinne,* discretion in the broad sense)[16].

The authority has discretionary power when a relevant provision provides: "if X, you may/can do Y". The exercise of discretionary power consists in the free – within the legal limits – choice of legal consequences which are provided for in this part of a norm which contains rights, duties or other legal effects. According to the mechanism of "norm action" (*die Normwirkung*) the legal effects are constituted as a result of occurrence of certain facts provided for in that norm.

The discretion can be connected with the competence to choice of kind of behaviour (*das Entschließungsermessen*) or with the competence to choice of kind of legal consequence (*das Auswahlermessen*). Some elements of discretion can be found in a construction of *Beurteilungsspielraum* (margin of appreciation) which is based on granting to the administrative authority the exclusive competence of free legal assessment of facts. This construction is manifested in a stage of legal subsumption. However from a formal point of view the operation of subsumption is separated from a stage of establishing of legal consequences. Therefore the margin of appreciation is excluded from the scope of discretion. Similarly to this construction the undefined legal concepts (*unbestimmte Rechtsbegriffe*) are as well the subject to the law interpretation and application (in the process of subsumption of facts), not belonging to the discretion. Strictly considering the German approach it is worth mentioning that also so-called *Planungsermessen* (discretion in the planning process) cannot be incorporated into the concept of discretion. Planning norms are analyzed as *Finalnormen*[17]. This kind of legal norms are characterized by the non-conclusive legal effects (like the principles

---

15 Cf. e.g. M. Künnecke, *Tradition and Change...*, pp. 78 ff; Ch. Starck, *Verwaltungsermessen im modernen Staat – Rechtsvergleichender Generalbericht*, in: *M. Bullinger* (ed.), *Verwaltungsermessenim modernen Staat*, Baden-Baden 1986, pp. 24 ff.

16 M. Bullinger, *Das Ermessen der öffentlichen Verwaltung – Entwicklung, Funktionen Gerichtskontrolle*, Juristen-Zeitung 1984, Nr. 22, pp. 1001 ff.

17 *W. Hoppe, Zur Struktur von Normen des Planungsrechts*, Deutsches Verwaltungsblatt *1974,* Nr. 17, pp. 641 ff.; M. Ibler, *Die Schranken planerischer Gestaltungsfreiheit im Planfeststellungsrecht*, Berlin 1988, pp. 36–40.

in the Dworkin's sense) which take the forms of programmes, plans, strategies, policies. The empowered authority is required to achieve the normative aims and objectives by a balancing of conflicting interests (e.g. public and private interests). The way and the result of the operation of balancing are not strictly determined by the law. Consequently the administrative authority has in this field a large scope of freedom.

3. Levels of intensity of judicial control of the discretionary administrative power

Judicial control of administrative discretion is the subject to very difficult conceptual and structural problems[18].

On the one hand there is a problem of delegation of powers by the legislator in order to flexible adopt legal norms via administrative rulemaking or administrative adjudication. In principle a court must accept the administrative action within the scope of delegated power in the same way it accepts legislation[19]. If the judicial control is exercised according to the criterion of legality, the court may examine the contested administrative competence behaviour merely in the light of specified legal patterns. When the administrative authority is entrusted with the task of achievement of public goals by means of law-applying, lawmaking or regulating decisions which are political and free in nature, the court must respect the discretionary choices as long as they fall within the limits of the legal system. In principle the courts are not empowered to substitute their own discretion for the discretion assigned to the administrative body. Since the administrative discretion is not generally reviewed by the courts on the merits, they may not substitute their own purposefulness or extralegal (e.g. political, moral) choices or assessments for these of the competent administrative authorities. In practice there are problems with the interference of courts with the process of application of the law in administrative matters which are strictly connected with the policymaking. According to the principle of separation of powers the courts are not authorized to such interference. It may be said that in principle the courts shall defer to extralegal choices of the administrative bodies provided that these choices are performed within the limits of the law.

---

18 See more broadly e.g. Ch.H. Koch Jr., *Confining Judicial Authority over Administrative Action*, Missouri Law Review 1984, Vol. 49, No. 2, pp. 210 ff.

19 F.H. Easterbrook, *Judicial Discretion in Statutory Interpretation*, Oklahoma Law Review 2004, Vol. 57, No. 1, pp. 4–5.

On the other hand the court is a guarantor of constitutional position of the legislature and the individual rights. The judicial authorities are empowered and required to determine the legally permissible boundaries of the interpretation and the application of the law by the administrative bodies. Since the discretionary powers may to be granted only on the basis of statutory authorisation and may to be exercised only within the legal boundaries, therefore the court is obliged to examine whether and to which extent these boundaries and basis are obeyed. The judicial control of administrative action is a necessary condition for implementation of the rule of law and for protection of the legislature's lawmaking supremacy. Furthermore the judicial review over administration is a crucial element of the system of the protection of individual rights.

The issue of intensity of judicial control of discretionary administrative power is strictly connected with the problem of internal division of the legality which remains the fundamental criterion for the control exercised by administrative courts. In the considered approach the legality is understood as a compliance of the administrative action with the law. The legal provisions determine formal and substantive requirements of the legality. On the one hand there is the legality with regard to the form of the administrative action. This category of legality embraces all procedural and formal conditions concerning the process of decision making. On the other hand there is the legality with regard to the substance of the administrative action. This kind of legality covers all legal requirements concerning the contents of decision. In the theory of French administrative law the first category of legality is defined as "*légalité externe*" (external legality) and the second – as "*légalité interne*" (internal legality)[20]. The German theory of administrative law uses in turn the analogous terms: "*formelle Rechtsmäßigkeit*" (formal legality) and "*materielle Rechtsmäßigkeit*" (material legality)[21].

Having regard to above-mentioned distinction it should be noted that judicial review of the exercise of administrative discretion must take into account certain limitations or reductions in the process of examination of legality of the discretionary actions. Indeed the exercise of discretion is a very special type of administrative action and therefore must be reviewed consistently with its special nature[22]. It is an indisputable fact that in many legal orders the judicial scrutiny of the discretionary administrative acts is confined merely to the verification of certain areas of the legality. This kind of limitation results from the essence of

20 See e.g. J.-C. Ricci, *Droit administratif*, Vanves 2004, pp. 144 ff.
21 See e.g. H. Maurer, *Allgemeines Verwaltungsrecht*, München 2011, pp. 256–261.
22 Ch.H. Koch Jr., *Confining Judicial Authority*..., p. 210.

discretion. The discretionary power implies possibility of choice between legally acceptable and equivalent solutions. Consequently in principle the court may not interfere directly in the contents of the contested discretionary act. In other words, some aspects or levels of the substantive area of the legality remain beyond the reach of judicial verification. It is therefore justified to claim that the judicial verification of legality of the discretionary administrative power is reduced in the sphere of substance of the controlled act.

Characteristic for judicial review of the administrative discretion is a gradation of the intensity of judicial control powers. There are several levels and grades of the intensity of judicial control.

The first level of judicial control covers the examination of existence of breaches of the formal law. A common feature of many legal orders is the full and unrestricted controllability of the formal and procedural requirements of the legality of discretionary acts[23]. The judicial scrutiny must be therefore concentrated on the searching for formal and procedural errors of the reviewed act.

Firstly, the court is empowered to quash, invalidate or declare null and void the discretionary act if it is defective because of lack or violation of the competence. The administrative authority acts outside its power (*ultra vires*) if it takes any decision or action which was beyond its legal authorization or fails to do something which was obliged to do[24]. The violation of the competence can consist in an exceeding the jurisdiction i.e. authority's acting beyond the limits of its power. It may take the following forms: exceeding the substantive jurisdiction (the authority has no power to deal with the kind of matter at issue); exceeding the territorial jurisdiction (the authority has no power to dispose of the matter which arose within a specified territory); exceeding the personal jurisdiction (the authority has no power to deal with the particular person concerned)[25].

Secondly, the court is entitled to interfere in the case of formal defects of the controlled act. This ground for judicial control encompasses the situation when the issued act is of a kind that the authority has no power to issue or when the issued act contains defects concerning its form.

Thirdly, the ground for judicial control is the procedural defectiveness of the administrative act. Regardless of whether the controlled act is bound or discretionary the court sets aside the challenged administrative act in the case of failure to obey procedure required by the law.

23 Cf. Ch. Starck, *Verwaltungsermessen...*, p. 35 ff.
24 Cf. A. Carroll, *Constitutional and Administrative Law*, Harlow – London 2007, pp. 314 ff.
25 J.-M. Auby, R. Drago, *Traité des recoursen matière administrative*, Paris 1992, pp. 329 ff.

The second level of judicial control is concerned with the inquiry whether the administrative body acted within the substantive (material) scope of its competence (authority). A subject of the judicial verification is the contents of the controlled act. According to above-mentioned remarks this stage of control is connected with the substantive (internal) legality. In many legal orders on the level of this kind one can observe the limitations of review intensity with regard to the discretionary administrative acts. This kind of level is internally differentiated.

In the French administrative law one can differentiate four grades of intensity of judicial control of substantive legality[26].

First grade embraces the control of observance of the legal and the factual basis of the administrative act (*contrôle des motifs*). An activity of the court is focused on the existence of the errors of law (*les erreurs de droit*) and the errors of fact (*les erreurs de fait*). The legal errors take place when the authority misconstrues or gives an incorrect meaning to legal rules (misinterprets the law applicable to the issue to be decided). However, it must be stressed that the defective legal assessments (legal qualifications) of the facts are excluded from the scope of these errors. In comparison with the legal defects the factual errors result from a breach of duty to make the sufficient, accurate, complete and truthful factual findings.

Second grade of intensity covers the evident errors of legal assessment of the facts with regard to the undetermined legal concepts (*les erreurs manifeste d'appréciation de la valeur des faits*) and the evident abuse of power or procedure (*le détournement de pouvoir ou de procedure*). The evident errors of legal assessment are a consequence of defective subsumption of the fact under the undetermined concepts in the matters which require the specialized knowledge and experience of the public administration bodies. In principle the courts are not empowered to verify the administrative legal qualification of the facts in the case of discretionary power. But in the above-mentioned situation the court exceptionally may verify whether the subsumption is illogical, grossly unjust or unreasonable. A similar approach is typical for the cases of the evident abuse of power or procedure. The abuse of power or procedure occurs when the administrative authority uses the competence (also in its procedural aspect) for purposes

---

26 See e.g. J. Koch, *Verwaltungsrechtsschutz in Frankreich. Eine rechtsvergleichende Untersuchung zu den verwaltungsinternen und verwaltungsgerichtlichen Rechtsbehelfen des Bürgers gegenüber der Verwaltung*, Berlin 1998, pp. 174 ff.; C. Lerche, *Landesbericht Frankreich*, in: J. Abr. Frowein (ed.), *Die Kontrolldichte bei der gerichtlichen Überprüfung von Handlungen der Verwaltung*, Berlin – Heidelberg – New York 1993, pp. 7 ff; M. Geurts, *Verwaltungsgerichtliche Kontrolldichte…*, pp. 55 ff.; B. Varadinek, *Ermessen und gerichtliche Nachprüfbarkeit…*, pp. 40 ff.

other than that which the legislator intended[27]. In order to determine whether the abuse of power has been committed the court must examine the motives of issuance of the contested act (e.g. the authority was motivated not by the public interest but by a personal one).

Both grades of the control are obligatory and the court has a legal duty to exercise them. This is the "minimal control" (*contrôle minimum*) or "reduced control" (*contrôle réduit*).

The third grade of intensity is focused on all errors of subsumption. On this level of control the reviewing courts are authorized to verify all legal assessments of the facts in a full scope and to substitute their own legal qualification for the qualification of the administrative body. This grade of control is also applicable to the matters in which the authority is vested with the special and exclusive competence to exercise freely the legal assessment of the facts (margin of appreciation). The control exercised on the first, second and third stages is called the "normal (ordinary) control" (*contrôle normal*).

The fourth and the last grade of intensity (so-called "control maximal"/*contrôle maximal*) is connected with the control of observance of the principle of proportionality. The court examines in this case whether the administrative action or its contents are adequate in relation to the facts, the legal conditions and the legal purposes. It may be said that then the judicial scrutiny is transferred into the realm of purposefulness. Therefore this extralegal verification is performed very seldom.

A different approach can be observed in the UK administrative law[28].

On the first level of control the courts examine all cases of illegality including primarily the defects of interpretation, subsumption and factual findings. As regards the illegality of the exercise of discretionary power one should be noted that it can result from a failure to exercise the discretion or from an abuse of discretion. The first situation occurs when the authority fails to fulfil a statutory duty of the exercise of discretionary power. The second situation takes place when the authority takes into account wholly irrelevant considerations or fails to take into account that which was relevant, or when the authority uses the power to achieve improper purpose (a purpose or objective which is not that for which the power was given).

On the second level of control the court is empowered to evaluate the contested act in the light of extralegal criterion of rationality (reasonableness). The

---

27 Cf. B. Schwartz, *French Administrative Law and the Common-law World*, New York 1954, pp. 200 ff.

28 See e.g. H. Barnett, *Constitutional and Administrative Law*, London – Sydney 2002, pp. 837 ff.; A. Carroll, *Constitutional and Administrative...*, pp. 314 ff.

judicial assessments are derived from the fundamental principles of logic or social morality.

The third level of control is actuated in the exceptional cases. In these cases the extralegal standards of proportionality and procedural propriety are applicable. These latter are emanated from the rules of natural justice (which are rooted in the common law system).

In the German administrative law the intensity of judicial control of administrative discretionary power is a consequence of internal division of the legality into two kinds[29].

The formal legality (which covers the legal requirements of the competence, form and procedure) is examined without limitations. In turn the verification of the material (substantive) legality is reduced. The operations of interpretation, subsumption and factual findings are in principle reviewed in the full scope. Exceptionally the administrative subsumption is verified to a limited extent. This limitation is concerned with the administrative matters in which the administrative authorities have the exclusive competence to make the legal assessment of the relevant facts (*der Beurteilungsspielraum*). The competence of this kind is exercised freely within the limits of the law and the special knowledge and experience of the administrative body. The administrative court is not empowered to intervene in the sphere of professional, specialized and autonomous evaluations of the competent administrative authorities.

As already mentioned, the German concept of discretion is confined to the choice of legal consequences of the facts. Since these consequences are provided for in the concretised norm of substantive law therefore the control of exercising discretion is the matter of verification of material (substantive) legality.

The act of exercising discretionary power is a subject to reduced verification. The administrative court is merely empowered to review whether the administrative discretionary act (or omission to its issue) is illegal because the statutory limits of discretion (external limits of discretion) has been exceeded or because the discretion has not been exercised for the purpose of the competence (internal limits of discretion). The defective exercise of discretionary power takes place when the authority: a) fails the duty of exercise of the discretion at all (*Ermessensausfall* or *Ermessensunterschreitung*); b) violates the statutory provisions which are relevant to the exercise of discretion (e.g. constitutional or statutory regulations

---

29 See e.g. M. Geurts, *Verwaltungsgerichtliche Kontrolldichte...*, pp. 25 ff.; B. Varadinek, *Ermessen und gerichtliche Nachprüfbarkeit...*, pp. 40 ff.; M. Künnecke, *Tradition and Change...*, pp. 89 ff., 110 ff.

of substantive law) (*Ermessensüberschreitung*); c) abuses the discretion, i.e. uses the power to the achievement the purposes which are improper, prohibited or disproportionate (*Ermessensfehlgebrauch*).

The court is not allowed to carry out the directly verification of the contents of discretionary act. Substantive verification of the discretion and the substitution of judicial discretion for the administrative discretionary choices would have led to the court's adjudication in the administrative matter on the merits. Therefore, it is not disputed that the control of discretionary administrative acts is confined to the verification of formal legality and to the determination of substantive limits of the exercising discretion[30].

30 See more broadly e.g. M. Kamiński, *Mechanizm i granice weryfikacji sądowoadministracyjnej a normy prawa administracyjnego i ich konkretyzacja* (*Mechanism and limits of judicial-administrative verification and administrative law norms and their concretisation*), Warsaw 2016, pp. 629 ff., 747 ff.

Bartosz Wojciechowski
(Associate Professor, University of Lodz, Poland, The Supreme Administrative Court of Poland Judge)

Marek Zirk-Sadowski
(Professor, University of Lodz, Poland, The Supreme Administrative Court of Poland Judge)

Justification as the limitation of the discretionary power of the administrative judge[1]

Abstract: The subject matter of this article is that any decision should find its justification in the current law. In this case, judicial discretion involves choosing the appropriate forms of arguments and finding a balance between the applied interpretative rules and the principles of law when it is not possible to read the meaning of a specific legal provision literally.

Keywords: justification, judicial discretion, legal argumentation

A peculiar feature of modern legal systems, which are characterised by the rule of law, is the tendency to avoid subordinating law, in particular administrative law, to acute political and economic goals. Such an objective is achievable only through the protection of the relative autonomy of the legal culture, which can protect against the instrumentalisation of the standards of the protection of the rights of individuals. In the context of administrative law, therefore, we can observe a transition to the administrative model[2].

An autonomous system relies on a relationship between the law and the political system, in which the law is a source of values, which are not voluntarily granted to the citizen by the state. Law ceases to be a kind of instruction provided by a sovereign and, rather, becomes an emancipated mechanism for rationalising social goals and ideals in relation to the political system. Emancipation occurs in the sphere of the administrative law functioning within such an autonomous legal

---

1 This contribution was in part supported by a research project granted by the National Science Center (Poland), No. DEC-2013/11/B/HS5/04156 to the first author.

2 Cf. Ph. Nonet, Ph. Selznick, *Law and Society in Transition. Toward Responsive Law*, New York 1978, p. 16, E. Kustra, *Polityczne problemy tworzenia prawa* [*Political Problems of Law Making*], Toruń 1994, p. 35.

system, in relation to the political system or to the purposes of authority centres. The interpretation of the law in any case cannot allow for any threat to civil rights and freedoms. Moreover, in the autonomous system, the content of the law is agreed in the judicial interpretative discourse, independent from political power; therefore, the justification of legal decisions, both in creating and applying the law, demands formal compliance with the law and, accordingly, there exists a "test of the legality" of the acts of creating and applying the law. As a result, a transition occurs from administrative law as a kind of instruction to administrative law as a set of norms created in the process of making judicial arrangements of its contents.

In the autonomous legal order, the legitimisation of legality as a kind of cultural value is carried out mainly by guaranteeing by law the protection of certain fundamental values. The autonomous values of law constitute specifically human rights and the democratic institutions of the rule of law[3]. Neil MacCormick rightly points out, however, that the thoughtless following of certain patterns of behaviour shared in the society should be regarded as activities of heteronomous character, although nothing stands in the way of autonomously recognising the standards of conduct shared in the society[4]. According to the Scottish thinker, a distinction should be made between the following:

a) rules – which are conventional in nature and are, therefore, specific to the law (in MacCormick's belief, they play the role of interpretative schemes)[5];
b) norms and preferences – which belong to the normative order[6]; and
c) shared standards of propriety, decency and good behaviour[7] – which are quite loose wordings defining behaviour.

---

3 M. Zirk – Sadowski, *Ideologie wykładni prawa administracyjnego* [*Ideologies of the Interpretation of Administrative Law*] [in:] L. Leszczyński, B. Wojciechowski, M. Zirk-Sadowski, *Wykładnia w prawie administracyjnym* [*Interpretation in Administrative Law*], Warsaw 2012, System Prawa Administracyjnego, vol. IV, p. 175.

4 N. MacCormick, *Institutions of Law. An Essay in Legal Theory*, Oxford University Press 2008, pp. 255–256.

5 Ibidem, p. 76.

6 In relation to the moral sphere, par excellence MacCormick very clearly emphasises the importance of autonomy; see N. MacCormick, *Institutions of Law*, *op. cit.*, pp. 249–252.

7 N. MacCormick, *H. L. A. Hart*, Stanford University Press 2008, p. 56; these standards of conduct are sometimes referred to by MacCormick, being somewhat inconsistent in the application of his nomenclature, as conventions and, therefore, the sense of the term "conventions" should always be clear to the reader according to the context in which it is used.

The latter could be considered as the contents of the "positive morality of a group"[8]. The point here is that the difference between such standards, which are understood as the "positive morality of a group", and morality would be associated to some extent with the concepts of heteronomy (standards) and autonomy (morality par excellence) of action[9].

Wherever a judge does not approach the process of applying the law in a strictly formalised and bound manner, there comes to the fore the discretionary power of the judge. The judge is not then faced with the task of carrying out a simple, rational subsumption but is authorised to balance between a great many alternatives to deliver substantive judgements. The judge can then decide between two contradictory decisions (e.g. granting or not granting the right) or, in a disjunction, can choose among numerous acceptable solutions. The concept of "discretion" is also used in the sense of "assessment" when it comes to a valuating adjudication, which constitutes the nature of judicial discretion and a margin of decision granted to the judge. In contemporary Anglo-Saxon literature devoted to "judicial discretion" it is stressed that this issue should be discussed in a broad context that allows for taking into consideration semantic and epistemic aspects[10]. Further, this allows for touching upon such issues, in this sense, as the knowledge of the social phenomena, the status of social ontology and the relationship between law and language.

From this point of view, the judge's discretion extends to both the horizontal and the vertical spheres of judicial activity. This range includes not only various fields of legal norms, which provide the judge with the freedom of settlement, but also varying degrees of legal qualification of the individual case. The freedom of the judge applies to the thinking process, assessment of the facts, interpretation

8 Ibidem, p. 67.

9 Ibidem, pp. 77 and N. MacCormick, *Institutions of Law*, *op. cit.*, pp. 255–256, where MacCormick clearly emphasises that the thoughtless following of certain patterns of behaviour shared in society should be regarded as activities of a heteronomous character, although nothing stands in the way of autonomously recognising the standards of behaviour shared in society. More on this topic can be found in a great analysis; see. K. M. Cern, *The Counterfactual Yardstick. Normativity, Self Constitutionalisation and the Public Sphere*, Frankfurt am Main 2014, pp. 67–86.

10 See D. Galligan, *Discretionary Powers: A Legal Study of Official Discretion*, Oxford 1986; M. I. Vila, *Facing Judicial Discretion. Legal Knowledge and Right Answers Revisited*, Dordrecht – Boston – London 2000, p. 14 ff.; *Judicial Discretion in European Perspective*, ed. O. Wiklund, 2003; B. Wojciechowski, *Dyskrecjonalność sędziowska. Studium teoretycznoprawne* [*Judicial Discretion. Theoretical-Legal Studies*], Toruń 2004, J. Andreoni, R. D. Madoff, *The Role of Judicial Discretion in Dispute Settlement*, "Boston College Law School Legal Studies Research Paper" 2008, No. 151.

of legal norms, determination of their mutual relationship and sometimes also to law-making. Judicial discretion applies to every form of judicial freedom, regardless of whether its origins can be traced to statutory authorisation or acquisition from the judiciary in a *praeter* or *contra legem* manner during the settlement of an individual case, which has not been precisely defined in the statute.

In this context, it is worth appealing to an aretic model of adjudication, whereby in addition to the content of legal norms and the analysis of the effects of the judgement, the judge is guided by his or her permanent dispositions, worked out by him or her in the legal practice, which are also based on an understanding of the objectives of the specific legislation and the general functions and social significance of the court[11]. The judge extends the decision-making grounds to add the content resulting from the reference to juridical virtues – created by judicial practice – such as courage, wisdom, temperament and, in particular, the virtue of justice. In accordance with its assumptions, the aretic model provides the possibility of combining stability with the flexibility of the law, if the judge has the authority, maturity, argumentative abilities and certain juridical virtues (and thus starts to resemble the judge Hercules). Moreover, the very process of adjudication constitutes a mechanism for the development, learning and maturity of judges, who are not "camels of justice" but sensitive subjects approaching each situation on an individual basis, seeking to combine hard evidence and legal arguments with the requirements stemming from the analysis of a specific situation. Such correction is enabled by the proficiency in referring to the principles and making use of functional interpretation.

In other words, the justification of legal decisions should be purposeful, taking into account the "openness" of the law to the needs and aspirations of the society and to morality that assumes cooperation in the society. Currently, the postulated value of interpretation is mainly in finding agreement (negotiating) between the interpretation of the legal texts containing administrative law and the fundamental rights of the individual. This promotes the activism of judges and a dynamic interpretation of the law, which means that the administrative authorities and

---

11 Here, I specifically refer to Lawrence Solum's virtue jurisprudence programme. Cf. *Virtue Jurisprudence*, C. Farrelly, L. Solum eds., Basingstoke 2008. L. Solum, *The Virtues and Vice of a Judge: An Aristotelian Guide to Judicial Selection*, "South California Law Review" 1988/61; *Virtue Jurisprudence: A Virtue-Centered Theory of Judging*, "Metaphilosophy", 2003/34/1–2; *A Tournament of Virtue*, "Florida State University Law Review" 2005/32; *The Aretic Turn in Constitutional Theory*, "Brooklyn Law Review" 2005/70; *Judicial Selection: Ideology Versus Character*, "Cardozo Law Review" 2005/26/2; *Natural Justice*, "The American Journal of Jurisprudence" 2006/51.

the administrative Courts must reach consensus on the general principles of law stemming from the Constitution as well as EU law and international law. Such an assumption is also justified by the principle of the democratic state of law, which shows that any decision should find its justification in the current law. In order to properly justify the judicial decision, it also becomes necessary to appeal to the "code of practical reason"[12]. As a result, the decision will be limited not only by the rules and principles resulting directly from the applied statute, but it will also comply with the complex rules which include the content of the law itself. In the context of "the revolution of law" taking place in the legal systems throughout Europe, based on the structure of the protection of fundamental rights, a crucial role is also played by the principle of proportionality, which becomes the primary contemporary justification and instrument for controlling the discretion of the legislature and the executive. It is referred to in the literature (not unreasonably) as the "methodological culmination of the current post-positivist and neo-naturalistic approach to the law which combines the positive and the natural law"[13].

The principle of proportionality is superbly placed in the broader framework of contemporary jurisprudence, because it forces one to change the views on what is legal, with regard to interference in the rights of the individual, as well as on what is proportional[14]. As mentioned above, such a perspective forces a proactive judicial approach, because it assumes the judge's axiological sensitivity in referring to the fundamental rights of the individual and the principles of the system, including those resulting from transnational law.

At this point, it would be instructive to refer to the decision of the European Court of Justice (ECJ) on Kücükdeveci, in which the Court ordered an appeal to the primary sources of EU law in order to justify the principle of equality and

---

12 R. Alexy, *Theorie der juristischen Argumentation*, Frankfurt am Main 1978, p. 234 ff. E. Hilgendorf, *Argumentation in der Jurisprudenz. Zur Rezeption von analytischer Philosophie und kritischer Theorie in der Grundlagenforschung der Jurisprudenz*, Berlin 1991, p. 115 ff. These rules are differentiated in the frames of internal and external justifications of judicial adjudication, cf. also J. Wróblewski, *Sądowe stosowanie prawa* [*Judicial Application of Law*], Warsaw 1988, chapter VI ff.

13 E. Engle, *The History of the General Principle of Proportionality: An Overview*, "Dartmouth Law Journal" 2012/10, pp. 1–11.

14 Cf. N. Emiliou, *The Principle of Proportionality in European Law. A Comparative Study*, Leiden 1996; T. Trimidas, *General Principles of European Law*, Oxford 2003, Chapters 3 and 4; M. Künnecke, *Tradition and Change in Administrative Law. An Anglo-German Comparison*, Berlin-Heidelberg-New York 2007, pp. 110 ff.

non-discrimination[15]. What was unique in this judgement was the recognition by the ECJ that when it comes to the principle of non-discrimination, its source is not provided for in Directive 2000/78/EC[16]. The Court noted that it belongs to *the general principles* of the EU, and thus it constitutes the category that belongs not to the secondary legislation (e.g. the EU legislation, such as the regulations or directives and international agreements concluded by the EU) but to the primary legislation – namely, to the law formed by the founding treaties (or amending treaties), general principles of law or, last but not least, common law.

From the point of view of our interests, the most interesting issue is the implication of the said judgement that opens up the possibility of a very broadly understood reference to "unwritten" and "non-EU" sources in a broader sense than just a reference to the EU law itself. Nevertheless, it should be noted that the principle prohibiting discrimination on the grounds of age has been considered a *general principle* of EU law, which is to have its *origin in the common constitutional traditions* of the Member States and in the international agreements binding them[17]. The Court, (a) pointing out "pre-sources" of the principle of non-discrimination (i.e. recognising that the latter exist), (b) which can be found also in non-EU international public law (its principles and the Universal Declaration of Human Rights and the constitutional traditions of the Member States), (c) concluded, at the same time, that the principle of non-discrimination "permeates" from the listed orders to the EU law, which is, after all, a part of the *international* legal community. Thus, the ECJ has widely opened the sources of the EU law to the axiological-normative references. From this perspective, two issues come to the fore.

First, it can be assumed that adjudicating with the use of *general principles* was presented by the ECJ as a particularly legitimised way of satisfying the principium of the rule of law of the applied EU law because, at its basis, there is to be placed – in the intention of the Court – normative unity, and within the latter – *a harmonized axiological pluralism* of the EU law with international law and with the laws of the Member States. Normative unity must, therefore, be viewed

---

15 Judgement of 19 January 2010, issued in case C-555/07 *Seda Kücükdeveci v. Swedex GmbH&Co. KG.*

16 Council Directive 2000/78/EC of 27 November 2000 establishing a general framework for equal treatment in employment and occupation (Official Journal EC L 303 of 27 November 2000, p. 16) enacted on the basis of then Art. 13 of the Treaty establishing the European Community, which in paragraph 1 established the legal basis for the adoption by the EU Council of "the measures needed to combat discrimination based on sex, race or ethnic origin, religion or belief, disability, age or sexual orientation".

17 Recital 21 of the grounds of the judgement on Kücükdeveci.

here as deontologically understood *prohibitive weights* for the plurality of values harmonised in such a sense that they never exceed these prohibitive weights[18].

Second, there is the issue of the legitimacy of the EU law – namely, that the possibility of justifying the common norms and shared values, as well as providing reasons in their favour, is of fundamental importance both for the reflective shaping of historically formed national identities and for the contemporarily constructed joint identity of the community of EU citizens. At this point, the principium of democracy comes to the fore. Justifications are designed to shape the area of normative activities which, although they are designed, on one hand, by sovereign legislators (understood as the political and legal institutions of the Member States), and, on the other hand, by the institutions of the European Union, in the area of mutually acceptable claims and justifications, they encounter the EU citizens as an elementary and, at the same time, the most crucial factor legitimising their decisions. Without indicating these reasons or without justifications approved by the three parties, compliance with the law cannot fully rely on gaining respect owing to the recognition of the law as worthy of respect, and the authority of the law can only be the authority of the sanction of coercion (force). In turn, these reasons may be recreated (reconstructed) only in a reflective attitude towards tradition, especially the tradition of the legal culture, understood as a constitutional culture rooted in the public political culture (namely, in the culture of public justifications).

Presenting rationality as a structure that gives sense to the activities undertaken within it allows for presenting the practice of law as a sphere of praxis which reproduces the values, categories of the description of reality and interpretative assumptions of certain types of rationality. This process is to a great extent influenced by the process of education and institutionalisation.

The use of the model of a creative action for the analysis of hard cases allows us to understand that the activity constantly transforms them. Action indeed requires description in terms of an active process, rather than static forms, and thus allows the judge to interpret and transform institutionally shaped knowledge (or, in other words, shared knowledge). Judicial activism is based on familiarisation with the

---

18 On the subject of "prohibitive weights" and the notion of political morality, see Karolina M. Cern, *Jürgena Habermasa koncepcja sfery publicznej – komunikacyjne kształtowanie opinii oraz woli obywateli, czyli idea samokonstytucjonalizacji* [*Jürgen Habermas' Concept of the Public Sphere – Communicative Shaping of Opinion and Will of the Citizens, Namely the Idea of Selfconstitutionalisation*], (ed.) P. Orlik, K. Przybyszewski, *Aktualność filozofii* [*Timeliness of Philosophy*], Wydawnictwo Naukowe Instytutu Filozofii UAM, Poznań 2012.

law, which depends on the ethical requirements posed to the legal discourse. The concept of the law as being such an object of cognition which is objective and purely external to the lawyer is, thus, rejected. Judicial activism, then, is based on the assumption that the law has many sources, of which the statute is only one. According to it, the law is justified by the authority of the nation, and therefore the will of the legislator can be for the judge only one of the benchmarks. The legal text only clarifies the law, which, however, is not exhausted in the legal provision, and the judge becomes the guarantor of such a broadly defined law against the arbitrariness of the legislator. The court is also presented here as an instrument that protects the citizen from the arbitrariness of the legislator. The result of the criticism of textualism is the emergence of a new conception of the role of the judge and the judging process. In this way, the judiciary becomes a reality because, by judging, the judges are given power over the integration of the normative meanings in the culture. In order to do so, however, judges must properly justify their decisions in a manner free from the argument of inertia (*Trägheitsprinzip*)[19], understood as a non-reflexive reliance on Court rulings rendered in similar cases, have a critical attitude towards so-called reticence and be guided by the principle of *summum ius summa iniuria*[20].

What becomes significant in this context in order to achieve the effect of the understanding and acceptance of the judicial settlement is a demand on the claim to justifiability[21]. According to this claim, everyone, when claiming something, has to believe it, yet it must be at the same time justifiable in order to be true, rational and correct. The claim to justifiability requires that the speaker is able to justify his or her claims at any time and in respect of anyone, unless he or she is able to provide an argument which justifies the refusal of justification. This rule is referred to as the "general rule of justification". The decision is justifiable if it is possible to find a justification for it – namely, to demonstrate arguability (in the strictest sense, in a strict sense or in a large sense on the grounds, respectively, of formal aletheic logic, deontic or normative logic or argumentation theory) of the ruling from the theoretical and/or axiological premises[22].

---

19 The principle of inertia: "rationality, as it is presented in law, is always a form of continuity"; therefore, "only a change must be justified". "Justification applies only to what is debatable and debated". Ch. Perelman, *Logika prawnicza. Nowa retoryka* [*Jurisitc Logic. New Rhetoric*], Warsaw 1984, p. 26.

20 M. Tullius Cicero. *De Officiis* with an English translation, W. Miller, Cambridge, Harvard University Press; Cambridge, Mass., London, England, 1913, *I, 33.*

21 R. Alexy, *Theorie der juristischen …, op. cit.*, p. 238.

22 J. Wróblewski, *Uzasadnienie i wyjaśnienie decyzji sądowej* [*Justifying and Explaining Court Decisions*], "Studia Prawno – Ekonomiczne" 1976, vol. XVI, p. 15 ff.

An optimally correct ruling must be inferred only by way of a rationalising justification of a choice between acceptable alternatives. The ruling should be constructed in such a way that allows control within respective instances (and thus to ensure verifiability and communication) of the judgement under appeal, which increases its clarity and acceptability and, further, the implementation of the sense of procedural fairness, as defined by John Rawls. The function of the justification of the judgement is expressed in the fact that its addressee – in addition to the parties themselves – is also the Supreme Administrative Court (although, for obvious reasons, any observations also apply to its justifications). Therefore, the case law of the Supreme Administrative Court also shows that the justification of the judgement of the administrative Court, in a situation where it is accompanied by the deficit referring to "the clarification of the legal basis of the decision", does not have the function of controlling its relevance, or a persuasive function, and is also far from carrying out the legitimising function. Accordingly, there is a disruption to its discursiveness, whose fundamental element is the justifiability of the judicial decision. In a situation where the body applying the law does not try to convince its "imaginable and indivisible" audience that the issued decision is rational, it does not undertake a comprehensive illocutionary act of justifying its decision. The objective of the justification is, in fact, to guarantee the absence of arbitrariness, eliminating the impact of purely personal preferences of the entity that applies the law, respecting the possibilities of defending one's reasons by the party and, finally, a chance to inspect the decision-making reasoning.

In our opinion, the opportunity to take into consideration in the interpretive practice so many important factors speaks against adopting the *clara sunt interpretanda* principle, while introducing a certain degree of interpretive freedom, which constitutes judicial discretion in broad terms. Consequently, one can speak here of a kind of "balancing" of the rules of interpretation, distinguished due to different contexts – namely, a linguistic, systemic or functional context – and, consequently, of balancing or weighing the settlement. The phrase "weighing" is used here in reference to Robert Alexy's concept of weighing law (*Abwägungsgesetz*)[23]. The conflict of the principles colliding in the process of argumentation underlines the need to understand the application of law as a model involving the weighing of the relevant principles and objectives. The object of weighing or balancing may be preferences, interests, goods, values or principles. Furthermore, the act

23 R. Alexy, *Theorie der Grundrechte*, Baden-Baden 1985, p. 146; J.-R. Sieckmann, *Regelmodelle und Prinzipienmodelle des Rechtssystems*, Baden-Baden 1990, pp. 223–240; J. – R. Sieckmann, *Zur Begründung von Abwägungsurteilen*, "Rechtstheorie" 1995, book 26, p. 46.

of balancing the principles includes a justified determination of the relationship between the priorities of the conflicting principles. Such a collision of principles or objectives results from the fact that different rules cannot be simultaneously complied with in a complete way in a particular case. The most general rule that applies to the act of weighing principles reads as follows: "The higher the degree of non-compliance or depletion of the operation of one principle, the higher must be in a given case the rank of the validity of another principle". The model of balancing principles corresponds clearly to the constitutional principle of proportionality, as mentioned above.

In such conditions, the solid element of the judicial practice of the administrative Courts is provided by the activities undertaken within the framework of the adopted jurisprudential strategies, whose value is expressed in taking into account the need to build the foundations for the possibility of carrying out the widest possible dialogue both in the constitutional and EU fields. The analysis of the judicature of the Polish administrative Courts justifies the claim that to the extent relating to the interpretation of law, the constitutional principles and the principles of the EU law bear significant importance, established already by a certain tradition[24], which causes the scope of the concept of law to be relatively wide and subject to the said balancing while adjudicating a specific case.

In this respect, it is worth noting that in accordance with Article 141 § 4 of the Polish Law on proceedings before administrative Courts, the reasons for a judgement shall include the provision of a brief picture of the state of the case, the charges of the complaint, the positions taken by other parties, the legal basis of the determination and its explanation. If, as a consequence of granting the complaint, the case is to be reconsidered by an administrative authority, the reasons should additionally include suggestions as to further proceedings. The fulfilment of the conditions set out in this legal norm is a guarantee that the administrative Court exercised due diligence when making a given decision, which allows, in particular, for assessing the validity of the reasons on which the decision is based. It is characteristic that in the Polish legal system, the scope of the examination of the case by the administrative Court is formed on the basis of the facts and the evidence, which is at the root of the contested administrative act and which is submitted in the files. The task of the administrative Court is, in effect, to determine whether the evidence gathered in the case file is complete, whether it has been properly

---

24 See more broadly W. Kręcisz, *Z problematyki uzasadniania orzeczeń przez sądy administracyjne* [*On the Issue of Justifying Judgements by the Administrative Courts*], [in:] *Uzasadnienia decyzji stosowania prawa* [*Justifying Decisions of Law Application*], ed. I. Rzuciło-Grochowska, M. Grochowski, Warsaw 2015, pp. 356–366.

assessed and whether it was sufficient for issuing the contested decision (see the judgement of the Supreme Administrative Court of 8 September 2011, II OSK 1301/11). Also of particular importance in any reasoning of a judgement is the indication of the legal basis for the settlement and its explanation. Proper written motifs of the judgement allow the litigating parties to familiarise themselves with the manner of reasoning and argumentation in the process of controlling the legality of the contested decision; at the same time, they reduce the impression of the arbitrariness of the rendered decision, especially in cases where the judge is allowed discretion. The resolution of the Supreme Administrative Court of 26 October 2009 adopted in full composition (I OPS 10/09) explained that the application of the legal provisions by the administrative Court also involves making such provisions a model of the control of the legality of an administrative decision or other action. It is worth noting that the legal basis of the decision and its explanation contained in the reasons of the judgement should refer not only to the content of the justification of the contested administrative decision but also to the allegations raised by the party in the complaint against such a decision (cf. the judgement of the Supreme Administrative Court of 23 November 2005, I FSK 408/05). In its resolution of 15 February 2010, the Supreme Administrative Court (II FPS 8/09) emphasised that when undertaking the control of the legality, the administrative Court may not uncritically accept the findings made in the administrative proceedings, particularly when these findings are challenged by a party to the proceedings. The position of the Court as to the correctness of determining the facts in a case of a dispute on this matter between the parties to administrative proceedings should include references to the arguments presented by both the administrative authority and the applicant, and should also explain why it considers the arguments of one party to be correct and others not. The Court should present the above analysis in a sufficiently detailed justification including those elements of the factual and legal states of the case which are relevant to its settlement. Any omission in this respect is a defect involving an insufficient explanation by the administrative Court of the factual and legal states of the adjudicated case, and therefore a failure which could have a significant impact on the outcome of the case (cf. the judgements of the Supreme Administrative Court of 25 November 2010, I GSK 1215/09, of 15 February 2011, II FSK 1832/09, and of 29 August 2012, II FSK 205/11). In other words, if the reasoning of the Court takes a vague form and does not show evidence of verifying the crucial elements of the factual and legal states of the case in a sufficiently detailed manner, there takes place a violation of Article 141 § 4 of the Polish law on proceedings before administrative Courts, which has a significant impact on the outcome of the case and prevents the judicial control of public administration. Court justification constitutes a restriction of arbitrariness and of unjustified leeway of the Court in deciding a given case. Although there is no single, objective measure for fulfilling that obligation, it is certain that its violation occurs when in a written justification of the rendered judgement, the circumstances, assertions and arguments relevant to the undertaken legal assessment have been omitted or considered only in part.

The obligation of proper justification is particularly important in a situation where the administrative Court must decide in respect of the merits. As an expression of the fulfilment of the requirements stemming from the right to the Court (especially in terms of the postulate of hearing a case within a reasonable time), significant changes have been introduced in the Polish Act on proceedings before the administrative Courts. One of the most significant changes designed to improve the conduct and strengthen the effectiveness of the administrative Courts' control over public administration is to grant to the administrative Courts in Art. 145a in specific and exceptional circumstances the power to rule on the merits of the case (Art. 145a § 1 "In the case referred to in Art. 145 § 1, subparagraph 1 (a) or subparagraph 2, where the circumstances of the case so justify, the Court shall oblige the authority to render a decision or order within a specified time limit, indicating the manner in which the case should be handled or determined, unless the determination was left to the discretion of the authority").

The remaining principle is still, naturally, the adjudication of last resort appeal, lying mainly in the possibility of setting aside by the administrative Court the contested decision of the administrative authority and obliging it to settle the case while taking into account the judgement of the Court. As a consequence, the analysed change grants to the administrative Court the right to issue a substantive decision, and not just to confine itself to setting aside the contested Act. The power of the Court will be excluded only when the provisions leave the decision to the discretion of the administrative body. Such authority of the Court, however, is carried out by the action of the administrative authority. In fact, the Court decides directly about the rights or obligations of the parties; however, in order to ultimately settle a given administrative case, it is indispensable to issue a decision or a ruling by an administrative body of the content of the settlement "imposed" by the administrative Court. Moreover, the Court, by deciding on the essence of the administrative case, would also oblige the administrative authority to give that settlement the form provided by the law – namely, a decision or a ruling, respectively.

Art. 145a of the Act on proceedings before administrative Courts grants to the administrative Courts the competence to specify in the judgement granting the complaint the manner of settling a case and even a future settlement, if the circumstances of the case justify so. This means that due to the judgement rendered under Art. 145a, the party becomes aware of its legal situation in terms of both substantive law and procedural law. It is also important that the new regulation prevents cases of non-performance of the Court's guidelines (Art. 145a § 2).

Consequently, the jurisprudence of the Supreme Administrative Court points out that the reasons for the judgement should be prepared in a way that results in indicating the reasons why the Court deemed the contested Act or omission of the administrative authority as consistent or inconsistent with the law. In this context, it is emphasised that restricting the justification of the judgement to citing a given legal provision or to vaguely relying on the views of doctrine or jurisprudence, without a simultaneous and thorough reference to the circumstances of the actual state of the facts, cannot replace the description of the logical operation resulting in the adoption of a specific direction of the interpretation and in the application of a given legal provision in the circumstances of the individual factual state of the adjudicated case and the adopted direction and method of settlement (cf. judgement of the Supreme Administrative Court of 11 January 2011, I GSK 685/09).

This is especially important when taking into account the previously indicated open and negotiating character of law, in which the important role is played by the act of weighing the principles and values, appealing to the purposes of the law and morality. In this context, N. MacCormick considers it necessary to clearly distinguish between the theory of the current positive law and the theory of the ideal positive law[25], and from this perspective, it must be kept in mind that the pursuit of the latter is performed by a discursive settlement of inherently highly controversial moral problems, articulated by autonomously issued judgements, which does not always or immediately (from the perspective of time) result in achieving consent in relation to them[26]. Therefore, MacCormick's position justifies a rather legalistic approach to making legal decisions[27], due to which, in his opinion, there is emphasised – to a much greater extent than in the case of other proposals – the relevance and role of making autonomous moral judgements, and on that basis pursuing a change to the actual form of law so that it approaches the ideal form.

The rules and principles which the judge should take into account are most often evaluative and are formulated in an abstract manner, allowing for covering

25 Ibidem, p. 257.
26 Ibidem, p. 259.
27 Ibidem, p. 261.

all potential situations, and pointing out what choice must be made, in a very general way. The directives and principles formulated in this way can be treated as rules of reference[28].

J. Wróblewski notes that such directives of the choice of consequence indicate that one should choose a "fair" or "good" settlement "corresponding to the principles of morality" or "complying with the rules of the natural law", referring thereby to extralegal values. The author points out that in a situation requiring such discretion in the decision-making, one must distinguish three points of view: legal, descriptive and theoretical[29]. From the legal point of view, we cannot talk about limiting the freedom of the judge because, by definition, it is placed outside the framework in which certain legal provisions govern the choice. However, from the descriptive and theoretical point of view, it should be concluded that the discretion of the judge is limited to such an extent that the judge feels bound by the prevailing ideology and to such an extent that this ideology provides him or her with specific directives. The descriptive and theoretical point of view requires providing a justification of the undertaken choice of legal consequences which is based on instrumentally or thetically relativised assessment.

---

28 J. Wróblewski, *Sądowe …*, *op. cit.*, p. 242 ff.

29 Ibidem, pp. 243, 250.

Iwona Rzucidło-Grochowska
(Ph. D., Judicial Decisions Bureau in the Supreme Administrative Court of Poland)

The role of judicial opinion in controlling the discretionary power in public administration[1]

Abstract: Controlling discretionary power in public administration by the administrative courts is also a matter of judicial opinion, not only one of judicial decision-making. From a practical point of view, the crucial role in this respect is played by the motives of the judicial decision, not by the ruling itself (by tenor).

Keywords: judicial opinion, discretionary power, judicial reasoning, legal argumentation

1. The possibility of verifying decisions, even those issued by organs enjoying discretionary power, is among the most important rights in a democratic state. The control exercised by the administrative judiciary is intended to directly review the conduct of the body of public administration in the field of discretionary power. This control takes place in several ways: deciding on cases when the organ did not undertake any action, or when the organ issued a decision.[2]

One of the crucial areas where such a control takes place is the administrative judiciary deciding on individual cases in order to verify actions taken by public administration – when a party disagrees with the decision of the organ. To present a claim in court, the party usually needs to obtain the justification for the organ's decision to refer to the arguments and findings in it. Because of this, administrative organs should justify their opinions (decisions) simply because of the possibility of having those decisions verified by court.[3]

2. Although the administrative courts control the discretionary power of public administration directly, other courts can also contribute to the control in two

1 The paper has been prepared as an result of the research grant within the programme "Diamentowy Grant" (2012–2015).

2 The paper is based on the perspective of the Polish administrative judiciary, attempting to indicate the main problems in terms of judicial control of public administration's discretionary power.

3 On the role of motives for an administrative organ's decision, see also Jan *Zimmermann*, *Motywy decyzji administracyjnej i jej uzasadnienie*, Warsaw 1981.

forms. The first is by issuing judgements in cases containing an administrative element (which the Supreme Court of Poland does as part of its duties), which establish patterns of argumentation, followed afterwards in other cases by the administrative bodies. They are willing to be self-limited mainly for pragmatic reasons – anticipating that (if the decision becomes a subject of judicial review), the court will adhere to its previous standpoint. In this way, even in the legal orders that (like Polish administrative law) do not recognise precedents in a strict sense, the administrative courts' judgments may have quite a broad and substantial impact beyond the frames of particular cases. The second way is to decide cases that – though not connected directly with administrative matters – can affect the decisions of the administrative bodies, limiting the actual scope of their discretionary power. This pertains in particular to judgments of some sorts of prejudicial power (in terms of factual findings and/or interpretations of law), based upon various legal grounds.

The forms of interdependence between the grounds of judgments and the conduct of administrative bodies (of an indirect nature) are only sketched here. The main focus will be placed on direct correlations between the judiciary and administration in exercising discretionary competence.

The administrative judiciary has several tools for controlling the operation of public administration – e.g. adopting resolutions, deciding on individual cases, etc. The subject of the paper refers to cases initiated by individuals, not by organs (which is possible in the higher court – the Supreme Administrative Court of Poland). In the Polish judicial system there are two levels: the voivodeship administrative courts and the Supreme Administrative Court, where the latter assesses adjudications of lower courts. As a result, exercising discretionary power by administrative bodies is controlled in the highest instance only indirectly, by reviewing the voivodeship courts' decisions (direct control).

To start with, it is worth pointing out that the Supreme Administrative Court may influence the practice in terms of discretionary power also through resolutions – i.e. decisions setting out abstract patterns of interpretation of particular rules. As a standpoint adopted in a resolution is binding upon other courts, it also shapes (indirectly) the practice of administrative bodies – which, due to the aforementioned pragmatic reasons, are likely to use self-restraint with their discretionary power, adjusting it to the standpoint expressed by the Supreme Administrative Court.[4]

---

4 For more on the influence of resolutions on the practice of the application of law process see: Mateusz Grochowski, *Uchwały Sądu Najwyższego a jednolitość orzecznictwa.*

3. The control of the public administration's discretionary power is not reflected in the ruling itself (in tenor). In fact, the content of adjudication says little about the case, indicating only the final outcome of control (approval or lack of acceptance for the organ's decision). From a practical point of view, the crucial role in this respect is played by the motives of an administrative court decision (depending on the terminological assumptions, they may be referred to also as the judicial opinion or, in some sense, justification).[5] Their significant role results from the following several reasons, to name a few.

Most importantly, judicial opinion is the principal area where the court can express its way of reasoning, especially by explaining the way of understanding legal or axiological problems of a case, and indicating the right and wrong elements in the conduct of the administrative body. All in all, the motives of a judicial decision enable the court to express its opinion and its arguments in a direct way, presenting its detailed standpoint with reference to the case. Consequently, although the motives are, in principle, (as opposed to the tenor) not binding, they play a principal role in understating the case and thereby establishing interpretative patterns for the administrative courts' further rulings.

Secondly, it should be pointed out that administrative courts play a special role within the judiciary. They decide cases in different ways to that of ordinary courts – assessing them not from the very beginning, but exercising only a review function (controlling the other authority's decision). The adjudication of this kind may take place chiefly by reviewing the written motives of the administrative decision, leading to a dialogue between the court and the organ. Its obvious area are the motives of the court's decision, referring to the arguments of the administration and providing its response to them (whether affirmative or critical). Only in this area can the court fully express its opinion on the details of the decision under control. As a result, as the control is most often based on polemic with statements expressed in a decision of administration, it can take place by justifying the courts' judgment.

The interdependence of a ruling itself and a judicial opinion is closely associated with the fundamental nature of the administrative judiciary, limiting

---

Droga do autopojetyczności systemu prawa? [in:] *Jednolitość orzecznictwa. Standard-instrumenty-praktyka*. Studia i Analizy Sądu Najwyższego, vol. I, ed. M. Grochowski, M. Raczkowski, S. Żółtek, Warszawa 2015, pp. 84–94.

5 See also: Iwona Rzucidło-Grochowska, *Uzasadnienie orzeczenia sądowego w świetle jednolitości orzecznictwa. Zarys problematyki* [in:] *Jednolitość orzecznictwa. Standard-instrumenty-praktyka*. Studia i Analizy Sądu Najwyższego, vol. I, ed. M. Grochowski, M. Raczkowski, S. Żółtek, Warszawa 2015, p. 62.

its role only to controlling administrative decisions and other acts, without fully deciding cases by itself. The concept of this control is, therefore, strongly discursive, involving a dialogue between a court and an administrative body. It changes the perspective of deciding cases and narrating about them in written motives. Therefore, it may take place principally within the most discursive (by its nature) element of judicial proceedings – the justification, discussing competing arguments and standpoints.

The third argument for the above thesis can be derived from the essence of discretionary power. Although the organ enjoys a certain scope of freedom, and in the frame of this freedom can undertake decisions, it is not completely free in this respect, but has to take into account several constraints established by the legal order. Compliance can be indicated almost solely in the written justification. Therefore, the motives of the organ's decision show that the decision has a legal basis and does not go beyond the framework of freedom granted to the organ. The administrative court is entitled to assess only whether the discretionary decision of the organ has been properly justified (in terms of the provision of a written argumentation), whether it is correct and whether it remains within the scope of competence granted to the administrative body by the legislation. The court, therefore, inevitably refers primarily to the justification that allows the reconstruction of the motives behind the organ's decision. Otherwise, any convincing and proper (non-arbitrary) judicial review would not be possible. Discretional competence, which by its nature leaves an organ with a broad scope of assessment, in most cases could not be reviewed without a proper explanation, given by the organ itself, of how it made use of its freedom and why.

What is more, the paper concentrates on written reasons, which – because of their durable form and the fact that they are able to be made public – can become available to multiple recipients (including those outside the particular proceedings). As opposed to an oral justification of a judicial decision (if it is not recorded), the reasoning set down in writing can be referred to at any time. For the purposes of control, it allows the reasons for judgment to be read, and for conclusions to be drawn, and this is possible in the broadest sense only in the case of written justification.

4. Judicial opinion may also – apart from being a part of controlling procedure – affect the power and autonomy of administrative bodies. This influence can take place both directly and indirectly.

The first way is apparent mostly when the organ receives a negative assessment of its activity and has to repeat the proceedings, either entirely or in a certain aspect. Then written grounds give it feedback on the particular case. In other words, in the most basic way, the court may include in the motives the assessment of the organ's action in a particular case. This control has a direct dimension – one decision of the organ – one justification of the court, relating directly to the action of the organ in a particular case. In this case, the role of the reasoning is that, especially if there is no approval of the organ's decision, it can indicate to the organ where it exceeded the scope of the discretion given to it, and why.[6]

Judicial opinion can also contribute to the control of discretionary power of administrative organs *in abstracto* and in an indirect way – when the same organ, or other organs in other similar cases, benefit from court statements contained in the judicial opinion. Organs decide to comply with the opinions previously expressed by the judiciary. Reading a judicial opinion in a similar case allows for (motivated pragmatically) some self-limitation on the discretion of the administrative body. The organ, as mentioned above, being aware of such an interpretation of the regulations that is shown in the grounds of a judgment, acts for pragmatic reasons (out of fear that their decision will be repealed due to a different interpretation than in the reasoning of the court), restraining itself in issuing decisions (they are not directly related to a court decision). The influence of this kind in particular concerns the situation when judgements of administrative courts are published. The possibility of harmonising administrative conduct is also feasible, to some extent, for the decisions of ordinary (non-administrative) courts – as indicated above in point 2.

A similar mechanism is noticeable within the judiciary in the formation of the judicial uniformity. It is an interesting phenomenon because the court, in general, does not have direct control over decisions of the organ, but does have an effect on it. What is important here is the rank of judicial decision (arising from the position of a court within the judiciary) and its publication. In addition, this effect arises *a priori* – before issuing a decision. This control is, therefore, not typical. Taking into account the possibility of control in the future and being able to predict its outcome (in light of the previously issued judgment), the organ is likely to adopt the same standpoint as the one expressed before in the court's justification. In this case, the control is performed by courts *de facto* – without any direct contact with a particular case. Justification therefore anticipates direct control, which always can be initiated, but its effect can then be positive for the organ.

6 On the differentiation between the administrative and judicial type of application of law, see Leszek Leszczyński, *Zagadnenia teorii stosowania prawa. Doktryna i tezy orzecznictwa*, Kraków 2004, Zakamycze, pp. 21–26. Taking the problem in more general and quite simplified terms, the latter is used as a means of control of the former, which leads to several theoretical and practical interdependencies.

The grounds for a judicial decision also provide an opportunity for another form of steering administrative practice (both in a general dimension, as well as in terms of specific cases). The justification, in addition to the "direct" grounds of a decision, may also cover the guidelines for an administrative body as to further proceedings (if, in the outcome of a review, the decision has been overruled), or providing general hints as to the areas that might be subject to overall improvement in the future. Guidelines of this sort are formulated when the court agrees with the complaint and returns the case to the organ for reconsideration. In this way, the negative assessment of the organ's decision may also have further consequences.

These guidelines serve the organ as a hint to resolve the case properly and have a binding character (a failure to take them into account can be subject to an effective claim to the court). These guidelines are not just a reflection of the court on the proceedings of the organ (which is the typical space for reasons), but because of their binding nature are also complementary to the ruling itself (tenor), being therefore a part of the court's decision. Despite this, they are contained in the judicial opinion, not in the ruling itself. Therefore, the judicial opinion carries an important element of the ruling related to the control of discretionary power of public administration. In addition, the judicial opinion also carries the entire ruling, in the sense in which the justification refers to the ruling, making it possible to learn about the adjudication without reading the ruling itself. Remarks of this kind have a dual nature – on the one hand it is obligatory for an administrative organ to obey guidelines given *in concreto*, on the other hand, however, they are the essence and natural consequence of the adjudication, supplementing the verdict. In other words, those guidelines are not only part of the court's opinion on the decision by the organ, they can also be part of an assessment carried out by the court (it could also be understood as the essence of the court's opinion on the organ's wrong decision). On the other hand, those guidelines are quite likely a separable part of the verdict, located however in another document – the grounds for judicial opinion.

5. The motives of a judicial decision play an important role in controlling the discretionary power of the organ also (as has already been mentioned) from the perspective of the theory of legal communication. The control of this power stems from the adoption, at least in part, of the concept of a communicative role of judicial opinion – considered as a message, or even a performative utterance, which addresses the specified recipients and affects them. It has an impact not only on mental experiences, but also on real behaviour in the legal sphere (if the court corrects the interpretation of standards by the organ, it tries to adjust its decision to interpret in the court's way). Such an assumption deepens the conclusions of the adopted control model, in which it is not the court that improves the organ's decision and actions, but the organ has to do it by itself – consequently the organ learns something about the case, though primarily it has to know how to resolve it.

The correct interpretation or way of proceeding is indicated in the judicial opinion. In the situation of control, discretionary power is limited to what the court has said in its written reasoning. This control is based, therefore, on the concept of justification as a message (feedback, containing an assessment of what the organ has done and what was reflected by the organ in its motives for the decision), used by an organ when re-examining the case. Even if the organ does not consider the case again, but its decision was accepted, that also brings benefits because it strengthens the organ's opinion with new arguments, or even the argument that the way of thinking by the organ was accepted by the court in a binding way.

6. As it follows from the foregoing, the burden of controlling discretionary power in public administration lies, in fact, on the judicial opinion, and not on the ruling itself. This control, in light of using the judicial opinion as a tool, has many aspects and dimensions.

Discretionary power in administrative law can be understood as a situation in which an organ is vested with a broader scope of freedom in choosing an option of how to resolve the case (freedom given by the legislature)[7]. This margin of discretion is very important, as it makes the process of the application of law more flexible and easy to match the situation.[8] The administrative court that assesses the organ's action also enjoys certain freedom in choosing the proper interpretation and taking the right option in the same areas so another interpretation means lack of acceptance for the decision of the organ. Thus, the scope of discretionary power of an administrative body may depend, in fact, on the possibility to verify and change the organ's decision by the court.[9]

The role of the written motives of judicial decision is, in the case of controlling the discretionary power of administrative organs, different to that of the case of verifying other types of the organ's actions. The judicial opinion should meet higher standards. First of all, it should be precise and richer in arguments, to

---

7 See A. Jakubowski, *Władza dyskrecjonalna organów zakładu administracyjnego na przykładzie uczelni wyższych* [in:] *Dyskrecjonalność w prawie administracyjnym*, ed. K. Ziemski, M. Jędrzejczak, Poznań 2015, pp. 267–268.

8 See also: wyrok NSA z 19 marca 1981r., SA 234/81, ONSA 1981, nr 1, poz. 23; E. Ochendowski, *Prawo administracyjne. Część ogólna*, Toruń 2009, *passim* and Jan Zimmermann, *Prawo Administracyjne*, wyd. II, Kraków, pp. 309–313.

9 A. Jakubowski, *Władza…*, p. 270.

prevent any doubts that the court has arbitrarily intervened in the discretionary power of an administrative body. If discretionary power that is intended to guarantee the freedom for the organs is then limited by the court, the border between controlling and deciding cases by the court in its own clearly becomes very thin (and, at the same time, not compliant with the discussed model of administrative judiciary, not allowing the substitution of organs in making decisions). The written judicial opinion therefore makes it easier to verify whether this border has not been transgressed by the court and – even more importantly – to provide the court with a chance to self-control its reasoning (while specifying it for the purpose of written grounds).

Summing up, discretionary power belongs to the sphere of decision-making, but also to the domain of justification. The control of a discretionary organ's decisions is exercised not by questioning the decision itself, but by investigating whether the decision has been justified by the organ (in the form of written motives), and whether these motives have been produced properly. Therefore, the motives of the organ's decision are of crucial importance. The court assesses the organ's decision as set out in the judicial opinion (justification). Therefore, this communication plays a crucial role in controlling discretionary power, expressing the court's assessment as to whether the organ remained within the frames of discretionary power vested in it by the legislation. What is also noteworthy, through the justification the court may exchange opinions upon the case with the organ (of course, with the court taking the dominant position). Thereby, judicial opinion enables discourse in the application of administrative law, at the same time providing useful empirical material for determining its content and features.

Part III

Andrzej Korybski
(Associate Professor, Maria Curie-Sklodowska University in Lublin, Poland)

Statutory interpretation and its role in administrative application of law

Abstract: The aim of this article is to describe and explain specific features of administrative application of statutes and other sources of statutory law across the legal orders of the EU member states. A special place is devoted to the Polish experience with the methods of statutory interpretation by the institutions of tax administration.

Keywords: legal cultures, statutes, statutory interpretation, rules of interpreting statutes

1. Statutory interpretation: cultural and systemic limits

The notion of statutory interpretation belongs to the fundamental categories of contemporary jurisprudence. It refers to the process of interpretation of statutes whose origin is the parliament as a legislative power entity. Statutory interpretation that meets the criteria of the above definitions can be observed both in common law and legal orders based on civil law culture. A role of the concept of statutory interpretation is predominantly (though not exclusively) to describe the processes of application of law. These concepts, however, can also be used to construct normative doctrinal models that indicate how entities which apply law ought to interpret statutes in order to eventually issue correct decisions concerning the application of law[1]. Despite these similarities, doctrinal statutory interpretations vary across different legal cultures. The differences pertain to both the objectives and the substance of statutory interpretation, as well as particular solutions and methods of statutory interpretation contained in normative acts passed by parliament.

---

1 More on this issue in: A. Korybski, Application of law as an Object of Study: Key Concepts, Issues and Research Approaches, (in:) A. Korybski and B. Liżewski (eds.), Application of Law. Selected Theoretical Problems in Decision Making Perspective, Maria Curie-Skłodowska University Press 2015. See also: A. Korybski and L. Leszczyński, Stanowienie i stosowanie prawa. Elementy teorii (Legislation and Application of Law. Elements of the Legal Theory), Lex a Wolters Kluwer business 2015, p. 13–16, 134–149.

The understanding and methods of statutory interpretation are influenced predominantly by relevant legal culture which positions statutory interpretation and public implementing bodies within public government structures and the proper social context. The varied understanding and methods of statutory interpretation also result from different state system solutions adopted by particular countries. This also pertains to statutory interpretation across the member states of the European Union.

Key differences in understanding of the substance, methods and aids of statutory interpretation in Europe stem from different legal cultures which have shaped the so-called English legal order (in England and Wales) on the one hand and legal orders of the remaining EU member states on the other. Statutory interpretation in continental Europe is shaped within the framework of statutory law system i.e. the supremacy of Constitution and statutes enacted exclusively by parliament. One of the fundamental principles of statutory interpretation in these countries is a competence-based and – to a large extent – institutional division between legislative processes and their results (i.e. legal acts containing legal norms) and processes of application of law with their outcomes (i.e. legal decisions in individualized cases). This distinction is not observed in common law legal orders because of the precedent activity of courts. An elaborative presentation of statutory interpretation in statutory law systems is the focus of the next part of this article. This part includes preliminary remarks on characteristic features of statutory interpretation in Anglo-Saxon legal systems, with particular attention paid to root causes for the differences in understanding, methods (approaches), rules and institutional aids of statutory interpretation in common law culture.

Statutory interpretation in legal orders based on common law culture is understood in two ways. In its narrow understanding it pertains to all legal acts enacted by parliament (jointly referred as parliamentary legislation). In its broad meaning, statutory interpretation refers not only to parliamentary legislation, but also to legal acts enacted by other public bodies, inclusive of executive and public administration organs and institutions.

In legal systems based on the British model of political regime (the so-called Westminster model of government)[2] the part of legislation narrowed down only to parliamentary acts (i.e. statutes) is often referred to as primary legislation. For statutory interpretation it is significant to define the objective of statute as an act

2 See G. Rivlin, Understanding the Law, Oxford Univ. Press 2009, pp. 19–90. See also more on state and legal order principles in the UK in: D. Kelly, G. Slapper, English Legal System, 2nd edition, US New York and Oxford Univ. Press 2009. See also H. Barnett, Constitutional and Administrative Law, 10th edition, Routledge 2010.

of Parliament. The statute's content is normally shaped in the process of balancing interests within the parliament and its political surroundings. This means that parliamentary legal acts are politically influenced and often strongly impacted by so-called "legislative intention" which is a result of political compromise or consensus. Defining the objective of legislation and other directions of parliamentary legislative activity is of fundamental importance for so-called "Purposive Approach" as one of the key approaches in interpretation processes, and for the selection of appropriate interpretation measures, including legislative history.

Acts enacted by parliament must be differentiated from legal acts enacted by executive bodies (such as orders, regulations etc.), jointly defined as secondary legislation[3]. They also must be differentiated from non-legislative acts, issued by executive and administrative bodies in order to execute parliamentary legislative or to carry out a public administration task or action. The key subject of statutory interpretation is constituted by statutes passed by parliament as the legislative branch of government – as part of the Westminster system of separation of powers. Interpreting acts of parliament is, in general, not a task of the parliament and executive bodies, but of the judicial branch of government i.e. courts – as courts have the formal power to interpret legislation.

The judiciary interprets statutes to apply them in particular cases, which have not been sufficiently and precisely written in the text of the statute. A subject of the normative concept of statutory interpretation does not pertain to the elements of the act of law which are not subject to interpretative doubts in accordance with the *clara non sunt interpretanda* principle. Therefore, so-called "Literal Rule" is applied as a key tool in interpretation. Interpretation comes into play in situations where a text of the given act contains ambiguous wording. Legal acts may contain ambiguities and uncertainties, because common language, as a basis for the legal terms, is ambiguous and changes its meaning over time. A need for statutory interpretation may also result from the fact that lawmaker is not able to foresee all the social situations and behaviours which are to be regulated by the given act of law. Acts of law often contain not only ambiguous or unclear words and expressions, but also linguistic and stylistic mistakes which hinder an appropriate and precise interpretation of the provision at hand. New phenomena and technologies may also lead to difficulties in the application of binding legislation.

---

3 The principles of interpretation of secondary legislation acts are based on rules of the statutory interpretation in the narrow sense of this notion, although the specific constructs of the secondary legislation has been taking into account and confronting with the supremacy of Parliament (see: J. Holland, J. Webb, Learning Legal Rules, Oxford Univ. Press 2013, 8th edition, p. 296–297.

Imperfections of the text of legislative act may also result from the fact that act itself is a product of need for compromise/consensus, or the need to cater limited goods to special interest groups.

Statutory interpretation of acts of primary legislation is performed predominantly by courts in the process of applying statutes to particular cases. Due to the above-mentioned imperfections of acts of law passed by parliament, the practice in common law has offered so-called Interpretation Bills, which are in fact collections of the most important and generally applied interpretation guidelines[4]. Interpretation Bills contain rules of interpretation directed predominantly to courts as statute interpreters. Rules of statutory interpretation presented in Interpretation Bills are formally binding, and their rejection of courts is possible only when courts declare their content as a violation of the constitutional order. In reality, the scope and range of application of Interpretation Bills is becoming increasingly extensive. Public administration bodies also use these bills in order to prevent possible lawsuits following some decisions of these bodies.

Apart from the rules stipulated by Interpretation Bills, judges have also developed some supporting rules for the process of interpreting statutes – as a result of their rulings based on doctrinal comments and judicial reviews. The rules are not formally binding for judges. Moreover, some of the rules are not only guidelines for correct interpretation of legal acts, but also supply arguments to justify the decisions by judges. These rules stem from judicial practice and are often described as traditional canons of statutory interpretation. Judges may apply commonly accepted rules of interpretation to interpret not only statutes, but also acts of secondary legislation and the so-called delegated legislation (such as regulations of administrative bodies). Moreover, in issues regulated by the EU law judges apply the so-called purposive approach derived from the judicial review of the European Court of Justice. This means that domestic courts are obliged to apply the Purposive Approach when they resolve matters regulated by the EU law.

4 The Interpretation Bill in the U.K. (Interpretation Act 1978), encompasses the fundamental terminological solutions concerning words and phrases commonly used in statutes, as well as semantic rules like "singular includes plural", "he includes she" etc. The corresponding act in Australia is the Acts Interpretation Act (1901) which contains similar interpretation rules as well as the rules for defining the scope of interpretation, the meaning of common statutory terms and phrases, the impact of time and space on the meaning of words and the principles of interpretation of terms, phrases and linguistic expressions which describe the legal instruments of secondary legislation. Similar Interpretation Bills also function in Canada, Malaysia, Hong Kong, New Zealand, and Ireland.

However, rules and instructions contained in Interpretation Bills are of fundamental importance for statutory interpretation. In the doctrine of statutory interpretation there are four key interpretation rules: earlier mentioned Literal Rule and Purposive Approach, and the two next interpretation tools: the Golden Rule and the Mischief Rule[5]. An initial stage of statutory interpretation is always the Literal Rule, according to which the words and phrases used in statute should be interpreted in accordance with their ordinary and natural meanings, as used in the ethnic language (also as the language used for official purposes). The auxiliary rule here is that one may go beyond the ordinary and natural meaning of given word only if the lawmaker introduces another and precise meaning of the word. A large part of detailed linguistic directives of the Literal Rule are contained in Interpretation Bills.

Application of the Literal Rule for statutory interpretation may in some situations lead to absurd conclusions or unjust results that are clearly contrary to the interpretation planned by parliament. In such situation it is justified to resort to the remaining interpretation rules. If there is a clearly absurd conclusion resulting from the interpretation the interpreter must firstly use the Golden Rule which identifies the meaning of words and expressions used in the provision from perspective of the entire act under interpretation, and within the constraints defined by intention of avoiding the clearly absurd conclusion. In practice, the Golden Rule is about verifying the legislator's intention or the regulatory function legislator assigns to the act under interpretation. A significant task of the interpreter is to ensure coherence of interpretation i.e. achievement of the same results of interpretation of the act's provisions which pertain to the same issue. The interpreter, therefore, fixes the shortcomings or mistakes made by legislator during the drafting and editing stages[6].

The Golden Rule is often treated as a "lighter" or less explicit form of the next interpretation rule i.e. the Mischief Rule. The Mischief Rule clearly refers to the legislator's intention behind the introduction of the act to the country's legal order. Prior to its application, the problem to be solved by the legislator must be identified. This requires the interpreter to look into the documentation of the legislation history, including the parliamentary justification of the act. The Mischief Rule facilitates elimination of not only absurd interpretation of the particular provision, but also the elimination of clearly unjust interpretations contradicting the

---

5 More on this issue in: C. Elliott and F. Quinn, English Legal System, Pearson Education Ltd. 2015, 10th edition, pp. 49–73. See also J. Holland, J. Webb, Learning Legal Rules, op. cit., pp. 257–304.

6 In: C. Elliott, F. Quinn, op. cit., pp. 53–55. See also J. Holland, J. Webb, op. cit., pp. 258–261.

legislator's intentions. The literature on the subject also points at a certain disadvantage of the Mischief Rule resulting from its origins. This Rule was established in 16th century when the position of the British parliament was not yet clearly based on the principle of the supremacy of parliament, and legislative activity of parliament was limited and undoubtedly subsidiary to the common law. Today's position of parliament is entirely different, and its legislative activity has a much broader range. It is also important to note that the contemporary parliament has its own general policy of legislature. Consequently, the intentions of legislator must be interpreted not only with reference to a single legislative act and the problem it addressed, but also from a broader perspective encompassing the general policy of legislature in a given state. That is why the Mischief Rule is often treated as less appropriate now that legislative situation is quite different[7].

Due to above-mentioned disadvantages of the Mischief Rule in interpretation practice, the Purposive Approach is playing an increasingly important role. Additionally, one must emphasize the growing importance of EU legislation and the rulings of the European Court of Justice for activity of the domestic courts. EU law interpretation implemented by this court is clearly based on an approach which focuses on giving effect to the purpose of given legislation in context of the supreme European freedoms. Consequently, over the recent decades we have been observing the birth and development of the Purposive Approach to statutory interpretation. The approach is applied not only to the context of European law, but also to pure domestic legislation. The scope of its application in statutory interpretation can nowadays be compared with the importance of targeted-functional interpretation applied in continental Europe.

An important part of Anglo-Saxon concept of statutory interpretation is the question of interpretation aids. Some of these aids are specified by provisions of the statute, including the provisions of Interpretation Bills and statutory definitions. The other aids (particularly with reference to the Literal Rule) stem from the repertoire of rules of ordinary language, and are adjusted to the needs of legal language of acts of law. Both these groups of aids are defined in the doctrine as internal aids. The remaining aids are referred to as external aids. The internal aids are applied predominantly by the Literal and Golden Rules. In Anglo-Saxon legal orders, the use of interpretation aids is subject to certain presumptions. This means that when it is possible to draw conclusions based on analogy across two related legal orders (e.g. the domestic legal order and the legal order of European human rights), the effect of the rule which limits the interpretation of the domestic

---

7 Cf. C. Elliott, F. Quinn, op. cit., p. 56.

statute may be suspended. An example here may be the rule deriving from Roman law i.e. "*Lex retro non agit*". In principle, it excludes the effectiveness of act on the events preceding the entry into force of act. However, if there is an act of international law which provides for retro-action in precisely defined situations, the application of the Roman principle becomes suspended. Another constraint results from the principle stipulating that statutes must not change the regulations of common law. The next principle stipulates that statutory law cannot lead to the removal of any issues which have so far been under court jurisdiction. Another principle obliges courts to interpret unclear statutes (for example statutes which create crimes) in the most favourable way for human beings.

Among the internal aids, an important role has recently been played by explanatory notes issued along with statutes. In the English legal order the obligation to issue statutes with explanatory notes has been in force since 1999. However, the obligation to explain regulations and solutions offered by the act does not apply to secondary legislation. The group of internal aids also includes comparisons between the interpreted provision and other similar regulations of the same act of law or its title and titles of its parts. The linguistic means and directives of interpretation are in fact the canons of statutory interpretation developed so far. In principle they are convergent with the doctrine of statutory interpretation in the legal orders of continental Europe (e.g. the following directives: "*Eiusdem generis*","*Expressio unius est exclusio alterius*", "*Noscitur a sociis*", "*In pari materia*", "*Reddendo singula singulis*", "*Generalia specialibus non derogant*" etc.)[8].

The external aids used when the Mischief Rule is applied include predominantly the historical setting of legal regulation of the issue at hand, comparative study and analysis of other legal acts devoted to the same or similar issue. Moreover, this group of interpretation aids also includes dictionaries with definitions of both ordinary and specialist/professional language. The interpreter of the statute may also use official reports and transcripts of parliamentary meetings (official reports, Hansard in Great Britain etc.). The meanings of words and expressions used in a given act may also be defined by subsidiary reference to a historical practice of resolving issues regulated by the act and the provision at hand. Most of the above-mentioned external aids are aimed at identifying the intention of the legislator passing the act. The group of external aids is not treated by doctrine as an enumeration of a set of means and interpretation directives. The aids described above are examples of the ways to uncover the legislator's parliamentary intention[9].

8 In: C. Elliott, F. Quinn, op. cit., p. 61.

9 For an account of different aids see for example C. Elliott, F. Quinn, op. cit., pp. 63–68.

In light of the above information, therefore, courts are the crucial organs which shape the practice of statutory interpretation in Anglo-Saxon legal orders. The framework of their practice, however, is set by the stipulations of parliament contained in the binding Interpretation Bills. These ramifications are binding from public administration bodies and their decision-making practice is also influenced by court rulings in cases resolved by the legislative activity of parliament. A characteristic feature of the decision-making practice of public administration bodies is subjecting administrative decisions to court scrutiny (including their decisions of legislative character).

2. Statutory interpretation in legal orders based on civil law culture

The role of statutory interpretation in legal systems of the countries of continental Europe is directly defined by the position of statutes in the hierarchy of sources of law. The hierarchy, in principle, does not include court precedents as a source of law, and courts do not have legislative competencies. Statutes as acts of legislation are issued solely by the parliament and in terms of their legal force are only second to the Constitution. Consequently, statutes must be compliant with Constitution and normative acts of law issued by the executive branch and public administration can only be issued on the basis of an empowerment expressed in a relevant statute – in order to facilitate the exercise of the statute's provisions.

In legal literature devoted to legal culture of continental Europe's countries, a frequently indicated constitutionality control mechanism (different than the ones applied in the Anglo-Saxon legal culture) is the verification of compliance of statutes with the Constitution, and verification of legality of other normative acts (i.e. their compliance with statutes). In principle the investigation of constitutionality and legality of acts of law is the task of a special court – the constitutional court. As far as the investigation of legality of acts other than statutes is concerned (in particular acts of law issued by local governments), particular continental legal orders have their specific solutions[10].

In some countries there are special solutions pertaining to the legality of executive acts accompanying the statues, including legal acts issued by local governments. They allow for the control of the acts by higher-level executive bodies (more on these solutions will follow in the next point of this article).

---

10 See: L. Leszczyński, Zagadnienia teorii stosowania prawa (Selected Problems of the Theory of Application of Law), Zakamycze 2001, p. 52–53. See also: A. Korybski and L. Leszczyński, Stanowienie i stosowanie prawa ..., op. cit., p. 167–169.

The processes of control of constitutionality and legality of acts of law have shaped the relevant, specific practice. The essence of the practice is the issuance of the so-called interpretation decisions by controlling organs i.e. decisions/rulings stipulating whether the provision at hand is compliant with the relevant higher-level act of law only if there is a correct interpretation thereof, as prescribed by the controlling body. A special role in the issuance of such interpretation decisions is played by the constitutional court which issued binding interpretations of statutes. The authority of the constitutional courts to issue such decisions is, however, sometimes questioned.

Due to the special position of the statutes the term "statutory interpretation" is very rarely used in legal literature. In turn, the general notion of "legal interpretation" is widely used and encompasses both the interpretation of the Constitution and the interpretation of statutes and lower-level acts of law. If any particular type of interpretation is discerned by the doctrine, it is usually the interpretation of the constitutional provisions. As a rule, the term "statutory interpretation" is absent in the representative legal literature. The term that is used is "interpretation of law", but the basic rules of interpretation are referred to the statutes[11]. Principles of the interpretation of law proposed by the doctrine predominantly pertain to interpretation of statutory provisions, although a broader impact of these principles is also referred to (i.e. interpretation of lower-level acts of law). The literature also points at the phenomenon of the so-called correspondence of the principles of legislative techniques and the principles of interpretation of law: certain principles of encoding normative content in legal provisions must be reflected in the appropriate, analogous principles of de-coding normative content from these provisions[12].

Secondary legislation can only be issued based on authorization contained in the statute and within the limitations of statutory regulation. Moreover, the control of legality of these normative acts is performed with reference to the relevant statutory basis (authorisation specified by the relevant provision of the binding statute). These acts are jointly referred to as executive acts as they are issued by

11 For example in the most representative Polish literature on interpretation of law. See: M. Zieliński, Wykładnia prawa. Zasady. Reguły. Wskazówki (Interpretation of Law. Principles, Rules. Instructions), Wydawnictwo Prawnicze LexisNexis 2002;

12 The term "correspondence between legislative techniques and rules of the law interpretation" was introduced to the Polish legal literature by S. Wronkowska and M. Zieliński. See: S. Wronkowska, M. Zieliński, Problemy i zasady redagowania tekstów prawnych (Problems and Principles of Editing of Legal Texts), The Government Office Press 1993, p. 5–31.

executive bodies (the central government and government agencies), as well as local government bodies. Another term to describe this group of acts of law is the term "sub-statutory acts" as in the hierarchy of acts of law these acts are positioned below statutes.

The authority to perform statutory interpretation, including the authority to investigate compliance of statutes with the Constitution, enables the relevant bodies to shape the legal order of their country. It is so because the doctrine assumes that bodies authorized to make acts of law at a certain level are also authorized to perform the so-called authentic interpretation of their provisions in the form of definition of legal terms used in the provisions. This also means that the supreme position of the legislative power in enacting statutes is not equal to monopoly of the lawmakers to shape the legal order. Parliament as the sole lawmaker creates the legal order's framework, yet remains under control and scrutiny of the constitutional court. The parliament activity and its results – statutes – define the scope of lawmaker's regulation binding for executive and public administration bodies (including central government administration and local governments).

3. Specific institutional solutions of the binding statutory interpretation – the Polish experience

The Polish solutions pertaining to bodies authorized to perform binding statutory interpretation, the scope and form of interpretation can serve as a good example of seeking an optimal institutional model of statutory interpretation performed as part of administrative application of law. The solutions are evolving, too, stimulated by the changes in statutory regulations of the bodies authorised to interpret law, and the changes in the scope and set of interpretation instruments. These solutions also expose the separation of statutory interpretation performed by courts as part of the judicial process of application of law from the binding statutory interpretation performed by the relevant executive and public administration bodies.

Statutory interpretation performed by judicial bodies (courts) is used to decide upon an individual case (criminal, civil, or administrative). It is limited to the provisions of the Constitution, statutes and other sources of law equal to statutes (including, in particular, in international agreements ratified by the President on behalf of the Republic of Poland). It is only binding for the court which performed the interpretation as well as the parties to the relevant court proceedings i.e. the addressees of the court's decision.

In turn, statutory interpretation performed by executive and administration bodies is a reflection of the decision-making practice of these bodies. However, it is not always associated with a particular process of administrative application of law. This means that statutory interpretation performed by public administration and executive bodies does not need to be the operational interpretation of law in all cases, performed in a particular process of administrative application of law in order to issue an administrative decision. This type of interpretation may be performed to meet the needs of future processes of administrative application of law. Therefore, according to the terminology presented in the previous paragraph, it may be labelled as the so-called general statutory interpretation. Moreover, this type of statutory interpretation does not need to be limited to interpretation of statutory provisions; it may also be applied to the provisions contained in executive acts accompanying statutes (regulations, administrative legal acts) if the provisions constitute part of the legal basis for the given administrative decision. This interpretation may be of general or individual character.

General interpretation occurs when the executive body explains the normative meaning of the given provision/s for future administrative proceedings in a particular type of cases. This interpretation binds the administrative bodies subordinate to the interpreting executive body (typically – the relevant minister). The performance of general interpretation of the provisions is justified predominantly by the intention to maintain interpretative homogeneity across the bodies which issue administrative decisions based on the same statutory provisions. This is of large significance for the issues of certainty and predictability of administrative decisions for the citizens and other legal entities, especially due to the fact that in the Polish legal order the number of administrative decisions issued ranges between 10 and 20 million, (particularly in tax law cases which lead to issuance of a few million administrative decisions per year).

The individual interpretation is carried out by an executive body (or by its subordinate and authorised bodies) upon a motion by an interested entity who wishes their case to be resolved. This does not need to be a case based on an existing factual state as it can be also be based on probable future events resulting in the initiation of tax law proceedings. The entity which has received the individual interpretation may justly predict that the administrative decision taken in their case will be based on an individual interpretation carried out by the relevant administrative body.

In statutory law legal orders, issuing a general or individual statutory interpretation may only be carried out by the public or administrative bodies which have the appropriate authority to perform such interpretations. The scope of their authority – as regards the type of statutory interpretation, the interpreting entity and the branch of law – must be specified in the authoritative norm contained in the relevant act of law. Therefore, the scope of authority is decided upon by the parliament i.e. a legislative body. The division of power, in turn, means that administrative decisions (including decisions made on the basis of general or individual statutory interpretations), are subject to judicial control. Consequently, these individual or general interpretations are binding for public administration and executive bodies but are not binding for courts. The right of courts to deliver an independent interpretation of particular statutory provisions in order to decide upon a case is protected by the principle of independence of courts from other public authorities and the principle of court independence in the process of judicial application of law.

In the current state of the Polish legal order the authority to deliver a binding general or individual statutory interpretation rests with the Minister of Finance. The binding act of law (the Tax Ordinance)[13] obliges the Minister to ensure a consistent application of tax law by tax offices. This includes issuance of general interpretations of tax regulations if these regulations are unclear and lead to a lack of certainty of interpretation, and situations when tax administration bodies issue contradictory decisions. In particular, it may also include the situation when the authorized tax administration bodies issued discrepant individual interpretation of the same tax law provision.

The definition of authority to deliver individual tax interpretations in the Polish legal order has been evolving. In its initial shape the authority (granted to the Minister of Finance by the Act) was delegated by the Minister selected directors of Tax Chambers indicated in the executive provisions accompanying the Act with their geographical locations. After more than ten years of the model's functioning, institutional changes were introduced. These changes were associated with the creation of the National Tax Information; apart from the Minister of Finance (who was granted the authority to carry out tax law interpretations), the authority was also delegated to directors of tax chambers. The change was justified by the intention to ensure the consistency of tax law decisions.

The Minister of Finance was authorised to amend an individual tax law interpretation delivered by a Director of a Tax Chamber as he strived to ensure the consistent application of tax law and alignment of tax law decisions with the rulings of domestic courts (including the rulings of the Constitutional Court) and

13 Art. 14a of the Act of 29 August 1997 – Tax Ordinance (Official Journal 2012, item 749 with further amendments).

international courts (including the rulings of the Court of Justice of the EU). The Minister's actions in this area were driven not only by conclusions resulting from their analysis of court rulings, but also by information from tax administration bodies, taxpayers (including the Ombudsman and NGOs representing taxpayers), and from the media[14].

An individual tax law interpretation is delivered upon a taxpayer's request. The request may pertain to the existing factual state or to probable future events which produce legal consequences for the taxpayer. The taxpayer must file a request along with a declaration stating that the elements of the factual state he or she mentions in the request are not subject to ongoing tax law proceedings, tax office audit or any other legal control proceedings. The Minister of Finance is under no obligation to take a position and interpret a provision when the request regards events that are already covered by an ongoing tax law proceeding, control or audit or if the case regarding such events has already been resolved through a relevant decision by a tax administration or control body. The request for interpretation must also contain an outline of the requesting entity's position as regards the interpretation of the relevant tax law provisions.

The interpretation must be delivered without undue delay, no later than within three months from the date of receipt of the request by the Tax Chamber. If the Director of the Tax Chamber does not issue the relevant individual interpretation it is assumed that the binding position for the tax body is the one adopted by the requesting taxpayer in their request. This solution may therefore be treated as a means of exerting influence on the relevant tax authorities which as a result should not evade interpreting the requested provisions.

Individual interpretation contains an evaluation of the requesting entity's position and a legal justification of the evaluation. The contents of the justification are formed by an interpretation of tax law provisions and arguments in favour of the interpretation and its correctness. If the requesting entity's position is evaluated

14 Data from the Ministry of Finance indicate that, over the recent years, irregularities or significant discrepancies in interpretation were found in approximately 3% of all individual interpretations issued annually by directors of Tax Chambers that consequently forced the Minister of Finance to amend such decisions. At the same time the number of individual interpretations challenged by administrative courts and consequently eliminated from circulation by legally binding decisions was twice as high. This may be evidence of at least partial ineffectiveness of the control bodies scrutinizing individual tax law interpretations, and prove that there are discrepancies in interpretation of tax law statutes by courts and tax administration bodies. Cf. *Informacja z działalności Biur Krajowej Informacji Podatkowej za 2014 r.*, Leszno 2015, pp. 2–4 and 12–13.

as correct the interpreting administrative body may resign from issuing a justification. An indispensable element of the individual interpretation is to notify the requesting entity about their right to file an appeal to the relevant administrative court. An important function of individual tax law interpretations is the fact that it binds the relevant tax administration body with the interpretation and, consequently, ensures the predictability of decisions made by tax administration bodies – although the predictability may be weakened through a possible change of interpretation by the controlling body i.e. the Minister of Finance. If such a change takes place, the Polish tax provisions stipulate that the taxpayer's compliance with the individual interpretation later amended by the Minister of Finance must not deteriorate the taxpayer's situation. Moreover, the taxpayer's compliance with the general interpretation prior to its amendment by the Minister of Finance must not be detrimental to the taxpayer who, after all, based their legal activities on the general interpretation.

The legal construct of specific statutory interpretation performed by tax administration bodies presented above illustrates the special nature of interpretation in statutory law legal orders. In such legal orders, the judicial and administrative processes of application of law can be distinguished, which is not the case in common law cultures. The differentiation is justified not only by the type of bodies that issue legally binding decisions after carrying out statutory interpretation, but also by the possibility of delegating the authority to carry out binding interpretations of statutory provisions in such a manner that other decision-making administration bodies are bound by the results of the interpretation. The scope of relevance of such statutory interpretation, therefore, significantly extends beyond the interpretative capacities of courts and public administration bodies in the legal orders based on the Anglo-Saxon legal culture.

Details of the construct of this type of statutory interpretation may differ depending on shape and principles of particular statutory law countries. The Polish statutory interpretation solutions presented in this article reflect the specificity of the Polish doctrine of statutory interpretation. Importantly, the function of similar solutions is shared by all statutory law countries, as such solutions serve to ensure the predictability of decisions made in the process of administrative application of law, and, consequently, to ensure certainty of law and confidence in the state with its bodies and agencies. The function, therefore, leads to the results which in Anglo-Saxon legal culture are ensured by the *stare decisis* principle. However, it must be added that in statutory law cultures interpretation solutions have yet another function, linked to the distinct nature of such legal orders. The nature of this function is to strive to a consistent policy of application of law by executive and public administration bodies (e.g. by tax administration bodies). The foundation of this policy is constituted by a definition of the public objectives and tasks for particular public administration bodies (e.g. tax bodies and revenue control bodies) followed by achieving a state of desired decision-making consistency across the decisions made by public administration bodies throughout the process of application of law.

Leszek Leszczyński
(Professor, Maria Curie-Sklodowska University in Lublin, Poland; The Supreme Administrative Court of Poland Judge)

Precedential Practice in the Statutory Legal Order and Its Role in the Judicial Control of Administrative Decisions

Abstract: The paper consists of considerations on the role of precedential practice in statutory legal order that are followed by an analysis of the impact of precedential practice on the judicial control of the administrative activities, seen from the angle of its scope and effectiveness.

Keywords: precedent, judicial control of administration, statutory law

The paper[1] consists of two parts. The first one starts from considerations on the role of precedential practice in shaping the relations between legality, flexibility and uniformity of the application of law in statutory legal orders. These considerations are followed by an analysis of the role of references to precedents (previous decisions) in the unification of judicial practice and of the advantages, universal for all branches of law, of this way of achieving a practically accepted scale of its uniformity. The second part of the paper deals with an analysis of the impact of precedential practice on the judicial control of the administrative activities, as seen from the angle of its scope and effectiveness.

1. Precedents in Statutory Legal Orders

1.1 Axiology of the judicial application of law. The role of its uniformity

Precedential practice understood as a reference to previous decisions in somewhat similar cases, using its *ratio decidendi* as an element of the basis for the actual judicial decision, is not only absent nor indifferent in the axiology of the judicial implementation of law but it also visibly enters the complex relations between its various values. It

1 The paper has been prepared as an result of the research project (2013/11/B/HS5/03821) "Potential of Precedent Argumentation in the Polish Legal Order (A Theoretical and Comparative Approach)", granted by the National Science Center (Narodowe Centrum Nauki) in Poland.

concerns both common law and the statutory legal order though in the latter (where precedential practice does not shape the decisional processes in the most prominent way, playing rather supplementary role as a source of the normative basis for decisions) occurs in a different manner and on a scale, leading to the different results.

If we accept, after Jerzy Wróblewski, that the axiological system of application of law in the statutory legal order (appropriate for both judicial and administrative type of these decisional processes) combines such main values as legality (accordance with the law), rightness (references to moral values) as well as certainty and uniformity (internal or "procedural" values)[2] we must admit that precedents, impacting the shape and role of all these values, are the most closely and directly connected with the value of uniformity of judicial practice. That is why one may distinguish the precedential type of unification of the application of law (in the context of the processes, reasoning and the decisions as their results) especially in the field of judicial practice (court jurisdiction) from its other types and sources.

It should be stated that the uniformity of application of law, placed in the frames of legal axiology as an element of a rational balance between all these values (but especially as an element of balance between legality and flexibility of judicial deciding), might be achieved in various ways and through various instruments.

Some ways leading to uniformity originate from the legislative activity in spite of fact that legislators play a kind of "double game" in determining the scale of discretion, either strengthening or weakening it, weighing in that way their own responsibility for the legal order as a whole.

To enlarge the discretion and to promote the value of flexibility of the application of law, they use special legislative means, including the formation of the general principles of law[3], general reference clauses.[4] Other open axiologically or linguistically normative constructs[5] play a crucial role.

---

2 J. Wróblewski: *Wartości i decyzja sądowa* [Values and Judicial Decision], Wrocław 1973, p. 42 ff.

3 For more information on the role of principles in making the implementation of law flexible see R. Dworkin: *Law's Empire*, London 1990, p. 209 ff., M. Atienza, J. Ruiz Manero: *A Theory of Legal Sentences*, Dordrecht 1998, passim R. Alexy: *A Theory of Constitutional Rights*, Oxford 2002, p. 51 ff.

4 See J. W. Hedemann, *Die Flucht in die Generalklauseln. Eine Gefahr fur Recht und Staat*, Tubingen 1933, passim, L. Leszczyński: "Legislative Policy and Judicial Practice. Discretion in the Case of General Clauses", (in:) *Politics of Law and Legal Policy. Between Modern and Post-modern Jurisprudence*, eds. T. Biernat, M.Zirk-Sadowski, Warszawa 2008, pp. 273–291.

5 See: H. Ehmke: *Ermessen und unbestimmte Rechtsbegriffe im Verwaltungsrecht*, Tubingen 1960, passim,: K. Engisch: *Einfuhrung in das juristische Denken*, Stuttgart 1975,

Trying to narrow down discretion, they may act through such instruments as substantial strictness of the norm encoded in the regulations (uniformity connected with "maximum-legality"), special legislative constructs such as "statutory definitions" of the given terms (limiting discretion in the semantic interpretation of law) as well as enacting special procedural institutions leading to "self-restriction" of the judiciary (like various types of instructions coming from higher judicial instances, among which one should emphasize the role of the binding general resolutions of "supreme courts", addressed to the judiciary as a whole).

All of them have, however, rather limited efficiency from the point of the legislature. Substantial strictness of regulations is limited by the generality of rules (their non-casuistic character) while the impact of legislative definitions is weakened by the failures in their accuracy as by features of both legal and general language. The supreme courts' resolutions do not have to follow entirely the legislative intentions (politically motivated in the autocratic orders), usually mixing their contents with judicial point of view, represented by these courts more or less in the context of the needs of judicial practice.

The first two methods are quite universal in their implementation in various types of legal orders, while the third one is connected rather with autocratic regimes, tangling the judicial practice (to a smaller or bigger extent) in political (and ideological) teleology and axiology. That is why the third method of unification of judicial jurisdiction is usually removed during the process of democratization of state.

The third method was used in Poland. Before 1989. the Supreme Court issued general instructions on the application and interpretation of law, binding on all courts[6]. Before 1997 the Constitutional Tribunal enacted general resolutions on the interpretation of statutes, binding on all courts and administrative bodies of authority[7]. Both instruments unified effectively the legal reasoning in the process

---

p 45 ff., B. Hoffmaster: "Understanding Judicial Discretion", *Law and Philosophy*, Vol. 1, No. 1, 1982, passim, L. Leszczyński: "Legal Certainty and Judicial Discretion in the Statutory Legal Order" (in:) *Legal Rules, Moral Norms and Democratic Principles*, eds.: B. Wojciechowski, P. W. Juchacz, K. M. Cern, Series: Dia-Logos. *Studies in Philosophy and Social Sciences*, Vol. 15, Frankfurt am Main: Peter Lang Edition, 2013, pp. 283–299.

6 The Supreme Court's instructions were introduced as instructions of the administration of justice and judicial practice under Article 24 of the Act of February 15, 1962 on the Supreme Court (*Dziennik Ustaw* [Journal of Laws] 1962, No. 11, item 54). In 1985 they became instructions on the interpretation and application of law, and this system was abolished by the Act of December 20, 1989 (*Dziennik Ustaw* [Journal of Laws] 1989, No. 73, item 436).

7 The Constitutional Tribunal's interpretative resolution was introduced under the Act of October 10, 1991 (*Dziennik Ustaw* [Journal of Laws] 1991, No. 109, item 470). I

of application of law, but they were recognized in the process of democratic transition of the state as contrary to the principles of rule of law and of the independence of the judiciary. That resulted in their removal, either at the very beginning of the transformation (as it happened in 1989 with the instructions of the Supreme Court[8]) or a little later when the new Constitution was enacted (as it happened in 1997 with the interpretative resolution of the Constitutional Tribunal[9]).

1.2 The precedential way of unification of judicial practice

Some judicial practice unifying instruments exercised by the judiciary in the application of procedural regulations of legislatures, exist and function in democratic legal orders. The most prominent examples of them are the resolutions of the enlarged panels of the highest judicial instances (taken by a panel of 7 judges, by the chamber or by the full panel of the court)[10]. These concern motions of regular judicial panels or by the president of the court. They are binding, however, to a smaller degree than the previous "instructions" of the Supreme Court, since the manner of changing them is easier (a new motion brought to the enlarged panel may lead to a new resolution, sometimes taken by a larger panel).

The crucial questions of the uniformization of judicial practice deal, however, with the role of precedents understood as specific judgments in particular cases in which one may distinguish a part connected with the facts of the case (*obiter dicta*) and a part expressing a more general rule (*ratio decidendi*), influencing decisions taken in similar matters[11].

Article 5 of the unified text of the Act on the Constitutional Tribunal established the competence of the Tribunal to issue universally binding interpretations of statutory acts.

8 On May 5, 1992 the Full Panel of the Supreme Court in its resolution Kw.Pr 5/92 decided that the instructions of this Court issued before December 20, 1989 are no longer binding (see: Orzecznictwo Sądu Najwyższego, Izba Karna [Decisions of the Supreme Court, Penal Chamber] 1993, item 1.

9 The resolutions have not been stipulated by the Constitution of the Republic of Poland enacted on April 2, 1997 (*Dziennik Ustaw* [Journal of Laws] 1997, No 78, item 483) as well as in the new Act of September 1, 1997 on the Constitutional Tribunal (*Dziennik Ustaw* [Journal of Laws] No. 102 item 643).

10 Articles 264–269 of the Act on Proceedings Before Administrative Courts [Prawo o postępowaniu przed sądami administracyjnymi] of August 30, 2002, *Dziennik Ustaw* [Journal of Laws], 2002, No. 153, item 1270, (hereinafter referred to as "LPAC").

11 See: R. Cross, *Precedent in English Law*, Oxford 1968, p. 25 ff., R.J. Aldisert, *The Judicial Process. Readings, Materials, Cases*, St. Paul 1976, p. 50 ff., J. Levin, *How Judges Reason. The Logic of Adjudication*, New York 1992, pp. 158–174.

The significance of the references to the previous judicial decisions taken in similar cases, functioning in the contemporary statutory legal orders, opens a debate on the question whether precedents (even understood in a "softer" way if compared with the *common law*) should be treated as optimal (the most optimal) instruments of unification of processes of application of law taking into account the principle of rule of law.

Generally speaking, there is no doubt that precedents in the statutory legal orders where there is no *stare decisis* rule and references to previous decisions ("soft precedents") play rather a supplementary role in the decision-making process[12]. Besides, the role of precedents (as well as the impact of precedential practice on the uniformity of application of law) depend on various factors. One of the most important ones (besides the type of a political regime or a situation of significant social changes), being vital for the judicial review of administrative decisions, is the branch of law (private vs. public law, civil vs. penal and administrative law) and the type of application of law, indicating crucial differences in administrative and judicial decisional processes (the independence of the judiciary in doing justice vs. managerial features or strong political involvement of some administrative activities).

There are several general advantages of strengthening the role of precedents as an instrument of the unification of the judicial application of statutory law. Firstly, the precedential practice in the contemporary statutory orders leads to uniformity in application of law in the most pluralistic way (based on "the strength of arguments" of many competing actors participating in the "judicial debate"). It is, as

---

12 This issue has been discussed in Polish theory of law for years. See, for example, A. Stelmachowski: *Prawotwórcza rola sądów* [Law-making Role of the Courts], "Państwo i Prawo", 4-5/1967, J. Wróblewski, *Precedens i jednolitość sądowego stosowania prawa* [Precedent and Uniformity of the Judicial Application of Law], "Państwo i Prawo", 10/1971, p. 521 ff., M. Zirk-Sadowski: *Precedens a tzw. decyzja prawotwórcza* [Precedent and so called law-making decision], "Państwo i Prawo", 6/1980, L. Morawski, *Czy precedens powinien być źródłem prawa?* [Should the Precedent be a Source of Law] in: *W kręgu problematyki władzy, państwa i prawa* [Around the Problerms of Authority, State and Law], ed. J. Malarczyk, pp. 187–202, L. Leszczyński, *Precedensy jako źródło rekosntrukcji normatywnej podstawy decyzji stosoania prawa* [Precedent as a Source of Reconstruction of the Normative Basis of the Decision of Application of Law], [in:] *Prawo a wartości* (Law and Values], ed. I. Bogucka, Z. Tobor, Kraków 2003, pp. 149–162, T. Stawecki, *Precedens w polskim porzadku prawnym. Pojęcie i wnioski de lege ferenda* [Precedent in the Polish Legal Order. A Concept and the Conclusions de lege ferenda] [in:] *Preecedens w polskim systemie prawa* [Precedent in the Polish Legal System], ed. A. Śledzińska-Simon, M. Wyrzykowski, Warszawa 2010, pp. 59–98.

a matter of fact, also a democratic way (even if the judges are not directly elected by the people), since judges are appointed (or at least accepted) by the elected bodies of authority (presidents, parliaments, etc.) and may decide jointly with the elected laymen[13]. Secondly, the precedential practice brings a judge-made output based on juridical discourse (not political one, as in the case of legislatures) and contributes to the making of the application of law effective and predictable based on a professional (substantially competent) input. Besides, the precedential way of deciding on a case is "located" in the direct neighborhood of its particular facts, which ties argumentation with a specific and precisely defined "need of a problem to be solved" within the framework of a slightly generalized *ratio decidendi* of a case (already established or in the process of establishing). And thirdly, precedential arguments expressed in the justification (reasons and motives) of the judicial decision should not only be treated as particular arguments of a judgement but also as the ones related to the arguments accepted by more or less developed lines of jurisdiction, contributing more effectively in their unification.

Lack of traditions of strong references to previous decisions, lack of the *stare decisis* rule or lack of a developed theory of the precedent in jurisprudence and in the statutory orders may weaken these advantages and slow down the development of this practice. However, in the long run, this should not be an obstacle to a gradual acceptance of the practical role of precedents.

It should be underlined that the presence of precedential practice in statutory orders (contrary to the *common law*) is based on the assumption that references to the previous decisions do not have to happen in each case (a "may-formula" instead of "must-formula"). Nevertheless, if such a reference becomes part of the parties' arguments, lack of any reference to the indicated judgements is usually not accepted on appeal, if any. This reference means, therefore, additional (validational and interpretational) argumentation in building the normative basis for a decision being actually taken, accomplished only if the pragmatically justified "needs of the case" demand it.

Speaking on the alternative effects of dealing with the way in which the previous judicial decisions are used in the decisional processes one should say that the differences depend on many factors. These include the type of practice used as an object of reference, the level of decision taken as a precedential judgement or the way in which the reference is actually made.

13 As it happens in the Polish legal order, which operates without the jury system but with the participation of laymen who support the judge in criminal cases heard by 3 person panels or 2 judges in 5 person panels (see Article 28 of the Criminal Proceeding Code of June 6, 1997 (*Dziennik Ustaw* [Journal of laws], 1997, item. 555).

To play a vital role in the decisional practice, the "precedential argumentation", presented in the reasons (motives), should clearly show why and in what manner (scope, interpretative context, etc.) the particular *ratio decidendi* has been adapted to the case in question and to the arguments used in its justification. The so called argumentative or discursive way of justification of judicial decision[14] gives much bigger chances to make the court's position clear in relation to the existing precedent or to highlight the role of a precedent in a particular decision as well as, in consequence, to shape a potential new precedent or to make a modification of the precedential line of jurisdiction, easy to be identified in other decisions that will follow.

Uniformity resulted from the precedential way of unification, strengthened by a discursive way of justification of the decision, based not on the "argument of force" but on the "strength of arguments", is slowly but surely achieved in the judicial practice. Such practice, contrary to the formal ways of unification of judicial practice, demands definitely more efforts from the judiciary playing the role of the subject responsible for finding and implementing the previous decisions as precedents. The uniformity achieved this way, being of a juridical (not political) character, is more stable and efficient in deciding (especially in hard cases), enabling judges at the same time to make necessary modifications of the line of jurisdiction (without the involvement of the politically motivated legislature).

The need of the case adjudicated offers in effect an opportunity to bring the judicial process closer to social expectations, treating the uniformity of jurisdiction on the one hand as one of superior values of application of law and, on the other,– as an important element of the social perception of judicial practice.

2. Judicial review in administrative activities (a case of the Polish legal order)

The above mentioned features of the precedents and precedential practice in statutory legal orders match the phenomenon of the judicial review of administrative activities. The combination of these features with the normative model

---

14 See: M. Zirk-Sadowski, *Wykładnia i rozumienie prawa w Polsce po akcesji do Unii Europejskiej* [Interpretation and Understanding the Law in Poland after Accession to the European Union] [in:] *Polska kultura prawna a proces integracji europejskiej* [Polish Legal Culture and the Process of the European Integration], ed. S. Wronkowska, Kraków 2003, pp. 94–96. On the reasons in administrative decision-making process see: J. Zimmermann, *Motywy decyzji administracyjnej i jej uzasadnienie* [Motives of the Administrative Decision and Its Justification], Warszawa 1981, p. 80 ff., 116 ff.

of control in this order shows some limitations, but it does not exclude the role of the judiciary (administrative courts) in shaping its scope through the unified precedential practice. That also applies to the present Polish model introduced in 2004[15], usually restricted to the compliance of the decision with the binding legal rules (competence, procedural and substantial ones), avoiding strict intervention in the discovery process as well as in the contents of decision.

2.1 Scope of control

Although judicial control of administrative activities is preceded by the internal appellate (substantial) control of a higher instance administrative body, affirming, quashing or remanding a decision back for to the original judicial body[16], it is the judicial control of administrative activities that brings administrative processes to the commonly accepted standards of the rule of law. That is why the issue of the scope of that judicial control is so important. Naturally, the role of precedents within this control must also be taken into account.

Article 1 of LSAC provides that "Administrative Courts shall administer justice through reviewing the activity of public administration and resolving disputes as to competence and jurisdiction between local government authorities, appellate boards of local government and between these authorities and government administration authorities". The scope of control has been defined in Article 2 of

15 The reform came with the implementation of two statutory acts: Act of July 25, 2002 on the System of Administrative Courts (*Dziennik Ustaw* [Journal of Laws] 2002, No 153, item 1269, hereinafter called "LSAC" and the statutory act mentioned in footnote 8 (i.e. Act on the Proceedings Before the Administrative Courts – "LPAC"). It should be stated, however, that the judicial control of administration has quite a long tradition in Poland. Its beginning is connected with the Supreme Administrative Tribunal operating between 1922 and 1939 and with the restoration of that control on September 1, 1980, when the Supreme Administrative Court started to operate in spite of the communist assumption of the lack of mistakes in administrative activities and no conflicting relations between various branches of the state apparatus. The reform of 2002, enforced in 2004, established a two instance court system. The judgments of 16 voivodship (district) courts are controlled (through cassation claims) by the Supreme Administrative Court which besides regular judgments, also makes general resolutions (by a panel of 7 judges, by the Chamber or by the Full Panel of the Court) based on the motion of a panel composed of 3 judges.

16 According to Article 138 of the Polish Code of Administrative Procedure (Act of June 14, 1960, *Dziennik Ustaw* [Journal of Laws], 1960, No. 30, item 168 (hereinafter called CAP).

this act under which "The review referred to in Article 1 shall be performed from the point of view of conformity with law, unless otherwise provided by the act".

Directing judicial control of public administration activities towards the criterion of conformity of this activity with a norm regulating the competence, the procedure and the contents of administrative decisions[17], even if deals with various aspects of administrative activities (or non-activity), strongly connects control with a formalized criterion of the legality of such activities. The concept of a wider scope of control depends on the understanding the notion of "conformity with the law" by administrative courts and on their jurisdictional consequence, the element of which might be a precedential practice (using the previous judicial decisions).

The control of the competence of the administrative organ which makes a decision usually comes first. It may be performed by way of regular court control of the decisional process as well as through the judicial decision on the competence claims brought to the court before such an administrative decision is taken by a body which has some doubts concerning its own competence in the matter[18].

Judicial control is strongly connected with the review of the observance of the procedural rules in administrative decision-making processes, regulated both in the CAP (being the most general normative act) and in separate regulation (e.g. the Tax Ordinance of 1997[19]), It embraces also the failure to act by an administrative body and protraction of the decision-making process[20]. Among the procedural rules the observance of the rules determining the way in which the administrative body establishes the facts of the case seems to be one of the most important once, since administrative courts, which do not find facts themselves (except an optional reference to the documents), review the obligation of the administrative bodies to establish facts precisely at their own initiative.

The control of the substance of the administrative decision touches the most difficult and sensitive issues of that model of review, which goes beyond the concept of legality (formal compliance with the letter of the law) of the administrative decision. On the other hand, however, this limits the scope of judicial intervention.

---

17 See: T. Woś, H. Knysiak-Molczyk, M. Romańska: *Prawo o postępowaniu przed sądami administracyjnymi. Komentarz* [Law on Proceedings Before Administrative Courts, A Commentary, Warsaw 2009, pp. 29–34.

18 Article 4 of the APAC.

19 Act of August 29, 1997 on teh Tax Ordinance, *Dziennik Ustaw* [Journal of Laws], 1997, No. 137, item 926.

20 Article 3.2. 8 of APAC.

The first issue touches upon the discretion (free recognition, Freie Ermessen[21]) given to administrative bodies by the legislators for the purpose of running the activity based on the execution of political goals and resulting from external motions or at the own initiative of the administrative body. The latter makes judicial control even more restricted, especially if the right to administrative action is regulated without specifying clear conditions.

The second issue deals with judicial control of rightness of the administrative decision and it is based on the criteria expressed but not defined in the legislation. These are brought by the notion of general clauses such as references to social interest, just interest of citizens[22] or other vague and axiologically rich criteria like rules of social coexistence or public interest. They are connected in the process of application of administrative law with political values, in relation to which the courts control the way in which general clauses are implemented (e.g. the balance between general axiology and individual values or interests by means of weighing the same[23]) rather than precisely define the content of individual values.

The judicial review, which embraces these issues, might be performed through the control of rationality of administrative action. This, in turn, touches upon the evaluation of the social dimension and effectiveness of decision-making processes in terms of consequences and coherence of administrative reasoning. The both aspects might deal with the abuse of administrative discretion or with the way this discretion is justified in writing in a document which specifies the reasons for administrative decisions. The written justification, following practically each decision (except the one that fully realizes the motion and does not touch upon the rights of others) has to include a statement of facts, applied proofs and reasons why other facts and proofs had not been recognized as well as the explanation of the legal base of decision[24].

Since judicial control cannot lead to replacing a court's decision with an administrative one (the court control might bring the acceptance of the decision or its reversal due to violation of procedural or substantive law[25]), the core of this

---

21 See, for example, G. Schmidt-Eichstaedt: *Ermessen Beurteilungspielraum und eigenverantwortliche Handeln der Verwaltung*, "Archiv fur Offentliches Recht", 1973, No. 2, *passim*.

22 Article 7 of CAP.

23 See: R. Alexy: *A Theory of Constitutional Rights*, Oxford 2002, p. 66 ff., 102 ff., R. Sieckmann: *Zur Begrundung von Abwagungsurteilen*, "Rechtstheorie" No 26, 1995, p. 46 ff.

24 Article 107. 3 of CAP.

25 An fairly exceptional judgment on the invalidity of a decision results from the most serious errors listed in CAP (see Article 156 of CAP).

control should focus on the review of the administrative interpretation of all three types of rules. That is why the reversing of the administrative decision should be accompanied by a precise instruction of the court which points out how the decision-making process should be proceeded and what should be taken into consideration in the interpretational reasoning.

Taking the case of Poland, due to the ineffectiveness of this aspect of judicial control (instructions and even a fine that can be imposed by the court for such disobedience[26] are not necessarily effective in all situations), the April 9, 2015 revision of APAC[27] strengthens control and widens its scope in terms of the relations between the court's judgment and repeated administrative processes. According to one of the most important amendments[28], the voivodship administrative courts may not only instruct the administrative body but also order it to take a proper decision indicating the way the matter should be resolved. In the event that the administrative body fails to act accordingly, the court may confirm the existence of a right or duty, which effectively means taking a decision on behalf of this administrative organ. Practice will show whether this eliminates the "wandering" of the case between the court and the administrative body if that latter does not want (for various reasons) to follow the solution indicated by the court, which is the most visible sign of the inefficacy of the control function. This solution may, however, increase the rate of observance, which will signify a remarkable achievement.

The rather limited scale of the judicial review of the substance of the administrative decision, as indicated above, brings into light the significance of control of the interpretation implemented through the administrative process.

2.2 Interpretation as an object and manner of judicial control

The presentation and explanation of the legal foundations of the decision, which must appear in writing as the substantiation of the legal basis thereof allows for enlarging the interpretative aspect of the judicial review, making room for the use of the precedential practice as a means by which judicial control is performed.

Taking a wide approach to the concept of legal interpretation, embracing both the validation and derivation phases of this process, one would include in the object of the judicial review all segments of legal reasoning in the application of law. Such a holistic review would make control more efficient.

---

26 Article 154 of APAC.

27 *Dziennik Ustaw* [Journal of Laws] 2015, item 658 (there are 81 amendments introduced in this revision to various regulations of APAC).

28 Article 145a of APAC.

The control of the validation arguments would include the selection of competence, procedural and substantial regulations implemented as the basis for a decision. The judicial review should cover a wide selection of the sources the applied norm derives from in the administrative process. It should, therefore, embrace not only the selection of various state regulations (constitutional, statutory, executive, local, internally biding, etc.) and supra-state regulations (international or the acquis) but also the selection of previous decisions ("precedents") and extra-legal arguments ("open-clauses") implemented in the controlled processes as the sources of the reconstruction of the implemented norm.

As far as the derivative phase of interpretation is considered, judicial control should embrace the reconstruction of a single norm on the basis of a legislative regulation or other sources (including the way in which the meaning of the words was defined by the administrative body) as well as the construction of the final basis for an administrative decision. If the reconstruction of the norm gives priority to the linguistic and systemic arguments (especially if they are taken form legislation), the final construction of the basis should definitely include, besides systemic ones, also functional and axiological arguments, giving them priority if the contribution of the precedents and open clauses is considerable. Taking axiology into account and earmarking the sphere of administrative discretion, the judicial control may reach a point of the axiological edge or border of the legal system (somehow going beyond the criterion of compliance with the law), which may translate into a somewhat lower effectiveness of this control. Even if such aspects are more difficult for the courts, it should not weaken the courts' involvement in the process of control of administrative interpretation of the general clauses in light of legal principles, in treating the legal principles as a universal standard of this control, or in a deeper interference in teleological and functional rules of interpretation by public administration. That would give rise to an argument against the implementation of the typical "legalistic" control of interpretative discretion. These "enlarged" fields of control, sometimes limiting control to the point of making the policy by the courts, would rather match the whole review with the *omnia sunt interpretanda* formula. All that in effect, apart from anything else, would bring the implementation of administrative law closer to the universal standard of substantial rule-of-law practices.

Therefore, to enlarge the scale of control and to strengthen its effects the courts as "courts of law" should concentrate on the precise and thorough control of all segments of administrative interpretation of law to equalize the efficiency of control with the political strength of administration. It is actually its additional function, since the features of administrative law and administrative type of the decision-making process create a wide scope of discretion in general, moving it towards political axiology and to the instrumental treatment of the requirements of the rule of law.

2.3 *The role of precedential practice*

The modifications of the model of the judicial review of administrative activity, depending on legislatures do not usually bring quick results, enlarging the scale of control and its effectivity. The remedy in both spheres might be brought by the judiciary with the implementation of gradual changes that embrace all aspects of legal reasoning of administrative agencies.

The efficiency of such an enlarged review (within the framework of the "legalistic" model of judicial review of administrative activity) would be strengthened if the administrative courts operated through a stable, consistent and uniform jurisdiction, showing their independent and crucial role in a democratic rule-of-law state. This assumption takes the significance of precedential practice into a consideration, if one treats this practice as a valuable and effective way of unification of jurisdiction. This would also apply to the field of judicial review of administrative activities, even if its effects are stretched over a longer period of time than that coming directly from the legislature.

The main features of statutory legal orders, including the fact that the *stare decisis* formula which does not operate and that precedential law-making is rather not accepted here, do not make the implementation of the precedents impossible. Their use, if properly proportioned in the relation to the legislation, do not weaken the functionality of that order. If administrative courts take advantage of the implementation of precedents in their practice by emphasizing interpretation as the object and a means of control, proposing interpretative precedents placed within the terms of reference of statutory law, the effectiveness of this intervention will be strengthened. One of the reasons is that the judicial impact through the interpretative precedents on the administrative practice is softer and does not cause a direct conflict between jurisdictional and legislative arguments.

The focus on the interpretative significance of the reference to the previous decisions of administrative courts, and primarily of the Supreme Administrative Court, might, in effect, strengthen the administrative type of the application of law, bringing more juridical arguments to the decisional process and to the contents of the administrative decisions as well as reduce the influence of political arguments, what in consequence would match the features of administrative activity with the unified judicial standards of the rule of law.

Anna Kalisz
(Associate Professor, Judicial Decisions Bureau in the Supreme Administrative Court of Poland)

Communication in Legal Decision-Making and Public Administration Discretionary Power[1]

Abstract: The paper emphasizes that in times of globalization and multi-centric European legal culture the issue of communication arises from the need of mutual acceptance. An increasing role of mutual acceptance on the individual level is displayed not only as the ADR methods recommended for administrative disputes, but also in judicial control of administrative decision and administrative discretionary power.

Keywords: rule (state) of law, communication, decisional process, administrative discretionary power

1. Society has been constantly experiencing an alteration in social mechanisms, values and norms – a social change[2]. However, various theoretical schools emphasize different aspects of such change; the law – in its *sensu largissimo* meaning – does not remain indifferent to it. Every "social turn" is either inspired or – more frequently – followed by a "legal turn" since law is an inseparable dimension of social relations. It means legal concepts and legal institutions both on one hand induce changes, on the other react by supporting, preventing or fighting them. The law is not an isolated phenomenon and does not operate (act or react) by itself or in a social vacuum. It is strongly determined by state actions, but also by on-going social trends. Thus, social change can be also considered from the perspective of *telos* and functions of law and law may be viewed as well as *sui generis* communication between and within different elements of culture, society and state.

1 The paper had been prepared as a result of cooperation in the process of realization of the research grant DEC-2013/11/N/HS5/04212, entitled: "The influence of judicial decisions on the discretionary power of public administration in the law application processes" financed by the National Science Center (Narodowe Centrum Nauki).

2 Further reading *inter alia*: P. McMicheal, *Development and Social Change: A Global Perspective*, Sage Publications 2011, p. 12–14; D. Perrons, *Globalization and Social Change*, London-New York 2004, p. 2–4.

Legal scholarship distinguishes a variety of functions of law[3] and contains at least a dozen of approaches that connect the concepts of law and culture. It also has been teeming with various theories on what law is. Since there is a lack of one clearly leading ontological concept[4] that a definition of law as such may be based on; the noteworthy ones are those, which depict law as a result of the processes of a negotiating, horizontal, argumentative and communicative nature. Even such an extremely brief "map' allows to make an assumption that the majority of significant contemporary conceptual theories picture law as a form of communication[5] within a society. The common starting point for all of such communication-based concepts is a decreasing and/or diminished position of the state.[6] Despite its strong liaison with law the role of the state has changed and experiences quite a reversal. It is not as dominant as it used to be over the past several centuries– nowadays a state itself is a partner in negotiations or a coordinator rather than a body superior to other social actors.[7]

However, the state – at least from the internal perspective – does not exist as one body. It acts through its institutions, offices and agencies – the authorities that make up its public administration. Thus, public administration and administrative (substantive and procedural) law – as an expression of the state – do not remain indifferent to social changes in their action. In recent decades they have responded, in particular, to the challenges such as globalization and European integration[8] and a part of this response is to broaden and outline an area for

3 More: A. Kociołek-Pęksa, *Cele społeczne kreowania norm prawnych* [in:] P. Chmielnicki (ed.), *Pochodzenie, tworzenie i efektywność prawa*, Warszawa 2014, p. 49. On "functions of law" in general – I. Bogucka, *Funkcje prawa. Analiza pojęcia*, Kraków 2000, passim.

4 *Vide*: J. M. Kelly, *A Short History of Western Legal Theory*, Oxford 1992, passim; M. Piechowiak, *W poszukiwaniu ontologicznych podstaw prawa*, Warszawa – Poznań 1992, passim oraz J. Oniszczuk, *Koncepcje prawa*, Warszawa 2004, passim (mainly the chapters II, III, IV i V). Cf. J. Stelmach, R. Sarkowicz, *Filozofia prawa XIX i XX wieku*, Kraków 1999, passim.

5 Which is also an undefined notion, also in the context of legal liasons and considerations -: W. Cyrul, *Wpływ procesów komunikacyjnych na praktykę tworzenia I stosowania prawa*, Warszawa 2012, p. 21 and further.

6 It is necessary to emphasize though, strong current tendencies date back to the nineteenth and twentieth century referring to law as a product of a nation's culture and as embedded in the daily practices of its people and disapprove the vision of law as the court-created and applied distinct cultural system.

7 L. Morawski, *Główne problemy współczesnej filozofii prawa. Prawo w toku przemian*, Wydanie II, Warszawa 2003, p. 131.

8 See: C. Harlow, *Global Administrative Law: The Quest of Principles and Values*, The European Journal of Internationa Law 2006, vol. 17 nr 1, pp. 187–214. In Polish:

communication on several levels: in relation to courts, to other administrative structures and to individual recipients of the legal norms.

2. The aforementioned communication approach to law states it – regarding many particular differences between various concepts as well as unavoidable simplifications – as a set of utterances considered to be a form of action, particularly with regard to its intention, purpose, or effect. Speech (in the sense of communication) acts are distinguished by different intentions[9] as well as by the relation between a sender and a receiver (a recipient). A monologue is a speech act by a single character of narrative or active nature; a discourse – an interactive communication dealing with some particular topics and involving an exchange of arguments[10] and a dialogue – which is a notion on the border of a discourse – is a multi-dimensional, dynamic and context-dependent process of creating a mutual agreement. Hence, dialogic relations have a specific nature: they can be reduced neither to the purely logical (even if dialectical) nor to the purely linguistic aspects. "Dialogic relations presuppose a language, but they do not reside within the system of language."[11] Such classification is significant and may also be referred to the decisional processes within the law at different stages.

Communicative concepts of law do not solely deny its multi-dimensional nature, however they are strongly linked to the idea. A multi-level approach to law[12]

N. Półtorak, *Europeizacja prawa administracyjnego* [in:] R. Hauser, Z. Niewiadomski, A. Wróbel (eds.), *System prawa administracyjnego*, t. VII, Warszawa 2012, p. 2–31.

9 *Vide*: locutionary, illocutionary, and perlocutionary acts by J. Austin, *How to do Things with Words*, Oxford University Press 1962, passim. Differently: J. Searle, *Speech Acts: An Essay in the Philosophy of Language*, Cambridge 1969, passim.

10 Various types of a discourse – an *analytical*, a *normative*, or an *empirical* – see: R. Alexy, *A Theory of LegalArgumentation. The Theory of Rational Discourses as Theory of Justification*, Claredon Press, Oxford 1989, p. 180 and further.

11 M. M. Bakhtin, *Speech Genres and Other Late Essays,* Austin Texas,1986, p. 117.

12 In Polish jurisprudence see: K. Opałek, J. Wróblewski, *Zagadnienia teorii prawa*, Warszawa 1969, p. 328. Cf. K. Opałek, *Problemy metodologiczne nauki prawa*, Warszawa 1962, p. 109 i nast., K. Opałek, *Przedmiot prawoznawstwa a problem tzw. płaszczyzn prawa*, "Państwo i Prawo" 1969 z. 6, p. 983–995; J. Wróblewski, *Prawo i płaszczyzny jego badania,* "Państwo i Prawo" 1969, nr 6, p. 996–1006; J. Wróblewski, *Zagadnienia wielopłaszczyznowości w metodologii współczesnej teorii prawa*, Studia Prawnicze 1969, z. 21. Cf. G. L. Seidler, *W poszukiwaniu systemu wszechstronnej analizy prawa*, Annales UMCS 1967, XVI. Sectio G, p. 1–22; L. Leszczyński, *Profesora G.L. Seidlera koncepcja wielopłaszczyznowej analizy prawa*, Annales UMCS 2014, LXI, 1, Sectio G, p. 95–105; A.Peczenik, *Płaszczyzny badania prawa*, "Państwo i Prawo" 1968, nr 2. See also: "external" and "internal" point of view theory: H. L. A. Hart, *The Concept of Law*, Oxford 1994, passim.

seems to be a great complementary adjunct to the aforementioned conceptual theories of law as a form of communication.

Such concept divides law into several phases (stages): a political, a juridical one, and also psycho- and sociological ones. The political stage covers *inter alia* public debates and discourses leading up legislative and reformative processes. It involves the issue of deliberative democracy[13] and a discourse-resulted law. The linguistic structures of communication are used to establish a normative understanding of society.[14] The juridical aspect focuses on law *de lega lata* – law viewed as binding legal sources providing norms (normative utterances worded in the legal language that have a normative proposition as their content). The psycho- and sociological stages refer to the *micro*- (individual) and *macro*-(collective) consequence of "law in action"[15] and to an attitude towards it. On such a stage the goals (*telos*) and functions of law are confronted with its results and its social reception as well as a notion such as "legal culture" or "legal consciousness". Each stage serves various *telos* and different functions, so the modes of communication within them vary in forms and – in particular – actors.

It also shall be stressed that the idea of understanding law as a form of communication and multi-dimensional phenomenon corresponds, not only by the prefix "*multi*", with multi-level governance[16] and *multilevel* protection both, of the rule

---

13 Further reading: J. Cohen, *Deliberation and Democratic Legitimacy*, [in:] A. Hamlin (ed.), *The Good Policy. Normative Analysis of the State*, Oxford 1989, p. 17–34; J. Bohman, W. Rehg (ed.), *Deliberative Democracy. Essays on Reason and Politics*, Cambridge 1997; J. Elster, *The Market and theForum: Three Varietes of Political Theory*, [in:] J. Bohman, W. Rehg (ed.), *Deliberative...*, op. cit., p. 3–33. Also: A. Gutmann, D. Thompson, *Democracy and Disagreement*, Cambridge 1996, passim; J. Fishkin, P. Laslett (ed.), *Debating Deliberative Democracy, Philosophy*, Politics and Society 7, Oxford 2006, passim.

14 J. Habermas, *Theory of of Communicative Action*, vol. I, Boston 1981, passim. R. Alexy, *Theorie der juristischen Argumentation. Die Theorie das rationalen Diskurses als Theorie derristischen Begründung*, Frankfurt am Main 1991, passim.

15 For such theory that examines law as it is actually applied in society and in individual cases see – questioning the dominancy of linguistic aspect of law – R. Pound, *Law in Books and Law in Action*, American Law Review 1910 nr 44, pp. 12–36 and followers.

16 MLG – an approach in public administration theory and political sciences that originated from phenomenon of European integration. Vide: S. Piattoni, *Multi-level Governance: a Historical and Conceptual Analysis*, Journal of European Integration 2009 vol. 31 nr 2, pp. 163–180. Also: L. Van den Brande, *Building a European Culture of Multilevel Governance: Follow-up to the Committee of the Regions' White Paper* – www.cor.europa.eu. and https://neurope.eu/article/cor-charter-multilevel-governance-europe/.

of *law* and fundamental rights[17]. They allow – from the perspective of each of the phases – a more profound understanding and analysis of what current European legal culture[18] has been based on.

In times of globalization and multi-centric European legal culture[19] European states are governed at several levels. It also leads to the communication aspect being strengthened and multiplied: the legal system contains the domestic, the supra- and the international dimension and yet it shall be functionally and axiologically consistent. The communication issue arises from the need of mutual acceptance.

The acceptance of norms and decisions becomes a way of gaining legal force and a criterion for legal validity. It applies to many aspects – from the creation of international legal norms to the alternative methods of dispute resolving on domestic grounds.

The issue of communication within legal decision-making may refer to different kinds of its outcome. It may cover the "decisions"providing a shape of an abstract rule and general pattern (a procedurally accepted legal norm or principle) made in a legislative, precedential or –too a lesser extent –a customary way, as well as to the *sensu stricto* decisions passed upon individuals by courts or administrative authorities. Hence, the communication in legal decision-making splits into two aspects – legislative and decisional.

Also the multi-centric nature on its own demands a constant acceptance of rules, principles and standards in order to make them coherent with each other and with the idea of a rule of law as well as a social will of the democratic society. It maintains a balance within the relations of the European structures (such as the Council of Europe and the European Union) with national legal orders. Thus, there is a need and practice of judicial dialogue and cooperation within such a "community of law", even if it tends to be criticized, distorted or misunderstood by politicians and a part of society.

17 A. Kalisz, *Mediacja jako forma dialogu w stosowaniu prawa*, Warszawa 2016, p. 63. See also: K. Tuori, *European Constitutionalism*, Cambridge 2015, passim.

18 G. Helleringer, K. Purnhagen, *Towards European Legal Culture*, Hart Publishing Limited 2014, passim.

19 M. Zirk- Sadowski, M. Golecki, B. Wojciechowski, Multicentrism as an Emerging Paradigm in Legal Theory, Frankfurt am Main, Berlin, Bern, Bruxelles 2009, passim.

3. The size of this very paper does not allow to concentrate on both aspects that have been singled out – legislative and decisional, hence further consideration will be granted to the latter one, whatsoever.

A decisional process is a cognitive process resulting in the selection of several alternative possibilities. It is aimed to make a final choice – a decision. Legal decision making is a process of identifying facts; selecting (and interpreting) legal norms to be applied and establishing legal consequences[20] resulting with an external and binding decision passed by a state authority. Such process is an application of law.

The law may be applied by courts or by administrative authorities. In both cases they constitute measures undertaken by state bodies, by which these bodies decide on the rights and duties of individuals and other legal subjects. Such measures involve communication between various actors: individuals (parties), individuals and state authorities as well as authorities of different instances.

A decision may – except for cognitive and legal elements – be partly based on the values and preferences of the decision-maker which constitute a discretionary power. In this context the communication issue covers also the questions of decision-justification and control of decisions. The divergence emerges from the differences in the assumed functions, in the decisional bodies (courts, individuals/parties to *ADR* methods or administrative authorities) and in the liaisons between them (internal or external).

The courts play a particular role. They may be asked to review the validity of the *ADR* methods and also in a democratic state of law they are meant to control the public administration discretion and the decisions of administration bodies. The role of the courts and judicial control against the administrative discretion conferred upon government officials is to prevent it from being based on policy considerations, rather than in accordance with precise legal standards.

Each type of a decisional process has its own distinctions. The main difference is an attribute of independence of the judiciary – that public administration lacks – and fundamental common grounds – framing within the rule of law.

---

20 It need to be stressed that stages, such as: recognition of facts, recognition of law (namely: the sources of law that shall be applied to these facts); legal interpretation; legal subsumption, decision on legal consequence and – at the end – the justification (the grounds) are explicit parts in judicial paradigm of decisional process –vide: L. Leszczyński, *Zagadnienia teorii stosowania prawa: doktryna I tezy orzecznictwa*, Zakamycze 2004, passim. Administrative paradigm varies from it in details – A. Szot, *Swoboda decyzyjna w stosowaniu prawa przez administrację publiczną*, Lublin 2015, passim.

As for judicial application of law there are two main approaches to the decision making: a discourse turning into a monologue in classic litigation and a discourse turning into a dialogue while applying alternative forms of dispute resolution (*ADR*).[21]

The administrative decision making by its nature draws a thinner line between the legislative and decisional aspect. Administrative application of law splits into many forms, but the proceedings are focused on passing and executing an administrative act – an action in which the public administration stands against a citizen. Thus, primarily it rather fits the monologue or "discourse turning into a monologue" pattern. The paradigm of administrative proceedings has to differ from the judicial one since it does not take place before the neutral and impartial court of law, but in other governing bodies. Such procedures are meant to implement a state executive function and establish efficiency, consistency, responsibility, and accountability. Consequently, it may seem there is naturally less space for discourse and dialog, unless it is a component of common axiological base.

There are some significant opposite tendencies though. Public administration[22] and administrative law are strongly related to the notion of rulership, but they also affect and/or interact with social reality.[23] The etymology of such notions, not accidentally, goes back to the Latin verb *administrare* which is placed somewhere between "manage" and "serve".They have its own functions arising from and connected with their executive role.

However, the public administration – as a product of history and culture[24] and a significant social and legal phenomenon – has been evolving. Particularly in recent decades, certain standards have been shaped and developed with a great influence not solely of jurisprudence but also of the judiciary.[25] Thus, the aforementioned judicial dialogue does not stay irrelevant also to administrative proceedings and decisions.

---

21 *Interalia*: J.T. Barret, J. Barret, *A History of Alternative Dispute Resolution: The Story of a Political, Cultural and Social Movement*, San Francisco 2004, passim; T. Sourdin, *Alternative Dispute Resolution*, Pyrmont 2008, passim.

22 R. Basu, *Public Administration: Concepts and Theories*, New Delhi 2004, 2–10.

23 The sociological approach to jurisprudence dates from Roscoe Pound's – idem, *The Limits of Effective Legal Action*, International of Ethics, 1917, nr 27, passim.

24 M. Elżanowski, *Nauka administracji teorią systemu administracyjnego jako systemu społecznego*, Studia Iuridica 1996 t. XXXII, p. 15.

25 Z. Niewiadomski [in:] R. Hauser, A. Wróbel, Z. Niewiadomski (eds.) *System prawa administracyjnego*, Warszawa 2012, p. 32.

It is riskworthy to state a thesis that the judicial and administrative decisional paradigms – while remaining different – have developed a certain level of convergence based on the principle of a democratic state of law.

The "right to a fair trial" has been a part of the human rights catalogue since its very early stages and remains an essential right in all countries respecting the rule of law.[26] It applies to civil, criminal but also administrative proceedings. It may be also described as a right to access to a competent, independent and impartial tribunal established by law and to a decision passed without undue delay. Despite it does not cover administrative authorities, the European Court of Human Rights has explicitly confirmed that the right to a fair trial applies not only to the judicial, but also to the administrative proceedings.[27]

In order to create effective, accountable, transparent and ethical administration the right to court and fair trial on administrative ground is followed by the analogous idea of good administration behaviour.[28] It places an obligation– in a soft law manner – on the administrative authority to act impartially, fairly, reasonably and without undue delay – which brings the standards of proceedings closer to those established in the judiciary. The convergent aspect is that they are both designed to protect individuals from the unlawful and arbitrary curtailment or deprivation of other basic rights and freedoms.

Concluding: not solely the law may be considered and examined from the perspective of communication between different elements of culture, society and state, but its communicative nature is also expressed in legal decision making within both aspects – legislative and decisional. For obvious reasons, it seems less complicated and less controversial to point out diverse "communication mechanisms" in judicial decision making. The discursive nature of adversarial litigation, neutrality and impartiality of courts, duty to justify an imposed ruling, dialogic nature of ADR may serve as an illustration. However, administrative decisional processes currently provide some space for mutual communication in order to *raise* the quality of public administration, to meet minor social changes as well as individual (citizens') expectations and to protect individuals from deprivation of their rights and freedoms. Increasing the role of mutual acceptance is displayed not only as the ADR methods recommended for administrative disputes, but also

---

26 See: Art. 10 of the Universal Declaration of Human Rights, Art. 14 of the International Covenant on Civil and Political Rights Art. 6 of the European Convention of Human Rights, as well as numerous state constitutions.

27 *Interalia*: C. Doebbler, Introduction to International Human Rights Law, CD Publications 2006, p. 107–108.

28 Enshrined in Article 41 of the Charter of Fundamental Rights of the European Union.

in judicial control of administrative decision and administrative discretionary power. The main standards for modern European public administration are based on a rational law-making process involving social participation (participating democracy) and reception of the standards created by the European Union[29] or the Council of Europe.

29 European Code of Good Administrative Behaviour that helps to buiding administrative culture of service, in which civil servants understand and internalise the principles of good administration and provides inspiration for certain similar texts in Member States of the European Union.

Marzena Myślińska
(Ph. D., Maria Curie-Sklodowska University in Lublin, Poland)

Mediation in the administrative and administrative court proceedings vs. discretion in the law application process – selected issues

Abstract: The objective of this article will be to indicate mediation proceedings as a way to introduce more flexibility to the process of application of administrative law in the Polish legal order in the context of the discretional nature of the administration's activities.

Keywords: mediation, administrative type of law application, mediation function, discretion.

Alternative forms of dispute resolution (hereinafter: ADR), including mediation, have become part of the implementation of justice in Europe, based on a statutory law culture. Even though the realisation of ADR assumptions takes place fully in the branch of civil law (as discussed in more detail below), consensual forms are also applied in other areas of the law; the specificity and legal conditioning of disputes arising between the parties to a legal relationship influence the extent in which they are used and the difference from their characteristic features. Additionally, the analysis of the contents of legal regulations found in the Polish legal system shows that consensual forms are not only used independently but also as a component of a procedure influencing the decision settling the dispute or ending the case. The essence of ADR is in the voluntary decision-making process aimed at the finalisation of a dispute by the parties themselves, by way of a mutually acceptable agreement/consensus. Irrespectively of the form of ADR, their application not only promotes a greater flexibility of the formalised law application process, but also the inclusion of parties to a dispute in the administration of justice (among other things, being the realisation of a civil society concept).

The obligation of administration agencies of being bound by the law (the rule of law – art. 7 of the Constitution of the Republic of Poland of 1997) refers not only to the seeing of legal bases for the taking of action in the contents of the laws in force, but also the requirement of their compliance with the laws. This rule does not mean that an administrative agency has no freedom in the law application process; however, it determines the framework of discretion for an administration agency, the basic manifestation of which is the administration's discretion and the filling of underspecified phrases with content[1]. Both of the indicated components entail flexibility improvement for the administrative activity, adaptation to the needs of a specific case thanks to the possibility to choose consequences of the existing situation (administration's discretion) or the evaluation of phenomena, evidence, facts (underspecified phrases). Therefore, the lawmakers assume the possibility of the existence of a field of consideration of agreement in the process of application of administrative law. Mediation, whose basic objective in this branch of the law is in the possibility of agreement upon the facts constituting the basis for a qualification decision seems to be consistent with the scope of discretion.

Therefore, the objective of this article will be to indicate mediation as a way to introduce more flexibility to the process of the application of administrative law. To this end, I will successively point out: the basic features of administrative law and the legal relationship under administrative law as a conditionality of the application of mediation, the essence of the application of mediation in the administrative type of law application, as well as the specificity of any performance of mediation functions by an entity playing the role of a mediator in disputes related to this branch of the law.

The discussion of above-mentioned topics requires drawing attention to the basic procedural assumptions of the decision-making process and principles determining the position of a mediator during the mediation. Features of the mediation are fully realised in the civil law that entails the equality of entities having a civil law relationship, the principle of the autonomy of parties and the freedom of contract principle[2]. The voluntary nature of the mediation, involving the need to express conscious consent to the participation in this form of dispute resolution, the autonomy of the conflict manifesting as the full authority over the dispute managed by the parties or the acceptability of the mediation reduced to the necessity of mutual consent both to the procedure of the mediation and the content of the agreement fully corresponds to these features. Additionally, anticipating the discussion contained in the next clause of this article, attention should be drawn to the impartiality, independence and neutrality of the mediator, as principles determining the normative and axiological pattern as well as the position of an external third party in the mediation. Impartiality is related to the obligation to abstain from favouring any of the parties to the dispute while

1 More in: M. Jaśkowska [in:] R. Hauser, Z. Niewiadomski, A. Wróbel, (ed.), *System prawa administracyjnego, p. 246.*

2 More in: G.. L. Seidler, H. Groszyk, A. Pieniążek, *Wprowadzenie do nauki o państwie i prawie, Lublin 2013, p.* 180.

the remaining principles involve the lack of potential influence on mediation functions performed by the mediator not only by parties to the dispute but also by external entities, as well as the impossibility of attainment of benefits from the subject matter of the dispute and the contents of an agreement.

In the context of the conditioning of mediation in administrative law, the conflict and the dispute primary for the examination of forms of the dispute overcoming mechanism show their specificity. The context of such examinations, including the perception of mediation as a form of resolution of disputes between parties to a social relationship from the perspective of the analysed branch of the law, implicates the application of mediation in disputes related to the authoritative settlement of individual cases by administration agencies. Therefore, mediation is linked to disputes belonging to the "external" area of administrative activities arising between the public administration agencies and entities whose case is settled by way of an administrative decision as well as the administrative courts control over such a decision[3]. An administrative decision is such a form of activity of the administration intended to have specific and individual legal effects and to model the rights or obligations of addressees in a binding manner. A decision is a principal unilateral action, and it constitutes a sovereign act that, combined with the fact that (in principle) it is the embodiment of *ius cogens*[4] standards, makes the consensual determination of its contents (and, therefore, the realisation of the ADR idea) difficult.

Parties to such an administrative law relationship (and, therefore, parties to the dispute) are administration agencies on the one hand and entities administered by them on the other hand. The inequality of entities participating in such a relationship is its immanent characteristic. Administrative agencies representing the state authority have the authority to model the legal situation of the other side of the dispute by enforcing the execution of the issued decision. This characteristic does not correspond to the equality of parties to the disputes typical for the ADR (being a perfect basis for the attainment of goals of mediation), which is a perfect conditioning of the realisation of the voluntariness, acceptability and autonomy of the conflict principle. The superiority of one side of a dispute resulting from the contents of regulations of the administrative law makes the realisation of the idea of a consensual dispute resolution more difficult. The situation of a dispute

---

3 The internal disputes arise between administration agencies themselves in connection with their organisational subordination (here: disputes over authority).

4 Among other things, more in: J. Borkowski, *Określenie administracji i prawa administracyjnego,* [in:] ed. J. Starościak, *System prawa administracyjnego,* Wrocław-Warszawa-Kraków-Gdańsk 1977, pp. 47–48.

in proceedings in administrative courts is a more convenient environment for the realisation of mediation principles. In this case, the claimant's position is equivalent to the position of an administrative agency whose decision is the subjected to the legality audit carried out by the administrative court. As W. Federczyk indicates, the dialogue leading to an amicable dispute resolution is more likely in such a disputable situation,[5] subject to the fact that such a dialogue is determined as the goal of the procedure, i.e. compliance with the law (both procedural and the substantive one) of the appealed decision of an administration agency, which limits the realisation of the idea of the consensual nature of mediation and the freedom of the parties.

Additionally, the specificity of a dispute in the administrative law entails the opposition of interests: the private interest and the public interest. With no detailed definition of both concept categories (that are not unambiguous in the Polish literature), attention should be directed to the fact that the difference is related to the evaluation of the current or future situation, and with benefits such a situation can bring about in the future. If benefits are perceived and refer to the realm of an individual, the private (individual) interest is indicated; however, if such benefits refer to a community or the entire society, we are dealing with the public/social interest[6]. The concept is realised every time in the context of the circumstances related to the facts. Therefore, the conflict of interests being the basis of the dispute is related to the opposition of goals and benefits of a party to the administrative procedure and objectives of the activity of the administrative agency representing the public interest (of course, in line with the above-mentioned rule of law). Conditions for the consideration of both of the distinguished interest categories (where an area for an agreement can be observed) in the issued decision are provided in the contents of art. 7 of the act of 14th June, 1960 – Code of administrative proceedings[7] (hereinafter: CAP). The legal standard resulting from it creates the obligation for an administrative agency to consider both the private and the public interest in its decision (and also in the conducted proceedings).

According to the literature[8], administrative law "covers standards that regulate the organisation and activity of state and local administration agencies, and

---

5 More in: W. Federczyk, Mediacja w postępowaniu administracyjnym i sądowoadministracyjnym, *Warszawa 2013,* pp. 61–66.

6 Among other things, more in: M. Zdyb, *Prawny interes jednostki w sferze materialnego prawa administracyjnego. Studium teoretyczno-prawne,* Lublin 1991, pp. 10–26.

7 Dz. U. [Journal of Laws] of 2016, item 23 consolidated text.

8 More about the definitions of the administrative law worked out in the doctrine in: Z. Duniewska Z., *Prawo administracyjne w systemie prawa,* [in:] R. Hauser,

relations between the citizens and administrative agencies"[9]. Therefore, the conducted mediation proceedings, in addition to the need to reconcile the public and legal obligation, have to take into account the administrative agency's mandate and its characteristics, as well as procedural standards and legal compliance of the issued awards (legality principle)[10]. Additionally, the "authoritative" nature of administrative law, the compliance with which is guaranteed by a system of legal sanctions, i.e. remedies within the scope of the administrative authority[11], is also significant. The said sanctions generate a direct influence on the process of establishment and application of the administrative law[12]. From the perspective of performance of mediation functions by entities in that area of disputes (more below), the politicisation directly influencing the operation of the entity applying the law, i.e. the administration agency that, in addition to the procedural order to make a decision, is bound with the management policy of the entity determined by its superior agency in the hierarchy[13].

When briefly discussing the characteristics of the administrative law determining the specificity of mediation in this branch of the law, one should draw attention to the formalised nature of the proceedings with an administrative decision as their final effect. The decision-making process of the administrative type of law application is based on the material model of decision making[14]. Mediation and alternative forms are close to the procedural model[15]. The decision-making process taking place in this form of dispute resolution involves the discursive determination of both the facts being the subject matter of the dispute and the contents of the decision ending the dispute and based on such facts. Therefore, the communication taking place as a part of the mediation demonstrates the features

---

Z. Niewiadomski, A. Wróbel (ed.), *System prawa administracyjnego. Tom 7. Prawo administracyjne materialne,* Warszawa 2012, pp. 73–102.

9 G. L. Seidler, H. Groszyk, A. Pieniążek, *o państwie i prawie, Lublin 2003,* p. 179.

10 More in: Z. Kmieciak, *Mediacja w polskim prawie administracyjnym,* [in:] ed. H. Machińska, *Mediacja w prawie administracyjnym,* Warszawa 2007, p. 38.

11 Among other things, more in: E. Ura, *Zagadnienia prawa administracyjnego i funkcjonowania administracji publicznej,* Przemyśl 2006, p. 23.

12 What finds its reflection in the contents of art. 7 CAP. See more in: Z. Niewiadomski (ed.), *Prawo administracyjne,* Warszawa 2007, p. 80.

13 More in: Leszczyński L., *Zagadnienia teorii stosowania prawa. Doktryna i tezy orzecznictwa,* Kraków 2004, pp. 20–21.

14 More in: J. Filipek, *Prawo administracyjne. Instytucje ogólne, part* II, Kraków 2001, p. 159.

15 More in, among other things: *L. Morawski,* Proces sądowy a instytucje alternatywne *(na przykładzie sporów cywilnych),* "Państwo i Prawo" 1993, No. 1, p. 13.

of a free convergence discourse; not being limited by the existence of formalised procedural rules, it allows for the direct exchange of information in the common language of participants in the interaction[16]. In the decision-making process of the administrative type of law application, the communication demonstrates the features of a transmission discourse, whose essence is in the exchange of information on the basis of system rules adopted in advance, with attention directed to the instrumental effectiveness of communications delivered by the entity applying the law with regard to the behaviour of their recipients (transmission discourse)[17].

Another issue that makes it possible to direct the attention to how the use of mediation by entities applying the law fits in the scope of the discretion is the indication of the place and its importance to the decision-making process of the administrative type of law application. To this end, one should direct the attention to the specificity of mediation procedures in administrative disputes, which lies in the fact that, in principle, conciliation is not an independent decision ending a dispute (as in civil disputes); in principle, it does not "free" an agency of the obligation to issue a decision qualifying the facts (considering the rule of law and legality principles). The "conciliation" of parties to the dispute is reduced to the agreement upon the facts, subsequently subjected to the evaluation of the agency applying the law and the qualification at the final stage of the decision-making process of the administrative type of law application. Therefore, one can conclude that the decision-making process of mediation is included in the first stage of the law application process, i.e. the determination of facts (therefore, it refers to the decision determining the facts). However, it should be noted that it remains important for further stages of the administrative application of the law. Validation conclusions and the choice of the source of the normative basis for the decision, its reconstruction and, finally, the decision determining legal consequences depend on its result. The agreement upon facts by way of the mediation proceedings subsequently subjected to qualification makes it possible to change the "orientation" of the first stage of law application because, in lieu of their retrospective determination, a party to the proceedings has an opportunity to direct more attention to its needs and interests and, in a way, give the facts some prospective value, which can influence the issue of a decision that meets that party's expectations to a greater degree. In the course of the mediation proceedings, a party has an opportunity to

16 W. Cyrul, *Wpływ procesów komunikacyjnych na praktykę tworzenia i stosowania prawa*, Warszawa 2012, p. 190.

17 More in: *ibidem*, p. 323. Differences in basic communication principles applied within the framework of discussed discourses are translated into distinct concepts of rationality and knowledge. More in: *ibidem*. p. 196 and the literature cited there.

subjectively present the information about the perception of facts and, after that, agree upon their common perspective with the other party to the dispute, i.e. the administrative agency. These remarks also seem to be current from the perspective of the mediation proceedings in administrative courts, specified in the contents of art. 115 and subsequent articles of the act of 30th August 2002 – the law of the administrative courts procedure[18] (hereinafter: LACP). The contents of the said regulation provide that the mediation proceedings are reduced to the direct confrontation of the positions taken by the parties, verification of their knowledge of the law and the joint search by parties to the dispute of a satisfactory consensus within the limits of the law[19]. Therefore, the administrative proceedings are a form based on the agreement upon disputable issues and ways to eliminate them; it has a servitorial goal in comparison with the court proceedings: the elimination of the action or omission that does not comply with the law[20].

To give a practical dimension to this publication, it is worthwhile to indicate the specificity of mediation functions[21] performed by the entity acting as a mediator that is (as mentioned already) reduced to the moderation of the discourse between parties to the dispute in order to put them on track to the conclusion of an agreement by themselves, subject to the rules of impartiality, neutrality and independence mentioned above. The dimension of these functions is determined in the legal provisions regulating mediation and also the rules of professional ethics that, in the Polish legal regime, are contained in the documents by which mediators are voluntarily bound (titled mediation standards, ethical codes)[22]. To

---

18 Dz.U. [Journal of Laws] of 2012, No. 270 consolidated text.

19 More in: R. Hauser, *U progu reformy sądownictwa administracyjnego*, "Państwo i Prawo" 2002, z. 11, p. 35.

20 See: J. Harczuk, *Okoliczności faktyczne i prawne jako element mediacji w postępowaniu sądowoadministracyjnym*, [in:] *Praktyczne aspekty stosowania przepisów, Materiały z konferencji naukowej, Iwonicz – Zdrój 18–20 października 2007 r.*, Rzeszów 2007, p. 136.

21 I understand the mediation function as a set of activities (targeted activity of the mediator) aimed at the attainment of the given goal of the mediation. More in: M. Myślińska, *Rola mediatora w porządku prawnym – analiza teoretycznoprawna*, Lublin 2015, Chapter II, Doctoral thesis.

22 Legal provisions do not regulate in detail the mediation procedure or the way of its execution by a mediator. The position of Z. Kmieciak is worth noting: in his opinion, the activities of the mediator in the context of a conflict between the private and public interests lead to the elimination of the margin of decision. The author even argues that "the greater the scope of discretional authority of the administration, the wider the application that mediation can have in dispute resolution". More in: Kmieciak Z.,

detail and, at the same time, anticipate further deliberations that will be limited to the analysis of the contents of the Polish legal regime due to the framework of this article, one should note that the general legal regulation of mediation in administrative law is limited to the indication of the subjective scope of mediation, the form in which the consensus is to be attained, the results it generates and also the competence to perform mediation functions[23]. Therefore, the indicated functions will not be exhaustive.

As mentioned above, mediation functions in administrative proceedings are performed by an administration agency (or an independent entity[24]) or a judge/court clerk in mediation proceedings in an administrative court[25]. Both the position and functions typically performed by the said entities differ from functions performed by mediators in the environment that is natural for mediation, i.e. civil disputes. In particular, administrative agencies perform a more active role than the mediator (by participating in the dispute resolution mechanism, they issue binding and arbitrary decisions ending the dispute) who, while remaining impartial, neutral and independent, cannot impose the contents of an agreement to the parties. Another difference is that it is not possible to bind a mediator with an instruction (which is typical for the operation of administration agencies)[26]; therefore, the performance of mediation functions in administrative law in the context of neutrality, independence and impartiality of the mediator requires a change of attitude towards the functions performed in the administrative type of law application.

An analysis of the contents of CAP regulations on the execution of agreements in proceedings in individual cases (art. 13 and art. 114–122 CAP) demonstrates that the essence of a mediator's tasks in general is reduced to the "undertaking of activities encouraging the parties to execute a settlement"[27]; therefore, it is

---

Mediacja w polskim prawie administracyjnym, [in:] H. Machińska (ed.), *Mediacja w prawie administracyjnym,* Warszawa 2007, p. 40.

23 More in: M. Tabernacka, *Negocjacje i mediacje..., op. cit.,* p. 40.

24 The possibility of the establishment of an independent expert to carry out the negotiations (no obstacles for the parties to choose mediation) is provided for in art. 19.10 of the act of 12th May, 2000, on the condition for supporting regional development (Dz.U. of 2000, No. 48, item 550). Among others, experts can appear in the form of a non-governmental organisation, a scientific authority, an eminent practitioner, etc. More in: Z. Kmieciak, *Mediacje i koncyliacje..., op. cit.,* pp. 62–63.

25 See: M. Tabernacka, *Negocjacje i mediacje w sferze publicznej, Warszawa 2009,* p. 45.

26 Additionally, as M. Tabernacka indicates, their performance of mediation functions is subject to particularly high standards of ethics. *Ibidem,* p. 47.

27 More in, among other things: A. Skóra, *Idea mediacji w polskim postępowaniu administracyjnym,* "Mediator" 2004, No. 2(29), pp. 53–54.

assumed that the performance of each of the mediation functions is permitted[28]. However, freedom is not unlimited in this area; its limitation is demonstrated in the characteristics mentioned above and the specificity of disputes included in this branch of the law. Provisions of detailed acts in this branch of the law indicate the functions in a similar manner. An example includes the content of art. 47.2 of the act of 13th October, 1995 – Game Law[29], art. 31.4 of the act of 17th May, 1989 – Surveying and Cartographic Law[30] or art. 79.3 and art. 81 of the act of 21st August, 1997, on real estate management[31], according to which the respective communal agencies, a geodesist authorised by a commune administrator, mayor, city president or the local appeal college shall aim at an amicable resolution, in this case in the form of a conciliation.

A more in-depth analysis of the contents of said regulations shows that the entity performing the role of a mediator in disputes related to administrative law performs the function that is informational (equips parties to the dispute with knowledge related to the essence of mediation), organisational (organises the time frame and space of the mediation process) and the function of an expert because of the obligation to explain the legal status of the case to the parties (implied in the light of the need for knowledge of the law). The basic cause of this situation is that mediation functions are performed by an entity specialising in the specified scope of the public sphere, determined by the mandate given to that agency. In turn, the fact that the result of the mediation proceedings (agreement upon the facts) influences the issue of an administrative decision being the manifestation of authoritative forms of the administration is not a convenient environment for the performance of the communication function and the dialogue between the

28 A thing worth mentioning here is the variety of mediation functions performed by the mediator throughout the mediation process. They can be divided into: 1) functions related to the organisation and progress of the decision-making process of mediation (i.e. organisational, procedural, stabilisation); 2) psychological, related to the influence or neutralisation of negative emotions in parties to the dispute (i.e. identification, catalyst, belaying, therapeutic); 3) informational functions, aimed at the communication of knowledge of mediation and the subject matter of the dispute to the parties (informational, educational, advisory, expert); and 4) the function related to the streamlining of the communication between the parties: communication function). More in: M. Myślińska, *Rola mediatora w porządku prawnym – analiza teoretycznoprawna*, Lublin 2015, Chapter II, Doctoral thesis.

29 Dz.U. of 2014, item 228 consolidated text, as amended.

30 Dz. U. of 2010, No. 193, item 1287 consolidated text, as amended.

31 Dz. U. of 2014, item 518 consolidated text, as amended.

parties based on the convergence discourse[32]. In the light of the said principles of legality, rule of law and formalised procedure, the performance of the function of a psychological nature, whose essence is in the diagnosis of actual interests and needs of the parties (identification and catalyst functions) is made more difficult. The same applies to the stabilisation function ensuring the balance between parties to the dispute due to the placement of an administration agency in a position that is superior in comparison with that of a citizen.

Basic mediation functions performed by a judge/ court clerk in the mediation proceedings in an administrative court, focus around the clarification of circumstances to establish whether the law was violated in the course of the previous administrative proceedings, to what extent such a violation occurred, what consequences it can have and what action is to be taken to remedy that violation[33]. The mediator's role is to equip the parties with knowledge of the legal status of the dispute to enable the claimant to qualify the violation of the law by the agency (which can lead to the discontinuation of proceedings) and enable the administration agency to notice the error and eliminate a defective deed or action and settle the case in a substantive manner[34] (art. 115 § 1 LACP, art. 117 § 1 LACP).[35]. Therefore, the informational function that, in the light of knowledge of the law

32 See: M. Tabernacka, *Negocjacje i mediacje…, op. cit.*, p. 46–47.

33 The professional nature of the entity performing mediation functions in the mediation proceedings in administrative courts is worth stressing in the context of knowledge of the law available to the judge/clerk and the administrative agency being party to the dispute with regard to the claimant. This disproportion is commented in the literature in the context of countering the idea of mediation and one of the principles of administrative court proceedings, i.e. the equality principle. More in: A. Drelichowska, *Model mediacji w postępowaniu sądowoadministracyjnym*, "ADR. Arbitraż i Mediacja" 2012, No. 2, pp. 25–40.

34 See: A. Skóra, *Nowe sposoby rozstrzygania sporów(Litigation) między organami administracji publicznej a osobami prywatnymi w świetle Rekomendacji Komitetu Ministrów Rady Europy Nr R (2001) 9 z dnia 5 września 2001 r.*, "Gdańskie Studia Prawnicze" 2005, t. XIII, p. 305; E. Cisowska-Sakrajda, *Postępowanie mediacyjne przed sądem administracyjnym*, [in:] *Arbitraż i mediacja. Praktyczne aspekty stosowania przepisów. Materiały z Konferencji Naukowej Iwonicz- Zdrój 18–20 października 2007*, Rzeszów 2007, p. 70; A. Miruć, *Mediator w postępowaniu przed sądami administracyjnymi* [in:] *Arbitraż i mediacja. Praktyczne aspekty stosowania przepisów. Materiały z Konferencji Naukowej Iwonicz- Zdrój 18–20 października 2007*, Rzeszów 2007, *p*. 195.

35 W. Ryms, *Postępowanie mediacyjne*, [in:] *Prawo o postępowaniu przed sądami administracyjnymi (zagadnienia wybrane). Materiały na konferencję sędziów NSA*, Warszawa 2003, pp. 45–46.

available to the judge and clerk, taken on the form of expert's knowledge, is the main function performed by the mediator.

Summing up the considerations contained in this article, one should note that mediation promotes a greater flexibility of the formalised decision-making process in the administrative type of law application, owing to the possibility of a consensual resolution of disputable issues related (mainly) to the facts of the case. By generating an area for agreement upon the facts (subsequently being the basis for the qualification decision), mediation proceedings become part of the basic role of administration's discretion. The freedom of such agreements is not unlimited; its framework is determined by the basic characteristics of administrative law and the administrative type of law application, including the principle of legality and the rule of law. These principles also determine the limits of freedom for the administrative agency/judge/court clerk performing mediation functions. Their performance requires a change of perspective regarding their realisation in comparison with functions performed in the process of the administrative application of the law and the consideration, to the greatest degree possible (determined by limitations of activity of the public administration and the nature of disputes in the said branch of the law), of procedural principles of mediation and the normative and axiological pattern defining the mediator's position in a dispute.

Wojciech Dziedziak
(Associate Professor, Maria Curie-Sklodowska University in Lublin, Poland)

Some Remarks on Good Law and Good Administration

Abstract: The paper concerns issues of good law and good administration, which are inextricably intertwined as one can hardly speak of any good administration without human-oriented law whose content is also good.

Keywords: good law, good administration, a human being as an objective of administrative actions.

1. Factors that shape discretionary measures in law application processes in public administration must be investigated prior to discussing symptoms of discretionary actions. At the very beginning one must point to good seen as a fundamental value on which law ought to be based. The value that is fundamental for law ought to be (must be) respected throughout legal order (both in legislation and the application of law)[1]. Pointing to good constitutes a clear and distinct position that may solve one of the fundamental problems, i.e. the range of discretionary powers in the administrative type of law application.

However, one must face the question what good is and how to understand its nature. So crucial is the question about good that it has never stopped inspiring humans. The same may be said about law. Hence, a belief has been held for over two thousand years, especially within the circle of European civilization and culture, also legal culture, which law ought to be good. Investigations into good are certainly difficult to pursue. Ancient thinkers used the word *Gigantomachy*[2] in order to express the gravity and difficulty of such undertaking, the complexity of which might only have been compared to investigations into the nature of existence.

However one might actually postulate that law should be good in present times, when a premise is widely accepted that law and morality should be separated – the

1 This paper shall not touch upon procedural aspects. Formal procedures are important, especially presently; however, mere procedures cannot guarantee law(s) whose content and material aspects would be good, nor can they guarantee good decisions in law application processes.

2 *Spór o dobro*, eds. A. Maryniarczyk, K. Stępień, P. Gondek, Lublin 2012, p. 7.

premise so characteristic for the classical legal positivism. Furthermore, within the context, where fashionable and influential intellectual trends negate universal values such as truth, justice, good, beauty, and human dignity. The answer to the above question must be a resounding 'yes'. Not only is it possible, but also necessary.

When it comes to the understanding of good (Greek *ἀγαθόν* [*agathón*], Latin *bonum*), one must point out that in philosophy good is analysed with respect to its metaphysical[3] sense (the way things are), moral sense, economic sense (usefulness of things), and aesthetic sense (perfection of things).

One may ask: why good? Why is good so significant? Why is a/the law to be good? Why are law application decisions (individual and specific) to be good? These are the questions that one must take a moment to contemplate because numerous justifications may be invoked in the answers.

A human is the only being (which was pointed out by Aristotle) that can distinguish good from evil, and, owing to this ability, chooses good. Let us quote the first sentence from the *Nicomachean Ethics*: "Every art and every inquiry, and similarly every action and pursuit, is thought to aim at some good, and for this reason the good has rightly been declared to be that at which all things aim".[4] A Latin fragment of this sentence – *bonum est quod omnia appetunt* – has become, and this should be stressed, a widely accepted axiom. At this point one may also quote the beginning of Aristotle's *Politics*, where he spells out that "every community is established with a view to some good"[5]. Hence, one may claim that aiming at good and interpreting reality with a view to good belongs to the nature of humanity. That is the feature that makes humans unique.

At this point, let us ponder over a fundamental paradigm of morality. Good is a paradigm of morality and morality aims at good. Doing good is the foundation of morality. It appears that good may also be said to be a paradigm, a permanent canon of law. Connections between law and morality are undeniable, doubtless, and obvious.[6] Therefore, good – to be precise, good in the moral sense – must

---

3 Good in the metaphysical sense is a common (transcendental) quality showing every being as a derivative from a creator or the Creator, and showing being as an aim of all pursuits – A. Maryniarczyk, *Dobro*, [in:] *Powszechna encyklopedia filozofii*, vol. 2, Lublin 2001, p. 614.

4 Arystoteles, *Etyka nikomachejska*, translated by. D. Gromska, Warszawa 2008, 1094 a.

5 *Idem*, *Polityka*, translated by L. Piotrowicz, Warszawa 2006, 1252 a.

6 One cannot separate (detach) law from morality. There are conceptually necessary connections between law and morality. Whenever law (legal norms) gets separated from morality (moral norms), the consequence is the arbitrary passing of legal norms.

also be assumed to be a fundamental value for law.[7] One may speak of a certain dependence of the notion of law and the notion of good.

At this point, it must be stressed that a statement concerning the Polish lawgivers making a distinction in these matters is not an erroneous one because a certain meta-axiology has been accepted in the Polish Constitution, through which a thesis 'has been expressed' on an indispensable link between law and morality. Let us wonder what hints to it. It is mostly visible through referring to good (good as a universal value referred to in the Preamble to the Polish Constitution, and the rule of the common good expressed in article 1 of the Constitution), i.e. the value that is a paradigm of morality. The connection is also visible in the rule expressed in article 30 of the Constitution, the rule of inalienable and inviolable human dignity that is an axiological basis for all constitutional order.[8]

Let us also cite a famous adage formulated by Celsus and relayed by Ulpian at the beginning of *the Digest of Justinian*: [...] *ut eleganter Celsus definit, ius est ars boni et aequi* – or as Celsus elegantly puts it, law is an art of goodness and equity (law is an art of good and rightness)[9]. This statement accentuates the morality of law and expresses a close connection of law and morality, a universal synthesis of law and morality, hence makes up a general directive showing good and rightness to be fundamental values for law.

It is also important that philosophical theory of good, traditionally also known as agathology, was – according to Henryk Kiereś – "superseded with axiology in modern times"[10]. Before the term 'value' became widely accepted, it was the notion of "good" (*bonum*)[11] that had been universally used. Therefore, good was 'superseded' with values – a change that has become universally accepted today.

---

7 However, one must remember that a view has been prevalent in philosophy that good in its metaphysical sense is the basis of all good. Cf. A. Maryniarczyk, *Dobro...*, p. 614.

8 More in W. Dziedziak, *O prawie słusznym (perspektywa systemu prawa stanowionego)*, Lublin 2015, pp. 93–107.

9 D. Ulpian, *Digesta* 1, 1, 1. pr.

10 H. Kiereś, *Agatologia czy aksjologia?*, [in:] *Spór o dobro*, eds. A. Maryniarczyk, K. Stępień, P. Gondek, Lublin 2012, p. 107.

11 W. Tatarkiewicz writes: "[...] the term «good» (in Latin *bonum*) [...] often surfaced in treaties from ancient times and Middle Ages: it meant approximately the same as «value» used by contemporary writers. It is still used frequently in Anglo-Saxon countries, actually even more often than the term «value»". – W. Tatarkiewicz, *Pojęcie wartości, czyli co historyk filozofii ma do zakomunikowania historykowi sztuki*, [in:] *Pisma z etyki i teorii szczęścia*, ed. P.J. Smoczyński, Wrocław-Warszawa-Kraków 1992, p. 75; also cf. A.B. Stępień, *Wstęp do filozofii*, 5th Edition, Lublin 2007, pp. 102–103.

If one may express a wider and deeper thought concerning good in its metaphysical sense, one could say that good is coded within the structure of reality, within the structure of the universe.[12]

Thus, law cannot be alienated from good. Law is to be (ought to be) aimed at good. So primordial is good as a category, that rejecting it, or accepting its opposite i.e. evil as a basis (foundation) would be totally incongruous and absurd as it would result in destruction, chaos and a collapse of social life.[13] Analogous problems might emerge if good and evil were to be intermingled or if evil was to be called good.

What is good which we are discussing, i.e. good in the moral sense?

Analysing good, one must say that a human is the good *per se* – a human is *bonum honestum*. We refer here to a classical philosophical distinction (separation of three great domains of good). The distinction is of an ethical nature, according to which a fair good (*bonum honestum*) is the first and foremost dimension of good. It is *bonum honestum* that is the foundation of morality. The fair good is the good of an objective aim. This is proper, actual good. The fair good is the "*good per se*".[14] A human being is the fair good, i.e. a good which is an objective, absolute aim. On the other hand, the utilitarian good (*bonum utile*) is the good of a means, a means for reaching a goal.[15] *Bonum utile* is an extra personal being that is a means to an end, which is a personal being (a human) – a goal *per se*. Being as a means to an end is being useful for a subject. A human being cannot be reduced to the level of *bonum utile*. If a human being chooses *bonum utile*, the goal is a benefit derived by a subject. The third kind of good is the pleasant good (*bonum delectabile*), i.e. good of a personal aim. This category takes account of the very function of desire; however, its aim is the very function of acting.[16]

---

12 Cf. e.g. M. Heller, T. Pabjan, *Stworzenie i początek wszechświata. Teologia-Filozofia-Kosmologia*, Kraków 2013, p. 146; M. Heller, *Granice nauki*, Kraków 2014, pp. 237–242. "Living in a universe saturated with GOOD is very different from living in a universe where good (it is unclear why good) occurs only because some man decided to do something which he called (nobody knows why) good". M. Heller, T. Pabjan, *op. cit.*, pp. 146–147.

13 Cf. J. Potrzeszcz, *Aksjologiczne podstawy stosowania prawa a prawo słuszne*, [in:] *Zagadnienia stosowania prawa. Perspektywa teoretyczna i dogmatyczna*, eds. W. Dziedziak, B. Liżewski, Lublin 2015, p. 118.

14 Cf. M.A. Krąpiec, *Człowiek jako osoba*, Lublin 2009, pp. 209–210; cf. *idem*, *Człowiek i prawo naturalne*, Lublin 2009, p. 16.

15 Cf. *idem*, *Człowiek jako...*, p. 210; also cf. A. Maryniarczyk, *Człowiek wobec świata. Studium z metafizyki realistycznej*, Lublin 2009, p. 121.

16 Cf. M.A. Krąpiec, *Człowiek i prawo...*, p. 16.

Whenever good is referred to as a fundament of law, we primarily refer to fair good, i.e. good that is to be achieved for its own sake, not for the sake of its utility (when it becomes a means to a further end) or a pleasure that is connected with it. The pleasant or utilitarian good may only matter when it is also the fair good, because the three categories do not have to be mutually exclusive, they can be complementary. Nonetheless, good is also connected with action.[17] Useful action or action for pleasure is good in its nature when it is at the same time correlated or coupled with the fair good. At the same time, we know that as the fair good, a human being cannot be reduced to the dimension of the useful or pleasant good. A human being is the good that cannot be treated instrumentally; it is necessary to treat humans in a non-instrumental way. A lawgiver cannot be motivated or directed solely by the utilitarian good as an aim, or the good of a personal aim. Similarly, those who apply law cannot be directed merely by *bonum utile* or *bonum delectabile*. Subjects creating laws and applying them must be directed by the fair good in their actions and proceedings; this category of good must be chosen while making decisions. This good is a proper measure. Human beings themselves constitute the fair good and thus require unconditional affirmation. A human being is the extra-utilitarian good. A human being is an aim in himself or herself.

To make things precise, one must distinguish from good as a goal, i.e. good in itself – we already know it is a human being – the fair good (*bonum honestum*), and the good of a human being, i.e. aspects that serve human development. More precisely, the aspects that serve a comprehensive and full development of a human being (biological, psychological and spiritual development). Administration is to organise and provide means and conditions that are to be attributed to full capabilities of human development. Naturally, such a development is connected *inter alia* with health, knowledge, education, work and being fairly paid, security and property.

On the other hand, what is the common good? Generally speaking one may say that an integral, thorough development of a human persona[18] and living in conditions appropriate to human dignity are the common good (*bonum commune*). Fulfilling individual potential develops and perfects an individual, but it also serves others. Personal development of a human being is a "non-antagonistic good"; it does no harm to the good of others. Hence, the law ought to facilitate doing such good. Definitely, a development of the personal forces of a human

17 Usefulness and pleasantness are referred to objects as well as actions.

18 Cf. M.A. Krąpiec, *Dobro wspólne*, [in:] *Powszechna encyklopedia filozofii*, vol. 2, Lublin 2001, p. 631.

being is the common good, as law is to serve a thorough development of a human being. A right to the integral development of a human being concerns their physical, intellectual, and moral development. The law cannot obstruct human development, e.g. in the cognitive aspect – unfortunately, the right to truth is occasionally breached and violated. Thus, the law cannot be a source of restrictions and deformities in human development. Human personal development as a category is not an expression of any particular thinking that is typical of certain philosophical trends, it is no abstraction. Normative regulations, particularly the Universal Declaration of Human Rights govern these matters.[19] Nonetheless, one primarily has to be in order to be able to develop. One has to exist. At this point, it needs to be highlighted that the right to live and the right to be born are the starting points.

The common good is explained and ultimately justified in the good of a human being. Human life (existence) is a condition for human good and is connected with development in all material and spiritual domains. It concerns development in an embryonic state, and further intellectual, moral and creative development in the further stages of life. For the content of legal norms, a lawgiver should or even must take into account the good as a basis for personal and communal existence. Laws which are passed by human beings are to serve the good of an individual and the common good.

The common good requires conditions that facilitate human development and guaranteeing their decent living within their society. Conditions need to be provided that are conducive to human beings obtaining optimum conditions for existing and living. Legal regulations are to set up structures and institutions that are to provide an opportunity for comprehensive development. One may say that it is about an institutional dimension in the sense of a means that fully guarantees for the subject a dimension that has been mentioned earlier. Hence, when the problem is addressed from this perspective – which might be called an object perspective – the common good is a whole, an entirety of conditions and institutions geared toward developing a human persona and making human life and development real. The law ought to support human beings in their development through appropriate regulations.

With regard to all the issues presented earlier, it needs to be repeated and accentuated that the common good is explained and ultimately justified in the good of a human being. Therefore, one must agree with Marian Zdyb, who says that "The content of the common good must always be perceived from an individual

19 Further analysis W. Dziedziak, *op. cit.*, pp. 65–66.

perspective, because a state, a society, a social group, etc., are necessary systems or might become such; however, they are also systems that are essential for the full development of a human being, and they are always relation-based entities".[20] A human being (person) is an independent entity that is complete and unique.

Let us accentuate that one cannot consider legislature to be autonomous from the good of a human. There is no common good of a community organised into a state without respecting the good of an every single human being.

2. Good is a fundamental constitutional value in the Polish law, and as such is spelt out in the very Preamble to the Polish Constitution as well as in Article 1 of the Constitution. The introduction to the Polish Constitution assumes the existence of universal values such as truth, justice, good and beauty.[21] This is expressed in the excerpt opening the Constitution: "Having regard for the existence and future of our Homeland, which recovered, in 1989, the possibility of a sovereign and democratic determination of its fate, we, the Polish Nation – all citizens of the Republic, both those who believe in God as the source of truth, justice, good and beauty, as well as those not sharing such faith but respecting those universal values as arising from other sources [...]". The Preamble also mentions "recognising responsibility before God or own consciences" of those who established the Constitution. These excerpts clearly show that the creators of the Polish Constitution departed from voluntarist, purely positivistic inspirations.[22]

It is difficult to state unequivocally whether the Constitution refers to the good in a metaphysical sense, or the good in a moral sense. Assuming that it is the good in the moral sense that the Constitution refers to shall implicate fewer complexities. However, let us remind and stress a dominant philosophical vein that postulated the good in its metaphysical sense as a basis for the understanding of any good. Let us accentuate that the Constitution speaks of the good being a universal value. Good is a universal value. However, how are universal values

---

20 M. Zdyb, *Istota decyzji*, Lublin 1993, p. 30.

21 More of the legal significance of the Introduction to the Polish Constitution can be read in. M.E. Stefaniuk, *Preambuła aktu normatywnego w doktrynie oraz w procesie stanowienia i stosowania polskiego prawa w latach 1989–2007*, Lublin 2009, p. 63–78; also cf. L. Garlicki, *Wstęp*, [in:] *Konstytucja Rzeczypospolitej Polskiej. Komentarz*, vol. V, ed. L. Garlicki, Warszawa 2007, p. 4–5.

22 L. Garlicki states the following with reference to the abovementioned fragment of the Introduction to the Polish Constitution: "[...] these excerpts point to a willingness to bind the Constitution with the system of norms and higher values (natural ones), i.e. positioned outside (and above) positivistic structure of norms and shaping the method of understanding and applying constitutional regulations". – L. Garlicki, *op. cit.*, p. 12.

to be understood? According to a dictionary definition, the word "universal" implicates common human values.[23] Universal values are not ephemeral, they are not transient. Neither are they relative. On the contrary, they are timeless (they exist independently of any historic period). Human beings do not set up, nor do they create universal values; however, they may recognise them. Unfortunately, its cognition may be erroneous.

Is the good which is mentioned in the Preamble to the Constitution an objective or a subjective value? Generally speaking, everything that is (exists) independent of an undertaking cognition subject, independent of their consciousness and pre-existing (independently of their views, will, emotions) is objective. On the other hand, everything that depends on the subjects undertaking cognition (their mind), either treated individually or collectively, is considered to be subjectively relative. Good as a universal value is of an objective character. However, how to justify the objectivity of good? According to arguments by Władysław Tatarkiewicz, one may generally point to three possibilities: 1) there is no good (there is no good or evil); 2) good is subjective; 3) good is objective. The first assumption is obviously "preposterous".[24] Hence, only the two latter possibilities remain: good is either subjective or objective. With reference to the above, W. Tatarkiewicz concludes that: "If a subjectivism is a false theory, objectivism must be the true one. There is no further need for a proof for the correctness of objectivism other than denying subjectivism. Hence, denying the validity of subjectivism, I am proving that good and evil do not depend on the subject, and thus I am proving objectivism to be true."[25] Were good to be subjective, it would depend on a subject.[26] However, it is not. As a universal value, good is independent of somebody's assessments, experience, views, and emotional reactions. Good is independent of a subjective judgement. It is irrelevant for the universal values who recognises them and whether everyone does. If somebody claims X to be good, it does not mean that good exists depending on the claiming subject. Consequently, one must assume that a human being cannot make themselves a gauge for the existence of good nor for its non-existence. A human being cannot position themselves above good. If God is a source of good, a human being may not treat this value as

23 Cf. *Słownik języka polskiego PWN*, ed. M. Szymczak, vol. 3, Warszawa 1995, p. 561.

24 The first position is also dismissed by W. Tatarkiewicz.

25 W. Tatarkiewicz, *O bezwzględności dobra*, [in:] *Dobro i oczywistość. Pisma etyczne*, ed. P.J. Smoczyński, Lublin 1989, p. 79.

26 T. Barankiewicz writes that values exist subjectively, i.e. they depend on the cognitive, emotional, or volitional sphere of a human mind. Cf. T. Barankiewicz, *Aksjologiczna problematyka prawa*, "Roczniki Nauk Prawnych" 2004, vol. XIV, z. 1, p. 50.

a subjective one. The very existence of good does not depend on a human being nor a state (or on a social agreement). Being a universal value, good cannot be based on subjective impressions. Moreover, it is cognisable. Having assumed earlier that it is a human being that constitutes the good, is it not an objective value? Also, having assumed that the good of a human being is essentially bound with their life and is connected with their development, are these not objective values?

Nonetheless, good is also connected with action, which has been mentioned earlier. Useful activities or pleasure-oriented activities are essentially good whenever they are aimed at a fair, objective purpose, provided it is correlated or bound with the fair good. Let us remember that it is a human being that is the fair good. It is a human being that is (supposed to be) an aim of action. Useful activity is moral whenever it serves and expresses affirmation for the good, which is a human being. A human being is a good and an aim (objective and absolute) that determines an appropriateness of the selection of a good as a means for aims and the very function of actions. The useful and pleasant good (*bonum utile and delectabile*) cannot be treated as aims in themselves. A lawgiver cannot reduce a human being to the dimension of a means. Should a human being be reduced to the dimension of the useful or a pleasant good, they will become an instrument, and thus reduced. After all, all human beings are the objective, absolute good and a means in themselves. As Tatiana Shauvin stresses: a human being "is a basis (grounds) justifying all legal rules and regulations".[27]

Good law is geared towards a human being both in the law-making process and in the application process. Law is to serve the actual good – a human being. A human being is an aim of all activities.

Article 1 of the Constitution spells out the rule of the common good. It may be assumed to develop good as a universal value pointed out in the Introduction. One must stress that the rule of the common good is a fundamental constitutional rule. This rule had been placed in the Constitution before other rules.[28] Unfortunately, the rule of the common good is not appreciated and is often misinterpreted. It has not been fully noticed and used by court and constitutional court jurisdiction. Placing the notion of 'a common good' rather than 'good of the common'[29] – as

27 T. Chauvin, *Homo iuridicus. Człowiek jako podmiot prawa publicznego*, Warszawa 2014, p. 7.

28 The category of a common good also surfaces in article 25, item 3: "[…] for the good of a human being and a common good", as well as in article 82 "[…] taking care of the common good".

29 Changing the word order expresses a qualitative change in this notion. Unlike in the Constitution of 1935 "a good of the common" (article 1, item 1 of the April 1935

it used to be in the April 1935 constitution – expresses the idea of a serving state (a state that serves citizens) in contrast to citizens serving the state. The common good is not in opposition with fragmentary good – personal good.[30] The good of a human being is a basic determiner for the common good. Protecting human rights is a fundamental obligation of the common good. Such protection takes for granted respect for every person as they are. The common good is the good of an individual and at the same time the good of a community.[31]

One may speak of a natural and a legal character of the common good. This notion has a long tradition that dates back to St. Thomas Aquinas and has long been firmly rooted in Christian social teaching. According to the literature of the subject, this justification for the meaning of this notion had been referred to throughout introductory studies that resulted in introducing the notion into article 1 of the Polish Constitution.[32] In his *Common good as a fundament of the Polish constitutional order* [*Dobro wspólne jako fundament polskiego porządku konstytucyjnego*], Marek Piechowiak proves the constitutional lawgiver to have accepted the concept of an objective rooting of the common good and axiological cognitivism; he also justifies the legal and natural character of this value.[33] This author adamantly claims that the common good is the foundation of the Polish constitutional order. According to him, this is the most important constitutional

---

Constitution reads: "Polish state is the good of the common, of all the citizens"), but instead "the common good" (article 1 of the 1997 Constitution: "the Republic of Poland is the common good of all her citizens"). Cf. W. Sokolewicz, *Rozdział I "Rzeczpospolita", artykuł 1*, [in:] *Konstytucja Rzeczypospolitej Polskiej. Komentarz*, vol. V, ed. L. Garlicki, Warszawa 2007, pp. 1–2; also cf. M. Piechowiak, *Aksjologiczne podstawy polskiego prawa*, [in:] *Prawo polskie. Próba syntezy*, eds. T. Guz, J. Głuchowski, M.R. Pałubska, Warszawa 2009, p. 112.

30 It is worth stressing that this thought dates back to Aristotle, who wrote that a state originates "in order to facilitate life and exists so that life was good". – Aristotle, *Polityka…, 1252 b*. A good life is a happy life. The Stagirite wrote thus in his book seven: "We need to answer the question whether happiness of every individual and happiness of a state are to be equated or not. There may be no doubt in this matter, though, because everyone will probably agree that they are to be equated". – *Ibidem*, 1324 a.

31 John Finnis writes that: "a common good is fundamentally the good of individuals" – J. Finnis, *Prawo naturalne i uprawnienia naturalne*, translated K. Lossman, Warszawa 2001, p. 189.

32 Cf. M. Piechowiak, *Prawnonaturalny charakter klauzuli dobra wspólnego*, [in:] *W poszukiwaniu dobra wspólnego. Księga jubileuszowa Profesora Macieja Zielińskiego*, ed. A. Choduń, S. Czepita, Szczecin 2010, p. 603–604.

33 See. *idem*, *Dobro wspólne jako fundament polskiego porządku konstytucyjnego*, Warszawa 2012, pp. 316–318 i 436–437.

rule and is in fact the rule of rules. Furthermore, he proves it is not just one of many but the prime rule, and not only from the editorial viewpoint. He reiterates that the common good rule is a paradigm for the whole state and all its elements. He stresses that the rule determines the primary aim of a state, relations between an individual and the state and the place of human rights in the constitutional order.[34] He also highlights the fact that: "[...] the rule of the common good (just like the rule of the dignity, albeit for different reasons) is not to be weighed against other values and rules".[35]

Analysing this paradigm of the understanding of the common good in the Polish constitution, and referring to the classical thought, Marek Piechowiak writes that: "the common good is a sum of social life conditions, specified in the vein of a political community, owing to which individuals, families, and other communities may develop and more easily reach their perfection".[36] Hence, as the first article of the Polish Constitutions reads: "the Republic of Poland is the common good of all her citizens", one must agree with Krzysztof Szczucki[37], that the Republic of Poland is "a sum of social life conditions, owing to which individuals, families, and other communities may more fully and easily reach their perfection".[38] This is the institutional and objective dimension of a common good. M. Piechowiak proposes the following wording, which one needs to agree with, for the norm-rule specifying a duty to implement values of the common good: "one needs to act so that a state, as far as it is possible, is comprised of a sum of conditions facilitating a full development of individuals and communities that they build".[39] Article 1 – as the Author points out further – "primarily spells out what the Republic of Poland is to be like and forms a basis for duties mostly addressed at subjects of the institutional type – subjects creating, interpreting, and applying law".[40] Hence, public administrative organs which are duty-bound (obliged) to shape a state and its laws in a way facilitating a human being and their development as well as communities that they create are addressees of the rule which is being discussed and

34 Cf. *ibidem*, p. 30.

35 *Ibidem*, p. 441.

36 *Ibidem*, p. 261.

37 K. Szczucki relies on assumptions made by M. Piechowiak in his paper '*The common good as the foundation of the Polish constitutional order*'. [*Dobro wspólne jako fundament polskiego porządku konstytucyjnego*].

38 K. Szczucki, *Wykładnia prokonstytucyjna prawa karnego*, Warszawa 2015, p. 263; also cf. M. Piechowiak, *Dobro wspólne...*, p. 266.

39 M. Piechowiak, *Dobro wspólne...*, p. 274.

40 *Ibidem*, p. 275.

is expressed in article 1 of the Polish Constitution. Naturally, the common good derived from article 1 cannot be understood from the utilitarian perspective. A sum of social life conditions does not mean a collection of individuals' interests. It is not an effect of a simple calculation aimed at increasing happiness of the majority, even at the expense of the minority.[41]

To conclude, one must reiterate that article 1 of the Polish Constitution expresses the essence of a state and points to its aim – i.e. a good of an individual in their community. The value of the common good is only noticed when one notices a separate value of every individual. A human being is the rationale for law. A human being – the good in itself – is to be (is) an aim of every legal regulation.

To sum up the considerations above, one needs to accentuate that a good law is in fact geared towards a human being. This idea is expressed in an ancient adage: *Hominum causa omne ius constitutum est* – A human being shall be a cause of passing all laws. Good law is geared, both in passing and in application, towards a human being. Good laws are to protect this good. It is to guarantee innate (inherent) rights. It is to facilitate and support development. It is to facilitate ever greater perfection.

It needs to be reiterated that human beings are the objective, fair and good and they are bestowed with inherent dignity, which is also innate, inalienable, and indestructible. This personal dignity cannot be purchased, as it is inextricably connected with a human being, for it is bound with the very essence of humanity. An individual possesses it because of the very state of existing.[42]

The law is to serve this good – the authentic good. It is a human being that is the aim of any action. A human being is an aim of law. Let us also add that the law is only good as long it has the "power of law", i.e. as long as it exercises and serves this purpose.

3. Let us go on to discuss discretionary aspects of law. What are these? Generally speaking, it is assumed that these are connected with various manifestations of a freedom of decision of the law-applying subjects. Literature sometimes interchangeably uses the terms "judges' discretion" and "judges' arbitrary decisions", as they are believed to be synonymous.[43] The term "judges' activism"

41 Cf. K. Szczucki, *op. cit.*, pp. 264–265.

42 Dignity is not something that is added to a human being; on the contrary, it is connected with the very fact of being human.

43 B. Wojciechowski, *Dyskrecjonalność sędziowska. Studium teoretycznoprawne*, Toruń 2004, p. 57.

is also frequently used.[44] Naturally, with respect to administrative law application, one ought to refer to the activism of public administration. However, may one presently use the term "activism" analogically to the court type application? Theoretically yes, although "activism" might be more connected (identified) with a freedom and arbitrariness, or simply with latitude of administration, which these days is unacceptable and has declined. Without detailed terminological ruminations, one must notice that activism or discretion is not guarantees of appropriate, pertinent activities; on the contrary, they may support totalitarianism or dictatorships of various kinds.

Throughout this paper, we shall use the term "discretion" understood as all manifestations of a freedom to decide. Nonetheless, knowing that freedom may be used in order to implement various ideas and values, we shall concentrate on directing it. We shall speak of the discretion of administration[45] understood as a freedom of an administration organ connected with the processes of law application, a freedom within the framework of law, and in exceptional and absolutely necessary cases, a freedom that breaches the framework of the statutory law. Within this broad understanding of discretion, breaching the framework of the statutory law would only be possible in exceptional cases, i.e. when within the framework of statutory law it is impossible to take a good decision. We refer to cases when legal regulations are highly faulty and imperfect; they are simply wrong, obviously wrong, and within the system of law, there are no rules, values, nor instruments that allow taking a good decision. Such breaching of the framework of statutory law should only be allowed to facilitate a good decision. By no means do we postulate unrestrained and arbitrary activities. Obviously, a choice connected with discretion is not arbitrary, but directed by the value of good. When appropriately understood, good directs and restricts an organ's possibilities to decide. Let us accentuate that good shows a direction and at the same time limits of discretionary powers of subjects applying law of the administrative type.

A freedom of decision is unavoidable in a law application processes. Some decision latitude (a freedom of decision)[46] is a universal feature (property) of such processes. An organ does not act purely mechanically as it has some larger

44 Cf. e.g. L. Morawski, *Kilka uwag w sprawie sędziowskiego aktywizmu*, [in:] *Dyskrecjonalność w prawie*, eds. W. Staśkiewicz, T. Stawecki, Warszawa 2010; A. Czarnota, L. Rodak, *Epistemologia, aktywizm sędziowski i dwie tradycje prawa*, [in:] *Dyskrecjonalność w prawie*, eds. W. Staśkiewicz, T. Stawecki, Warszawa 2010.

45 The term "discretion" has been lifted to administrative law from court disciplines.

46 Decision latitude is a manifestation of discretionary powers of public administration organs in their law application process.

or smaller latitude, often undercover space in its decision choices.[47] There are various sources of decision latitude, one of which is the fact that the law, due to its linguistic properties, is an unfinished project at every moment of its existence, to paraphrase J. Habermas.[48] Let us highlight that try as they might, lawgivers cannot eliminate a freedom of decision, primarily, because of so called natural sources of such freedom – legal language has "an open structure of meaning".[49] Furthermore, decision latitude may be, and very often is, broadened by a lawgiver through conscious and purposeful introduction of constructions such as general clauses, evaluative (estimative) phrases, or constructions of discretionary decisions. Hence, one may specify two types of discretion: natural and artificial. Broader or narrower ranges of decision latitude are, *inter alia*, connected with the interpretation latitude which has a source in the above-mentioned open structure of meaning of the legal language. Latitude connected with a fact-ascertaining decision is another such manifestation (so called free assessment of evidence is an element of discretionary power).[50] Moreover, latitude might be connected with a validation decision. One may speak of validation, interpretation, evidence, and even subsumption latitude[51], it may also be connected with ascertaining legal consequences.[52]

Decision latitude, as we have mentioned before is connected with administrative discretion and naturally, such latitude is consciously and purposefully designed by a lawgiver (overt latitude) and allows an organ some choice of a

47 This seems to be confirmed by the following statement: "The ultimate shape of actions by a public administration organ undertaken in a form that has been provided for in statutory laws not fully determined in the normative sense." M. Oleś, *Działanie organu administracji publicznej jako złożony rezultat realizowania wartości*, [in:] *Wartości w prawie administracyjnym*, ed. J. Zimmermann, Warszawa 2015, p. 70.

48 L. Morawski, *op. cit.*, pp. 93–94.

49 Natural sources of a decision's latitude also include a lack of possibility to regulate comprehensively all features of social relations due to their intricacy and a dynamic character of the social reality.

50 Further: M. Jaśkowska, *Uznanie administracyjne a inne formy władzy dyskrecjonalnej administracji publicznej*, [in:] *Instytucje prawa administracyjnego*, vol. 1, *System prawa administracyjnego*, 2nd edition, Warszawa 2015, pp. 268–270.

51 Cf. D. Danecka, *Dyskrecjonalność w dyskursie administracyjnoprawnym, czyli…?*, [in:] *Dyskrecjonalność w prawie administracyjnym*, eds. K. Ziemski, M. Jędrzejczak, Poznań 2015, p. 120; M. Jaśkowska, *op. cit.*, p. 271.

52 This is highlighted by A. Błaś and J. Jendrośka, who write: "The imperium of an organ inevitably clashes with the sphere of individual rights and freedoms in all phases of law application because all phases implicitly evoke a range of discretion in administrative activities". As cited in M. Jaśkowska, *op. cit.*, p. 266.

solution. Let us add that administrative discretion is one of many manifestations of a discretionary power, one may also say that it is a special form (one of many forms) of discretion.[53] Such a manifestation of the discretion of an organ provided for by law ought to be, whenever an organ adjudicates, used in such a way so as to facilitate a good decision. This might be called a predesigned discretionary choice. At this point, an organ may use the rule of purposefulness, naturally, with reference to facts in a case, which have been ascertained precisely and appropriately. At this point, an organ ought to refer to both *ratio legis* and to *ratio iuris*. A discretionary decision may also use referral clauses[54] and one may speak of directing latitude through the clause of the common good from article 1 of the Polish Constitution, understood as the basic constitutional meta-clause (meta-clause of the legal system). A referral to a justifiable citizens interest included in article 7 of the Code of Administrative Proceedings may be considered within the framework of a freedom of judgement, which needs to be understood as pointing to the good of a human being rather than benefits that might be achieved due to the criterion of rightness.[55] Let us stress that a freedom of judgement by no means refers to arbitrariness. Naturally, a decision reached within the framework of administrative judgement must be thoroughly and carefully justified. Such a justification ought to point to actual and legal premises, motivation behind a choice of a given adjudication, as well as its expediency.

To sum up the above deliberations, let us accentuate that discretion is connected with a choice, but the choice is not free as it is to be determined by the value of good. However, can good actually determine the direction and limits of discretionary powers of the subjects applying law in the administrative type? Can it be referred to administration and its decisions? Shall further investigation confirm this?

4. Investigating good administration, one needs to ask about an aim which it is to serve. What is the aim of administrative actions? Let us start from the very beginning, i.e. from the etymology of the word "administration". The word has at least several meaning, nearly all of which are nevertheless connected with its Latin stem, i.e. a fusion of *ministrare* – "to serve" with the prefix "ad"[56] which

53 Discretion is broader a notion than administrative judgement.

54 L. Leszczyński, *Zagadnienia teorii stosowania prawa. Doktryna i tezy orzecznictwa*, Kraków 2001, p. 45–46.

55 On the understanding of rightness and a right law: W. Dziedziak, *O prawie słusznym (perspektywa systemu prawa stanowionego)*.

56 Cf. J. Filek, *Co to jest dobra administracja?*, [in:] *Etos urzędnika*, ed. D. Bąk, Warszawa 2007, p. 18.

strengthens the element of serving or the executive character. Let us stress that the word "minister" is derived from the Latin *minister* meaning a servant (a helper, an executor[57]), whereas *Polish "ministerialny"*, i.e. referring to an office, stems from *ministerium,* which means servitude, an office, service.[58]

According to Janina Filek: originally "when administration was nothing but a tool of a ruler, it was mainly a service for their will. Starting from the enlightenment, its major task was managing state matters, so in essence service for the state. With time, as administration started to take account of citizens' positions in the field of the activities it undertook, it was its service for the society that became ever more prominent".[59]

Administration means service. But what is "service"? It is, *inter alia,* "acting for an idea, devoting to a case"[60], "taking care of someone's good"[61]. Positive ethical connotations[62] are also included in cognate terms, such as: "servitude", "to serve", "to do service". Writing about learning the virtue of service, Aniela Dylus highlights that service is an expression of love. The author states that; "Service as an expression of love may be heroic but also very mundane. It may simply consist in a meticulous involvement in one's professional work". She further adds that: "In the case of an officer, it means that a human being on the other side of their counter is not to be treated as an importunate petitioner, but as someone special"[63].

Administration is a service. But service to whom? A human being. Administration is to serve a human being, every human being, in particular, the weakest. There is no common good of a community organised in a state without respect to the true good, which we must remember is a human being. With reference to previous deliberations, whenever we speak of the institutional and subject dimension of the common good, the administration's role in providing conditions facilitating development of a human being, as well as their decent existence in a society, is simply fundamental. Providing conditions facilitating development of a human being largely depends on administration. We know that the fair good – a human being – cannot be treated as a tool for another purpose. In activities of

57 *Słownik łacińsko-polski*, compilation K. Kumaniecki, Warszawa 1979, p. 310.

58 Cf. J. Filek, *op. cit.*, p. 18; *Słownik łacińsko-polski*, ed. M. Plezia, vol. III, Warszawa 2007, p. 499.

59 J. Filek, *op. cit.*, p. 18.

60 *Słownik języka polskiego PWN*, vol. 3, ed. M. Szymczak, Warszawa 1995, p. 244.

61 Cf. A. Dylus, *Służba (publiczna): cnota zapomniana*, [in:] *Etos urzędnika*, ed. D. Bąk, Warszawa 2007, p. 28.

62 Cf. *ibidem*.

63 *Ibidem*, p. 31.

an administration, a human being cannot be treated as a means for somebody's benefit. Neither may a human being be treated as a means in social activities.

Jan Zimmerman adequately ascertains that: "The good of a human being (an individual) is connected with administrative common good [...]"[64]. The author begins his overview of the basic values in administrative law with the good of a human being (generally, one may assume "administrative law to be dealing with administration and it is administration that is its subject")[65]. Further, he accurately states that: "Administrative law is to serve the good of a human being, which might be considered to be its primary, and practically the sole duty and rationale. All other elements – administrative structures, connections between these structures, competences, forms of action, any control, etc. only serve this sole aim. [...] Seen as an overriding value, the good of a human being should always be taken account of in administrative law, irrespectively of internal divisions within this law. Paradoxically, constitutional law should also serve it as it is not passed for the sake of administration but in order to make sure activities by an administration with respect to a human being are orderly and efficient. Naturally, there are special regulations in administrative law that have been purposefully designed for the protection of a human being. They can be seen in the very Constitution where they manifest in respective freedoms and citizen freedoms (public subject rights). Obviously, they can also be seen in the Charter of Fundamental Rights of the European Union, as well as in bills of law and other acts of a lower rank. Hence, should a lawgiver introduce an ordinary norm that fails to facilitate the good of a human kind, the very constitutionality of such a norm may be questioned and so may be its conformity with European norms."[66]

Nevertheless, the theory of administrative law also features views that equate the common good with the public interest, and the good of a human being is translated into individual interest. The same author writes that public administration is "exceptional as it is run by the state (or a specially designated subject acting on its behalf) and implements the assumptions of the common good, i.e. public interest in order to bring benefits to all (a community, a state) [...]".[67] Jan Zimmermann stresses that the notion of the public interest is not sharp and adds that: "Hence, attitudes or actions beneficial to all (the society) are in the public interest, and on the other hand, activities detrimental to all contradict the public

64 J. Zimmermann, *Prawo administracyjne*, 6th Edition, Warszawa 2014, p. 119.
65 *Ibidem*, p. 29.
66 *Ibidem*, p. 118–119.
67 *Ibidem*, p. 30.

interest".[68] Moreover, he adds that: "As usual the problem is that interpretation of the notion of public interest depends on political elements and conditions".[69] However, the author claims, "that public interest does not have a general, comprehensively descriptive meaning and requires constant redefinitions and analyses, as well as ever changing evaluation, an assessment in a never-ending process taking place through numerous channels and mechanisms of a political, organisational nature, by means of state organs, administrative structures, independent opinion-forming circles and judicature".[70] In a paper by other authors, we read that: "Public interest is an emanation of the common good".[71] Jurisdiction of the Polish Constitutional Court also occasionally equates public interest with the common good.[72]

However, in this paper we do not equate common good with the category of interests and benefits. The notion of the common good is not a synonym of public, social, or general interest. Thus, one cannot equate good with interest. Furthermore, let us highlight that, whenever one refers to public interest, it is relatively often contrasted with an individual interest. However, in this paper we do not present any conflicts between the general good and a good of an individual. We connect a good of an individual with the common good.

On the other hand, interest is connected with the category of benefits.[73] One might even say that it is relatively reduced to benefits. Dictionary meanings also bind "interest" with benefit, profit, and things remunerative.[74] According to one

---

68 *Ibidem.*

69 *Ibidem.*

70 *Ibidem*, p. 307.

71 Cf. *Prawo administracyjne. Zagadnienia podstawowe*, ed. I. Lipowicz, 3rd Edition, Warszawa 2015, p. 37.

72 E.g. verdict of the Constitutional Court of 27th January 1999 (K 1/98).

73 Binding public and private interest with public and private benefit dates back to Ulpian. However, in modern literature of the subject W. Jakimowicz may be quoted writing: "«It is in an individual interest» or «it is in the public's interest» means that a given benefit derived from a given objective state is bestowed upon an individual, or alternatively, upon the whole society. Hence, an individual interest is a relation between an objective state and an assessment of this state from the vantage point of benefits that it brings or may bring to an individual; whereas a public interest is a relation between an objective state and an assessment of this state from the vantage point of benefits that it brings or may bring to the public." W. Jakimowicz, *Publiczne prawo podmiotowe*, Kraków 2002, p. 115.

74 *Słownik języka polskiego PWN*, vol. 1, ed. M. Szymczak, Warszawa 1995, p. 749.

definition, "interest" is a venture that brings a material gain.[75] Hence, one may claim interest to be bound with utilitarian thinking.

Good administration serves rather than rules or governs. Administration cannot pursue individual, particular, or party interests; obviously it must not pursue its own interests either. On the contrary, it is to favour the good of a human being over personal, individual, and particular interest. Let us remind ourselves that administration is to serve, which is connected with its duty to help an individual and support them in their development.

It is vital to understand that one can only speak of a good administration when the law itself is good with respect to its content and substance, and when administration actually acts on the basis of such law, naturally observing procedural demands. Good law is to be aimed at the fair good. Such law facilitates good actions of administration, thus making it a good administration. Undoubtedly, it is easier to make a good decision when the law itself is good with respect to its content, and procedures are fair and transparent.

On the other hand, whenever legal regulations are in conflict with good, they are simply bad; the situation for decision making becomes more difficult, sometimes extremely difficult. Apart from typical, sometimes even obvious decision-making situations, there are problematic situations, in which one needs extensive knowledge on what is really good for a human being to make a right decision.

A law-applying subject, in practice an individual, needs to probe carefully what is good for a human being, recognise it and read it. A decision to be made is to be aligned with this good. Clerks ought to fulfil their vocation through work, which is to be treated as a mission. They should undertake decisions that serve human life and development. Naturally, making difficult decisions in situations that are problematic is never easy and requires effort.

A clerk is to make good decisions, and a decision is an act of choice, an act of intellect and will. A decision is to be aimed at the good of an individual. If this is the case, a positive balance of costs and profits is not of utmost importance, it is not the point of administrative activities. A border between a good and bad decision ought to be clear. Unfortunately, a decision may also be bad. When is a decision bad? Whenever negating the fair good becomes its foundation. Negating this aim, excluding real good.

One must stress that an attitude of moral relativism is extremely dangerous in administrative work, which might also be connected with an extensive exposition to numerous interests and conflicts. It is frequently putting people and groups

---

75 *Ibidem.*

against one another, and neglecting the common good. It is a perception of law, a state as a set of structures reflecting a conflict of interest.

A subject applying law (a clerk), and in particular an individual (a thinking entity) is to act for the good of an individual, for the common good. They are to take account of the good of a pertinent subject and take account of the common good at the same time. Hence, acting for the good of an individual and at the same time for the common good is a primary rule for all activities of public administration organs. Referring to the common good never automatically excludes, nor negates, the good of an individual and their inalienable rights.

Let us come back to really difficult decisions, which are truly contentious issues. What if legal provisions that were to constitute a basis for decisions are amoral, or bad? Would consequently a decision based on them be bad as well? Ought an amoral, or bad decision to be taken? Or need one to seek a good, morally appropriate decision? Nonetheless, how is one to achieve it? One solution is to use teleological interpretation that takes account of both *ratio legis* and *ratio iuris*,[76] through systemic and axiological rules. Pro-constitutional interpretation is crucial (conformity with the constitutional meta-rule of law, a rule of the common good derived from article 1). Naturally, apart from a good interpretation, validation choices (validation decision) can also lead to a good decision, where the following might be used as decision bases: the constitutional meta-rule of the common good (article 1 of the Constitution), social justice rules (article 2 of the Constitution) and the rule of inborn, inalienable human dignity (article 30 of the Constitution). Appropriately understood referral clause – a just interest of citizens – shall be important here (article 7 of the Code of Administrative Proceedings). Other prior law application decisions (argument *per rationem decidendi*) might be important within a validation decision, so might sources of international law, or applicable norms of the EU law.[77] Latitude connected with a choice of consequences could also be exploited for the sake of making a good decision.

Nevertheless, what happens when there are no determiners allowing the making of a good decision in a constitution, normative acts, legal rules and regulations, nor in judicature? We are approaching the most difficult and a most contentious

76 Establishing the meaning of a legal provision (legal text) should always be connected with a referral to teleological rules, i.e. to the aim of a legal regulation, which is to be aligned with the aim of law. W. Jakimowicz in his *Wykładnia w prawie administracyjnym* accentuates the priority of teleological interpretation in administrative law, Kraków 2006.

77 It might be necessary to apply provisions of international law concerning basic rights and freedoms of a human being.

issue here. In such a case, a decision ought to be (is to be) good, hence based on the values that have not been expressed in legislature yet existing as external values in such a situation. The fair good – a human being and their personal dignity – precede law. They are primary with respect to statutory law. In such a situation, good shall be a category external to the legal system, influencing the final result of an organ's actions from the outside.

Administrative actions also have a moral dimension. They are not neutral with respect to values understood in a substantive way. One needs to bear in mind that a human being is a moral subject and a veneer of legal rules does not exonerate them from such a responsibility of remembering about this. A clerk must seek good decisions. They are to be open to a human being. This openness is a significant requirement of a professional attitude. Working in administration ought to be understood and treated as a service for other people. Consequently, if administration is to be a service, its actions cannot merely consist of a purely automatic, mechanical application of law.

Thinking about a good administration, one must pay attention to an appropriate selection of people for performing clerical functions. The process of training administrative staff is vital too. A clerk must have high personal and moral qualifications. At this point, one needs to refer to the ethic of virtues, which is experiencing a revival.[78] A decision-making clerk ought to be equipped with a number of virtues[79], firstly they need to exercise a virtue of prudence. Pursuant to the classical tradition, this virtue is a mind-related quality (cognitive) as well as a will-related one. Prudence is both an intellectual and a moral virtue, as it streamlines both the mind and the will in their co-operation, the effect of which is a prudent decision that takes account of good.[80] Prudence[81] allows recognising

---

78 Virtue might be understood as a "constant inclination and efficiency of will in doing good". Cf. A. Szostek, *Pogadanki z etyki*, Częstochowa 2008, p. 111. A virtue is an effect of some effort. An inclination breeds improvement in a given domain.

79 More on the aretological (personal) model in public administration in T. Barankiewicz, *W poszukiwaniu modelu standardów etycznych administracji publicznej w Polsce*, Lublin 2013, pp. 181–247. This author distinguishes prominent personal and moral features of a clerk: honesty, politeness, kindness, responsibility, and readiness to accept criticism. He also lists ancillary features, which include: reliability, diligence, and pursuance of professional development.

80 Cf. A. Szostek, *op. cit.*, p. 116.

81 Prudence is known to be one of the cardinal virtues (from Latin *cardo* – hinge), i.e. the ones on which other one might say hang. This virtue is sometimes called "a driver of all virtues" (*auriga virtutum*).

good and chose a means of reaching it. This virtue is especially important for doing the job of a clerk well and similarly, it is crucial for making good decisions.

To conclude, one needs to highlight that although the above investigations had to be rather general, rudimentary and primordial, the most significant issues seem to have been raised.[82]

The perspective of this paper gives the right to a good administration another, or as one may put it, deeper, fuller meaning. Typically, this right is exercised as a right to a good procedure, in procedural aspects, in the light of procedural law.[83] However, good administration cannot be only seen from the vantage point of procedural aspects. It is hardly possible to speak of good administration without good statutory, human-oriented law.

Any activities of administration should be altruistic and geared towards the fair good. A human being and their good, correlated with the common good, are to be the aims of administrative actions. Let us reiterate that it is service for a human being that is to be administration's aim. Good law is to guarantee innate (inborn) rights of a human being; it is to facilitate individuals' development, while a good administration is to support this development.

82 Investigations were mostly conducted from the philosophical and legal vantage point.

83 A right to good administration is presently expressed in article 41 of the EU Charter of Fundamental Rights and in the European Code of Good Administration passed by the European Parliament.

Part IV

Bartosz Liżewski
(Associate Professor, Maria Curie-Sklodowska University in Lublin, Poland)

European Convention on Human Rights as a decision-making argument in the administrative type of law application (theoretical analysis)[1]

Abstract: The article touches upon a niche subject of Polish administration organs applying the European Convention on Human Rights within the framework of the administrative type of law application. The paper attempts at analysing this issue, mostly on the basis of hypotheses and effects of administrative organs' practice.

Keywords: human rights, administrative decision, human rights, adjudication standards.

1. Introduction

The European legal order within the sphere of protecting human rights is mainly shaped by two organisations: the Council of Europe and the European Union.[2] Historically, the Council of Europe dates back earlier and presently comprises nearly all European states[3]. It was the Council of Europe that established the European system for the protection of human rights and the European Convention on Human Rights[4] (further ECHR or the Convention), which remains the most important source of law in the group of numerous conventions passed by this organisation. The European Union is primarily active in the sphere of

---

1 The paper had been prepared as a result of cooperation in the process of realization of the research grant DEC-2013/11/N/HS5/04212, entitled: "The influence of judicial decisions on the discretionary power of public administration in the law application processes" financed by the National Science Center (Narodowe Centrum Nauki).
2 The subject matter of protecting human rights is also connected with the work of the Organisation for Security and Co-operation in Europe.
3 The Vatican and Belarus are not member states of the Council of Europe.
4 The Convention for the Protection of Human Rights and Fundamental Freedoms was opened for signing in Rome on 4th November 1950. The Convention entered into force in 1953 and Poland ratified the act on 19th January 1993 (Journal of Laws, No. 61, position 284).

broadly defined European economic integration, within which human rights have gradually become an element of the legal order within the Union, firstly via the judicature by the European Court of Justice (presently the Court of Justice of the European Union) and now via the Charter of Fundamental Rights. Sources of law from both the above-mentioned orders became, albeit on different terms, sources of law for the states united in these organisations. Consequently, regulations in international agreements, orders, directives and decisions are or may become elements of a normative basis (legal basis) for decisions undertaken during law application processes in European states. They may be also used, in connection with the judicature of international courts, as arguments to substantiate decisions made during law application. Hence, they are used in a varied way in national decision-making processes.

In most cases, it is the court type of law application that is the major perspective for the problems of applying the ECHR within the national, i.e. Polish, legal order. Its resolutions are used as sources for reconstructing a norm (basis for law application decisions) or as arguments for substantiating a decision. Such interest stems primarily from the fact that the ECHR is more often employed in the judicature of Polish courts. Hence, a lot of research is done into functions of an argument from the Convention in the process of law application by the courts. However, conducting a similar analysis with respect to the administrative type of law application seems to be an equally interesting issue (albeit considerably less explored). The best part of the dissertation is devoted to the influence exerted on the sphere of administrative organs using material administrative law by the Convention and by the adjudication of the European Court of Human Rights that is based on the Convention.

2. Administrative type of law application

Administrative type of law application is typically juxtaposed against the court type presented collectively[5] or against a specific procedure (e.g. a court procedure)[6]. Naturally, this is justified *inter alia* by the rule of the separation of powers expressed in article 10 of the Constitution. Isolating court powers from the total structure of state powers shapes their autonomous dimension, which makes them independent and based on their own rules and regulations. Appointing courts as the third power determines providing them with competences which

5 Np., J. Wróblewski, Sądowe i pozasądowe stosowanie prawa – problemy teorii i praktyki, "Studia Prawno-Ekonomiczne" 1981, R. XXVI, p. 7–21.

6 J. Zimmermann, Polska jurysdykcja administracyjna, Warszawa 1996, p. 6–7.

executive and legislative powers lack, which grants these courts powers in their autonomous constitutional position, which consists in acting as the judiciary[7]. Due to this fact, the issue of the administrative type of law application being realised via organs of executive powers makes a separate subject for study. The issue shall be dealt with in a general manner as it is to form a basis for the major investigation problem, i.e. specifying the role of the ECHR used by administrative organs as an argument in their decision-making processes.

Administrative type of law application is based on the subjugation of the proceedings and addressees of decisions to an organ granted with competences necessary for making an administrative act or an administrative decision[8]. This is, to a large extent, a consequence of a specificity of administrative law norms, most of which are of the *ius cogens* character. This feature of administrative norms causes that "…their specific part may only be used (realised) by an authoritative act of a properly authorised organ"[9]. One must stress that administrative organs are not provided with sovereignty within the scope of adjudicating, nor are they independent in their relations with other organs. Such constitutional position results from a complex hierarchical structure of the organs belonging to the executive power and public administration. Each organ realises specific public tasks. The duty of an organ to obtain specific results within the framework of their competences gives an organ a vested interest in adjudication content not only because of realising public tasks but also because an organ may bear consequences of making an administrative decision in breach of law. The fact that an administrative organ is provided with imperative forms of action does not mean that realising these forms is not controlled. Such control from the vantage point of addressees of a decision is an example of realising a democratic rule of law. To this end, a hierarchical structure of organs has been implemented. Organs situated at a higher level control decisions brought under appeal by organs of a lower level. The control takes place within administrative structures and is complemented by the system of court control over administration, where sovereign administrative courts check the legality of administrative decisions being passed. Hence, the control is being asserted within two types of law application.

The very process of applying administrative law is exceedingly complex and it is typically understood as a sequence of an organ's actions aimed at making an administrative decision. It is inextricably bound with the specificity and the range

7 P. Sadowski, Władza sądownicza – sądy, [in:] Konstytucyjny system organów państwowych, (ed.) E. Gdulewicz, Lublin 2009, p. 212.

8 A. Korybski (ed.), Podstawy wiedzy o państwie i prawie, Bydgoszcz 2012, p. 153.

9 J. Zimmermann, Polska… op. cit., p. 7.

of administrative law matters, either approached as a subject or an object. Making an administrative decision is a basic and typical way to apply administrative law. Providing a form for a decision, material law determines competencies of organs as well as a necessity to pass an individual and external act which would specify rights and responsibilities for an addressee of a legal norm[10]. Nonetheless, one must bear in mind that there are some other untypical forms of applying administrative law apart from the above-mentioned typical ones. A mechanism for using a norm featuring a direct imperative or a prohibition makes a good example of such mechanisms. A subject breaching such a norm must take into account the consequences in the form of a fine as an administrative execution of sorts. Such a fine as an instrument of administrative power may be a consequence of a delinquency (e.g. exceeding a speed limit is breeching traffic rules by a driver). However, material administrative law provides for situations where imposing a fine is not connected with a delinquency. For instance, the Road Transportation Act[11] features articles 92a and 93 which impose fines on a business person for a failure to meet their duties or conditions in road transport. The fine is aimed at guaranteeing that business is done according to the proper standards and carriers respect orders and prohibitions specified in applicable acts of law. Guilt and a degree of being guilty are not premises for imposing a fine, especially because a person who is actually transporting goods is a driver employed by the carrier who bears the consequences.

3. Conditions for the European Convention on Human Rights affecting the process of law application in the administrative type

Theoretical deliberations should not merely focus on attempting 'how' the European Convention on Human Rights affects the process of law application in the administrative type, but also account for factors that condition such applications. This approach shall facilitate presenting a thesis on whether the practice of referring to the ECHR by administrative organs is frequent or incidental (thought one intuitively perceives it to be rather incidental), but more importantly, it shall allow to be understood 'why' a decision-making process happens in a specific way. Analysing these matters poses considerable 'technical' difficulties for an investigation, which has been described in the literature of the subject. A quotation

10 Ibidem, p. 23.

11 Road Transportation Act from 6th Sept. 2001 (J.L. 2013, item. 1414).

referring to a slightly broader context seems very topical for these matters: "Establishing a level for the use of international, mostly European regulations on human rights, is rather difficult in administrative practice. Lack of empirical data, as well as the fact that administrative decisions are not published, forces one to base their conjectures on fragmentary knowledge concerning facts, intuition and experience"[12]. One must unreservedly agree with this thesis. Hence, any theory of law analysis is also based on these hypotheses and assessing results of the actions by administrative organs treated as consequences of influences of the Convention and adjudications by the ECHR. The following arguments may be used to develop the above-mentioned thesis.

The first argument refers to the specificity of administrative law as a branch of law. The law is comprised of a collection of norms regulating structure and competencies of public administration organs, as well as legal relations established while these organs perform their managerial and executive activities[13]. This branch of law covers constitutional, material, and procedural norms, and is considered the broadest and most extensive branch in the Polish legal system. Focusing merely on the material aspect of administrative law, one may assert that its norms form a basis for adjudications concerning most domains of social relations. So diverse are these relations that they exceed the sphere of personal and political rights and obligations. For this reason, the subject range of the ECHR may at most refer to a small portion of administrative material law. Rights and obligations in the Convention are either indifferent or hardly related to issues from construction law, water law, social welfare, public roads or traffic rules. Even in domains where such laws might apply, their substantive range only inconsiderably refers to the very extensive sphere of nationwide legal regulations concerning specific subject matters. E.g. the right to study regulated in article 2 of the protocol No. 1 supplementary to the ECHR,[14] merely constitutes a small fragment, which is on a

12 L. Leszczyński, Prawa człowieka i orzecznictwo Europejskiego Trybunału Praw Człowieka w wykładni prawa administracyjnego, [in:] System Prawa Administracyjnego, Tom 4 – Wykładnia w prawie administracyjnym, (eds.) R. Hauser, Z. Niewiadomski, A. Wróbel, Warszawa 2012, p. 390.

13 Z. Muras, Podstawy prawa, Wydawnictwo C.H. Beck, Warszawa 2008, p. 127.

14 Protocol No. 1 to the Convention for the Protection of Human Rights and Fundamental Freedoms of 20th March 1953 entered into force for Poland on 10th October 1994 (Journal of Laws 1995 No. 36, position 175).

very general level of problems for which there are specific norms in acts belonging to the sphere of educational law,[15] or in acts concerning higher education[16].

The next argument refers to administrative organs shaping a specific practice for law application. A preference for 'the law of one's own centre of power in a state'[17] is a characteristic feature of such practice in the Polish legal order. Administrative organs of the 1st instance hardly resort to rulings from the ECHR and adjudications by the European Court of Human Rights, partly because of a high degree of detail in national regulations that they consider adequate for qualifying facts that form the basis for decision-making processes. The aspect of legal provisions being too detailed or too general may also explain why no practice of referring to rulings from the Convention has been established for the legal basis of administrative decisions (naturally, only if a given case requires it). This might be directly connected with a lack of suitable interpretation competencies. General provisions from the ECHR must be analysed together with verdicts of the Strasbourg Court and juxtaposed against provisions of Polish law. It seems that members of administrative organs of the 1st instance do not have sufficient competencies to reconstruct legal norms being used. The problem is on the educational level rather than the law application practice. Generally, such members (unlike a judge, a barrister or an attorney-at law who train in formal apprenticeships) frequently have problems with using all rules of interpretation appropriately, especially referring to extra-linguistic arguments or open criteria. On the other hand, such persons specialise in a definite fragment (defined according to its subject) of administrative law, which facilitates mastering this branch of law on a high level with respect to its details. Lack of interpretation skill is often compensated by many years of experience within a narrow domain of specialisation. Undoubtedly, administrative organs of appeal have greater interpretation awareness. This results from the fact that their decisions may be appealed against in administrative courts. This makes it necessary for such organs to analyse more deeply a direction and ways of

---

15 In the Polish legal system, norms of educational law are included in the Constitution of the Republic of Poland of 2nd April 1997 (Journal of Laws of 1997, No. 78, position 483 with subsequent amendments), in the Act of 7th September 1991 on Educational System (Journal of Laws of 1991, No. 95, position 425 with subsequent amendments), in the Act of 26th January 1982 Teachers' Charter (Journal of Laws of 1982, No. 3, position 9 with subsequent amendments) and in numerous orders accompanying these acts.

16 The major regulation is the act of 27th July 2005, the Law on Higher Education (Journal of Laws of 2005, No. 164, position 1365) and executive orders accompanying this act.

17 M. Zirk-Sadowski, L. Leszczyński, *Prawo administracyjne a regulacje praw człowieka. Wprowadzenie…* op. cit., p. 384.

administrative courts' adjudications, which gives them 'better contact' with court practice of law application, including interpretations. One must stress that courts use material rulings from the ECHR significantly more often on the validation level, and adjudication arguments by international courts are used universally in the interpretive processes.

4. The ECHR's influence on the law application process in the administrative type

One must make two statements writing about theoretical aspects of the process of applying administrative law. The first refers to the word 'influence'. Its use may imply various forms of its understanding, for instance, strictly speaking, one may think about referring to the ECHR in legal basis for administrative decisions; however, some intuition might suggest other types of the ECHR's influencing the decision-making process. The decision practice of Polish administration organs suggests the latter, broader understanding of such 'influence'. Practically, the Convention is hardly ever referred to as a source of universally binding Polish law for administrative decisions. Hence, the notion of 'influence' allows seeking further potential and other ways of using this agreement in the process of applying administrative law.

The second statement refers to treating the ECHR and adjudication by the European Court of Human rights as a self-regulating system. Creating standards for the protection of human rights, the Court is a single and indispensable organ for a correct reading of the meaning of human rights. Hence, 'It seems justifiable to state that the centre of gravity in the process of ascertaining the meaning of conventional laws is being considerably shifted from the Convention to the Strasbourg Court'[18]. Consequently, writing on the influence of the Convention, I also refer to the influence that the ECHR exerts on the administrative decision-making process in the Polish legal order. Taking these two statements into account, one may point to three major manners in which the Convention influences the decision making process in the administrative type.

Manner I – consists in referring to the provisions of the Convention and other international agreements in the legal basis for decisions made by administrative organs; a status of sources of law universally binding in the Republic of Poland.[19] It

18 B. Liżewski, *Operacjonalizacja ochrony praw człowieka w porządku Europejskiej Konwencji Praw Człowieka (studium teoretycznoprawne)*, Lublin 2015, p. 218.

19 Pursuant to z article. 87 section 1 of the Constitution of the Republic of Poland, 'the Constitution, acts of law, ratified international agreements and executive orders are

is a major determinant for the possibility of referring to international agreements in legal basis of an administrative decision. Obviously, 'it is only a legal norm or a complex of norms belonging to normative acts that are sources of law that may constitute legal basis for a decision'[20]. The sphere of citizens' rights and obligations may only be shaped by means of universally binding sources of law.

The remark concerning international agreements, other than the ECHR, has been made intentionally. To my knowledge, the convention is hardly referred to as a basis for administrative decisions, which does not mean that other international agreements cannot be referred to in this way. However, such a situation decidedly occurs most seldom. As a rule, the sphere of administrative actions includes decisions concerning subject and object rights and obligations of citizens in cases that typically belong to the sole domain of the legislator and whose details are regulated in normative acts of the national law. The fact that administrative law has such a broad subject range is the main reason why administrative decisions only narrowly overlap with the sphere that is covered by the regulations from the European Convention on Human Rights.

Regulations (articles) from the European Convention on Human Rights are very general and refer to significant issues concerning human beings' individual and political rights. This matter is also a subject of regulations in the Constitution of the Republic of Poland[21], where it is also regulated at a similarly general level. Consequently, general regulations from the European Convention on Human Rights and Polish Constitution are specified and developed in national acts of law. Therefore, it is provisions from acts of law and executive orders that are appropriately detailed and precise to constitute a legal basis for administrative decisions concerning human rights. Normative acts of the Polish law may be said to complete the ECHR provisions with content, including adjudication standards

---

the sources of law universally binding in the Republic of Poland'. Pursuant to article 88, section 3 'International agreements ratified following a consent in the form of an act of law shall be published in the mode applicable for acts of law. Rules and regulations for publishing other international agreements shall be determined in a special act of law.' Furthermore, article 91, section 1 states that 'A ratified international agreement constitutes an element of a national legal order and is applied directly after the publication in the Journal of Laws of the Republic of Poland unless its application depends on passing a specific act of law.

20 J. Zimmermann, *Motywy decyzji administracyjnej i jej uzasadnienie*, Warszawa 1981, p. 46.

21 This matter is regulated in chapter II of the Constitution of Republic of Poland of 2nd April 1997 (Journal of Laws of 1997, No. 78, position 483 with subsequent amendments).

for the protection of human rights established on the basis of these provisions by the European Court of Human Rights. In this context, referring to the ECHR's provisions in the legal basis for an administrative decision is not necessary, even though it might seem justifiable. An administrative organ seems more likely to resort to provisions from the Polish Constitution as a complementary source for reconstructing a norm. However, whenever constitutional regulations for rights and obligations are used jointly with the provisions from other acts of law, M. Szubiakowski points out a heterogeneous lack of compatibility in these two hierarchically different regulations, which may lead to situations that are unacceptable in a democratic rule of law. This author shows three situations and supports them with suitable examples. The first situation is duplicating a constitutional norm in another legal act, which is redundant and unnecessary as it could lead to doubts in interpretation unless a norm is duplicated verbatim. The second situation consists in complementing a constitutional norm with a constitutional norm, which practically lead to changes in understanding constitutional norms. The third situation occurs when regulations in other acts of law contravene the Constitution[22]. It appears that legislation that is faulty on the level of acts may result in difficulties in applying provisions regulating human rights and freedoms. One must expect that an administrative organ shall base its decisions on provisions from legal acts and a potential erroneousness of a decision might only be stated during control proceedings in court.

In the light of the above-mentioned arguments, one may imagine a situation in which the ECHR is referred to in a legal basis for an administrative decision. If an organ were to arrive at such a decision, the Convention would perform the function of a supplementary source for the decision basis. Nonetheless, referring to international treaties in a basis for a decision occurs considerably more often in fields where an administrative decision might be directly based on such sources (e.g. bilateral agreements). Cases concerning foreigners make the most prominent field of this kind. Provisions of Polish acts regulating this matter (the Act on Foreigners, the Act on Providing Foreigners with Help on Polish Territory, the Act on Polish Citizenship, the Repatriation Act), as well as executive orders complementing these acts are detailed enough to qualify any cases which might occur. At the same time, passing new and amending existing laws takes account

22 Cf., M. Szubiakowski, *Problemy współstosowania regulacji konstytucyjnej i ustawowej*, [in:] Wykładnia i stosowanie prawa administracyjnego, (eds.) D. R. Kijowski, J. Radwanowicz-Wanczewska, M. Wincenciak, Warszawa 2012, p. 62–69.

of normative solutions accepted in international law and adjudication standards of international courts.

Administrative decisions referring to provisions of international agreements also stems from referral acts. Such a construction was established by the Act of 29th March 1963, which in Article 10, section 3, directly refers to applying the Geneva Convention. Issues concerning citizenship, its obtaining and changing are regulated in bilateral agreements made directly by independent states. Bilateral agreements that Poland enters into also refer to legal help and legal relations in civil law, family, employment, and employment cases. Poland entered into such agreements with over twenty countries within and outside Europe. Provisions of such agreements constitute an obligatory legal basis for administrative decisions within the scope in which citizens of these states are covered by these provisions. Apart from bilateral agreements, Poland is also bound by multilateral agreements. However, as a rule, such agreements feature collision norms that determine preferred choices for legal bases. Such norms answer which law ought to be applied in collision cases.

Manner II – consists in a direct influence of adjudicating standard of the European Court of Human Rights on the content of administrative decisions. One may point to two major fields where this manner is applied. The first refers to the freedom of assembly. Standards for the protection of human rights concerning this freedom, regulated in article 11 of the ECHR, strongly and directly influence specific actions undertaken by administrative organs. One must take into account that administrative decisions concerning approvals for organising assemblies considerably exceed their formally individual and specific character. Such decisions mostly have a public dimension. Various social groups have a vested interest and they are widely discussed, especially when a decision is negative. Freedom of assembly is covered by specific adjudication standards of the European Court of Human Rights because it is vital in a pluralistic democratic society. These standards affect interpretations of the Polish Act on Assemblies. The verdict by the European Court of Human Rights in Mr Bączkowski's[23] case proved to be a milestone in implementing such standards. The Court ruled that refusing a permit for organising an Equality Parade in Warsaw, while providing such a permit to an opposing manifestation, was an example of Warsaw authorities breaching articles 11, 13, and 14 of the ECHR. The case was followed up on 26th January 2011 with the Parliamentary Assembly of the Council of Europe accepting Resolution

---

23 Verdict by the European Court of Human Rights of 3rd May 2007 in the Bączkowski *et al.* vs Poland case, plaint No. 1543/06.

1787 (2011) and Recommendation 1955 (2011) on executing judgements of the Court. These documents listed Poland among other countries which have greatest problems with implementing verdicts by the European Court of Human Rights. The documents also mentioned Mr Bączkowski's case. In consequence of such complex legal actions on the European level, Poland has changed the practice of its administrative organs. Hence, one may claim that adjudication standards of the European Court of Human Rights directly affect the content of decisions made by administrative organs. Undoubtedly, in previous years, a negative evaluation made by organs of the Council of Europe with respect to national decisions was an important factor strengthening such influence. Administrative organs had to take account of the standards formulated by the European Court of Human Rights for properly meeting the obligations resulting from the European Convention on Human Rights. Undoubtedly, the human right to freedom of assembly belongs to matters overlapping administrative law because a decision to provide consent for an assembly or a refusal of such consent may be evaluated from the vantage point of exercising this human right. Recent years have seen a tendency for the Strasbourg Court to broaden its adjudication standard[24]. The Court presents a view that decisions within the scope of allowing organisation of assembly should not remain solely within the domain of an administration organ; conversely, they also ought to undergo evaluations through court rulings[25].

A similar influence may be observed within the framework of prosecutor proceedings administered by a prosecutor. A prosecutor's office is a legal institution consisting in a hierarchical, internally coherent system of one-person organs. It is included in the group of legal protection organs[26] subjected to executive powers. Presently, the connection is stronger through combining the function of the Minister of Justice and the General Prosecutor. Hence, decisions made within the framework of prosecutor proceedings must be considered to be made in the administrative type of law. The sphere of prosecutor actions connected with accusation(s) of (perceived) crimes committed, specified in the penal code and other penal acts, directly refers to the sphere of individual freedom and

24 The Court's verdicts of 21st October 2010 in the Alekseyev vs Russia case, plaints No. 4916/07, 25924/08, 14599/09; of 12th June 2012 in the Genderdoc-M vs Moldova case, plaint No. 9106/06.

25 A. Bodnar, M. Szwast, *Wolność zgromadzeń publicznych w Polsce po wyroku Trybunału Konstytucyjnego z 18 września 2014 r.*, Helsińska Fundacja Praw Człowieka, Analizy i Rekomendacje, nr 2/2015, p. 9.

26 J. Bodio, G. Borkowski, T. Demendecki, *Ustrój organów ochrony prawnej. Część szczegółowa, 5. Wydanie*, Warszawa 2016, p. 213.

security. This right is guaranteed by article 5 of the ECHR and is also a source of numerous adjudication standards of the European Court of Human Rights. The dignity of a prosecutor's office and the significance of the right being protected require prosecutors to be familiar with and take account of these standards in their proceedings. A prosecutor is in direct contact with these standards within the framework of administering their duties related to an accusation in court. A prosecutor's awareness is, or should be, influenced by a necessity to refer to and take account of the provisions from the ECHR in the legal basis for decisions, and using them as arguments, while performing their accusatory duties, together with the adjudication produced through verdict justifications by the European Court of Human Rights.

Manner III – consists in a direct influence of adjudication standards of the European Court of Human Rights on the content of administrative decisions. Indirect influence is based on exerting the influence through the courts' adjudication. Polish administrative courts have often been referring to the adjudication by the European Court of Human Rights within the framework of court control over administrative decisions. According to data from the Central Database of Decisions of Administrative Courts, they have referred to the Convention in nearly 900 decisions since 1990. Based on convention regulations, adjudication standards included in verdicts of the European Court of Human Rights are primarily used as an argument affecting a clarification of the understanding of material provisions in Polish legal provisions, which also serve as a basis for administrative decisions. This is especially clear in domains of social care, education, prosecutor proceedings, and cases concerning foreigners' stay on the Polish territory. Consequently, provisions from the Convention affect the sphere of administrative actions only as a result of court verdicts that refer to the provisions from the Convention concerning the way of understanding provisions of the Polish material law. Administrative courts most often investigate breaching the Convention through administrative decisions. Investigations are instigated by charges included in a plaint.

One may also observe more complex situations where a verdict by the European Court of Human Rights shows interpretation of the Polish law made by a national court to be faulty, which triggers a change in national courts' law application practice and consequently affects the content of administrative decisions. Consider the Bugajny vs Poland[27] case, the European Court of Human

27 Bugajny et al. vs Poland, verdict of 6th November 2007, plaint No. 22531/05.

Rights focused on an established interpretation of article 98, section 1 of the Law on the Real Estate[28]. The administrative courts used this regulation to proclaim a selected road to be public on condition it was proclaimed as such in a local zoning plan. In effect, the owners' rights to compensation depended on local zoning plans. Administrative courts presented a view that the term 'for public roads' was to be understood as future investments concerning building public roads[29]. The European Court of Human Rights questioned this interpretation. The Court ruled that qualifying a road as public should depend on the way in which it was actually used rather than on a local zoning plan. Furthermore, the Court pronounced that an erroneous interpretation of Polish law was a source of breaching regulations on property derived from the Convention. In this case, Polish provisions conformed to the Convention, and it was only their interpretation that was faulty. Administrative courts accepted suggestions from the European Court of Human Rights on interpretation and changed their own interpretation practice, agreeing that any case of an owner being deprived of their property or even restricted in their ownership rights must be connected with compensation[30]. Interestingly, it is irrelevant whether a breach is physical or stems from a verdict by a competent organ. This significantly influences the decision practice of administrative organs.

The Convention influences administrative procedures much less. Article 6 of the Convention guarantees a right to a fair trial and considerably affects the correctness of administering court proceedings. However, the European Court of Human Rights also used this basis for evaluating the correctness of administrative proceedings.

In conclusion, one must state that the court type of law application is typically the major perspective for using the European Convention on Human Rights in the national legal order and using its provisions as a basis for reconstructing a norm (basis for law application decisions) or an argument for substantiating a decision. Weak direct and indirect influence of the Convention on decision-making processes may be observed in decision-making processes of administrative organs.

28 Law on the the Real Estate of 21st August 1997 (Journal of Laws 1997, No. 115, position 741 with subsequent amendments).

29 Cf. verdict by the Voivodeship Administrative Court in Warsaw of 18th January 2006, catalogue No. I Sa/Wa 2128/04, Lex No. 208965.

30 Cf. verdict by the Voivodeship Administrative Court in Lublin of 26th June 2008, catalogue No. S.A./Lu 326/08; verdict by the Voivodeship Administrative Court in Poznań of 7th July 2010, catalogue No. II S.A./P 219/10.

The ECHR is not referred to as the basis for administrative decisions. Administrative organs use the adjudication by the European Court of Human Rights to guarantee the correctness of their ruling, or adjudication standard, are implemented by administrative organs through adjudication of Polish administrative courts whose ruling takes into account adjudication standards of the European Court of Human Rights.

Anna Ostrowska
(Ph. D., Maria Curie-Sklodowska University in Lublin, Poland; Lublin Voivodship Administrative Court Assistant Judge)

Administrative promissory commitment in the perspective of discretionary powers of public administration body[1]

Abstract: This article analyses the principle of protection of legitimate expectations, which is rooted in common law legal systems, as well as in German and European Union law. It argues that, although in Poland this principle has not yet been articulated in any normative act, it is becoming increasingly significant among scholars of law and in the jurisprudence.

Keywords: the protection of legitimate expectations, administrative discretion, administrative promissory commitment, administrative promises

In the relationship between a public administration body and an individual some circumstances may arise that create on the part of the individual certain expectations as to the future activity of the body. This is important in that sphere of public administration in which the administrative bodies are granted by the legislature a certain degree of discretion – whether at the stage of legal interpretation or in the phase of choosing the decision. The principle of protection of legitimate expectations is rooted in common law legal systems, as well as in German and European Union law. In Poland, this principle has not yet been articulated in any normative act but is becoming increasingly significant among scholars of law and in the jurisprudence as an effective instrument for solving the fundamental conflict between the need to protect expectations of an individual as a result of activities of an administrative body and the need for the implementation of variable political purposes by that body. In other words, this principle in public administration systems of democratic states delineates the area where individual needs can be protected in the view of policy changes that are an intrinsic feature of governance.

1 The paper had been prepared as a result of cooperation in the process of realization of the research grant DEC-2013/11/N/HS5/04212, entitled: "The influence of judicial decisions on the discretionary power of public administration in the law application processes" financed by the National Science Center (Narodowe Centrum Nauki).

Undoubtedly, the issues of protection of legitimate expectations cover the problem of administrative promissory commitment that has not enjoyed too much attention from Polish scholars of law so far. Moreover, even among those of its scholars who have paid attention to the phenomenon of administrative promise as part of administration activities, there is no unanimity both as to the substance of promissory commitment and its constitutive features, or as to the scope of being bound by promissory commitment in the administrative model of application of law. Administrative promissory commitment is seen by some as a legal form of administrative activity that is distinct from administrative act[2], while others perceive it as a dependent form of administrative activity, which is an administrative act of special nature[3] or a special form of administrative contract[4]. There are also opinions that administrative promissory commitment has no nature of legal form of administrative activity whatsoever[5].

Contemplations by Polish scholars of law focused primarily on efforts to classify administrative promissory commitment within the category of legal forms of administrative activity. Without prejudice to the role of administrative promissory commitment in the development of theory of law, one must note, however, that it is of secondary importance from the point of view of recipients of public administration services, while such key issues as the nature of promissory commitments and their effects in the area of discretionary powers of administrative authorities have been kept on the wayside so far.

---

2 J. Łętowski, *Prawo administracyjne. Zagadnienia podstawowe*, Warszawa 1990, pp. 182 and 192, M. Stahl, [in:] Z. Duniewska, B. Jaworska – Dębska, R. Michalska – Badziak, E. Olejniczak – Szałowska, M. Stahl, *Prawo administracyjne, Pojęcia, instytucje, zasady w teorii i orzecznictwie*, Warszawa 2000, p. 361, M. Stahl, *Szczególne prawne formy działania administracji*, [in:] *System prawa administracyjnego*, Vol. 5, *Prawne formy działania administracji*, A. Błaś, J. Boć, M. Stahl, K. M. Ziemski (eds.), Warszawa 2013, p. 395, I. Lipowicz, *Dylematy siatki pojęciowej w nauce prawa administracyjnego*, [in:] *Koncepcja systemu prawa administracyjnego*, J. Zimmermann (ed.) Warszawa 2007, p. 359, J. Zimmermann, *Prawo administracyjne*, Kraków 2006, p. 535.

3 A. Wiktorowska, *Kierunki zmian w teorii prawnych form działania administracji*, [in:] *Koncepcja systemu...*, p. 384, Z. Niewiadomski, [in:] Z. Cieślak, I. Lipowicz, Z. Niewiadomski, *Prawo administracyjne. Część ogólna*, Warszawa 2011, s. 220–221.

4 E. Ochendowski, *Prawo administracyjne. Część ogólna*, Toruń 1994, pp. 110–111.

5 K. M. Ziemski, *Indywidualny akt administracyjny jako forma prawna działania administracji*, Poznań 2005, p. 63. J. Łukasiewicz, K. Kłosowska, *Słowo o przyrzeczeniu administracyjnym*, [in:] *Umowy w administracji*, J. Boć, L. Dziewiecka-Bokun (eds.), Wrocław 2008, p. 100.

The analysis of the scholarly opinion on administrative promissory commitment from the perspective of legal forms of administrative activity that was briefly outlined above does not lead to the formulation of coherent conclusions. Given the types of actions by administrative authorities, promissory commitment is a so diverse category that any attempts to classify it fail[6]. From the point of view of the relationship between an administrative body and the individual who is a recipient of its action, it is not essential whether the scholarly opinion recognizes administrative promissory commitment as an independent administrative legal form of public administration activity or not.

The literal interpretation of regulations on promissory commitments (promises) issued by administrative authorities in Poland, that are fragmentary and scattered across a number of legal acts, demonstrates that the legislature does not attach much importance to the standardization of procedures, forms and effects of those actions. Sometimes, promissory commitments are made in the form of administrative decisions[7], while in other cases – in the form of factual and technical activities[8]. Moreover, a number of activities not regulated precisely by the law, and undertaken by administrative authorities under the general rules authorizing the settlement of certain categories of cases, have also some features of administrative promissory commitments. These are so-called non-formalized promissory commitments.

---

6 More on the topic in: M. Chlipała, *Przyrzeczenie administracyjne w systemie prawnych form działania administracji*, RPEiS 2016, vol. 1, p. 164.

7 Promise of granting permission to a foreign national to acquire real estate – Article 3d of the Act of 24 March 1920 on the Acquisition of Real Estate by Foreigners (consolidated text: Journal of Laws of 2014, item 1380); decision on a promise to issue an entry visa for repatriation – Article 11 of the Act of 9 November 2000, on Repatriation (consolidated text: Journal of Laws of 2014, item 1392, as amended), promise of the concession – Article 60 of the Act on Freedom of Economic Activity (consolidated text: Journal of Laws z), promissory commitment to issue a permit for collective water supply or collective sewage disposal – Article 17c of the Act of 7 June 2001 on the Collective Water Supply and Collective Sewage Disposal (consolidated text: Journal of Laws of 2015, item 139, as amended), promise of a permission to establish an airport – Article 57 of the Act of 3 July 2002 – Aviation Law (consolidated text: Journal of Laws of 2013, item. 1393, as amended).

8 Promise of funding for research and development – Article 11 paragraphs 2 and 3 of the Act of 30 April 2010. Principles of Financing Science (consolidated text: Journal of Laws of of 2014, item 1620, as amended), antiquities restoration recommendations – Article 27 of the Act of 23 July 2003 on the protection of monuments and care of monuments (consolidated text: Journal of Laws of 2014, item 1446, as amended).

It should be assumed for the purpose of further discussion that administrative promissory commitment means an action of a public body, that holds a promise of future specific actions to be taken by that administrative body[9], i.e. to take some action or permit another entity to take a particular action (hereinafter referred to as a final act or final activity)[10]. Thus, this is a manifestation of the public body "being bound by oneself", especially in the sphere of discretionary powers[11]. A promissory commitment is usually granted when on the applicant's part there is no hindrance to obtain the final act (e.g. where an entity that applies for a promise of the concession to conduct business activity does not yet meet all the conditions of the concession). A public-law promissory commitment may be granted using various legal forms. Their kind is crucial from the point of view of interests of the addressee of the promissory commitment. It is so because it determines the extent and procedure for protection from authority's actions that are contrary with the promissory commitment, which is further discussed hereinafter.

First, one needs to refer to the basic, albeit a narrow category of administrative formalized promissory commitments, known collectively as "administrative promises" (Polish: promesy administracyjne; singular: promesa administracyjna). Formalizing means in this case that there is an empowering norm, and not only does it authorize granting a promise, but also determines its form, legal consequences of the issue thereof, its validity, and often the conditions to be met in order to be granted the promise.

Typically, a promise is granted subject to conditions that must be met by its recipient to make the promise capable do be fulfilled by the administrative body

---

9 W. Taras, *Zalecenie, ostrzeżenie i przyrzecznie administracyjne w systemie form działania administracji publicznej*, [in:] *Administracja i prawo administracyjne u progu trzeciego tysiąclecia*T. Bąkowski (ed.), Łódź 2000, p. 473.

10 This concept of public promissory commitment was applied in the bill on General rules of administrative law, which was, however, not enacted. Article 19 paragraphs 1 and 2 of the bill contained a provision according to which the public authority who has made a written promise to settle the case of any entity in a certain way, is bound by it, unless unlawful, unenforceable, extorted by giving false facts or circumstances, or where facts changed, which could not be predicted in advance, or the law changed in a way that prevents the promise to be fulfilled. And in the event the authority fails to fulfil the promissory commitment, the entity that has been granted the promissory commitment is entitled to execute it within a specified period, and if the entity had suffered a loss, it/he/she has a right to compensation under the terms set out in civil law.

11 Polish law contains examples of formal administrative promissory commitments granted in a situation where the authority is bound by law when issuing the final act, but – given the subject of this study, they remain outside the matters discussed herein.

in the future. These conditions are defined in the legal norm containing the power to grant the promise, or are formulated by the authority itself in the content of the promise.

Administrative promises take the form of administrative decisions, i.e. administrative acts issued in administrative proceedings in individual cases. These decisions are issued usually in those areas of administration, in which the legislature, by specifying the grounds to issue the final act, used general clauses or other indeterminate phrases[12], or where the legislature conferred on the bodies the authorization to act under administrative discretion, understood as a choice from among two or more legally equivalent solutions permitted by law[13].

The direct effect of a promise granted within those areas, in which the body has a certain margin of discretion, is to protect the interests of addressees of its final acts by ensuring the predictability of these decisions. The recipient of the promise gains a claim to demand from the body to act in the promised manner in the future, as long as the recipient meets the conditions specified therein. This feature of the promise is perfectly reflected in the provisions of the Act on Freedom of Economic Activity on the promise to grant a concession. The number of concessions granted is very limited, which is obvious given the fact that they cover business activities of strategic importance for the national economy. Thus, often several or even dozens of entrepreneurs apply for one concession. Thus, being granted a promise for the concession allows the awarded entity to take, often labour-intensive and very expensive, preparations to undertake the licensed activity without being exposed to the risk of losses in the event of failure to obtain the concession e.g. where another applicant is awarded the concession.

Of course, such an increase in the degree of certainty of the situation of the promise recipient entails further consequences, not only in the sphere of his/her/its interests, but also for the general public, as it contributes to the implementation

12 By way of example, it should be mentioned here: a promise of a concession to conduct business, or promissory commitment to issue a permit for collective water supply or collective sewage disposal.

13 Such a situation occurs when a legal norm does not explicitly define the legal effect of a certain factual situation, but clearly entitles the body to choose the particular effect. Examples of promises in the sphere of discretionary powers of public administration are: promise of a permit for the acquisition of real estate by a foreign national (Article 3d of the Act on the Acquisition of Real Estate by Foreigners), or promise of a concession to provide security services for the protection of persons and property (Article 17a of the Act of August 22, 1997 r. on the Protection of Persons and Property, consolidated text: Journal of Laws of 2014, item 1099, as amended).

of the general principle of citizens' trust in public authorities. A promise, by involving the entity to which it is addressed, engages citizens in the process of public governance[14], makes the addressee of its activity a partner, whereby it meets the postulate of good governance. By strengthening mutual trust between citizens and the authorities, a promise reduces feeling of alienation of an individual in the bureaucratic machine, where he/she is often regarded merely as another "reference number" or "case", and not as an individual person requiring individual approach.

A promise, within the period of its validity, generates for the issuing body a state of being legally bound, based on the fact that the body, when evaluating the application for the issuance of the final act, do not examine it in terms of the requirements set out in legal provisions[15]. The body only examines whether the facts relevant to the resolution of the case changed since the date of issue of the promise, and whether the recipient has met the requirements specified in the promise (if set out therein). This state of being bound will continue also where the final act is subject to appeal proceedings and administrative judicial examination. As long as the promise operates within the legal system, the presumption of its legality is valid. Due to the fact that the only party to the proceedings for the award of a promise is the applicant, the decision that is beneficial for him/her will not be subject to appeal in the administrative proceedings (unless the recipient is contesting conditions specified in the promise, on which the issue of the final act depends)[16], and therefore it will not be subject to appeal as part of administrative judicial proceedings. However, it is possible to eliminate the promise from the legal system on the initiative of the body itself under extraordinary measures (resumption of the proceedings or under annulment procedure), if strictly defined statutory conditions occur. Therefore, when conducting examination proceedings relating to the application for promise, the body should have in mind limited possibility of subsequent elimination of that act from the legal system.

This is a reason to perceive the functioning of promises within discretionary powers of administrative body also in a critical way, as an instrument that is

---

14 J. Łukasiewicz, K. Kłosowska, *op. cit.*, p. 103.

15 Cf. Judgement of NSA (Supreme Administrative Court) of 11 October 1996, II SA 2120/95 (OSP 1997, vol. 7–8, item 138).

16 If the promise recipient appeals only against some specific conditions of issue of the final act, that are set out in the promise, and the body finds that there were no grounds for granting the promise, then the body will only be able to issue a decision against the applicant if it finds that the contested decision blatantly violates the law or grossly breaches the public interest (Article 139 of the Act of 14 June 1960 – Code of administrative procedure (consolidated text: Journal of Laws 2016, item 23).

contrary to the objective of protecting the freedom of action of public authorities. It may be presumed that if the authorities reduce (or even eliminate) the scope of its discretion by granting a promissory commitment, then they give up achieving the fundamental goal of discretion granted to them, which is to ensure an individualized approach to the case, and also to be in accordance with the constantly changing public interest.

Such a conclusion would be too far-reaching, because discretion does not mean full, unrestricted decision-making freedom of the body. A decision taken by the body within its discretion is always determined by certain factors – both legal and factual. Indeed, the need for an individual approach is emphasized in the sphere of administrative discretion, but the importance of policies governing the performance of tasks by public administration is recognized too[17]. It is true that when making a promise for the future settlement of the case the body restricts its range of various options of solution provided for by the law to choose, but this promise can be seen as a manifestation of the exercise of discretionary authority rather than renunciation of power by the body. This is so because the body, before making the promise, examines the case, taking into account all relevant circumstances and values needing protection, and when making the promise it specifies the preferred direction of the decision. It cannot therefore be concluded that a promise so perceived is contrary to the nature of discretion in public administration.

As an argument against the reduction of administrative discretion as a result of a promise, one can also point out to a decrease in the flexibility of administrative action in the sphere of policy, the directions of which must comply with dynamically changing social and economic relations. Nonetheless, although this argument is still valid, it does not seem sufficient, considering the fact that promises, in Polish law, are issued for a pre-determined time, which does not exclude changes in policy, and this may only suspend their implementation at most.

It must, however, be noted that the functioning of administrative promissory commitment in the legal system raises more risk than making promises in the sphere of private law[18]. In private law, prohibiting a person, whose action results in expectations, to change his/her/its position, imposes the obligation to pay for his/her/its mistakes only on that person. In contrast to this, in public law, prohibiting the authority to change a decision or policy imposes the obligation

17 Cf. Ch. Hilson, *Judicial Review, Policies and the Fettering of Discretion*, [2002], Public Law, p. 112.

18 The matters of promissory commitments made in the sphere of civil law is regulated in Articles 919–921 of the Act of 23 April 1964 – Civil Code (consolidated text: Journal of Laws 2016, item 380).

on the whole community in a way that may be detrimental to the public interest. Perhaps, this is the reason why the institution of promise in Polish administrative law is used only in a few areas, as the legislature demonstrates consistent restraint in this scope.

The comments on the benefits and risks that are associated with the operation of promise in the system of public administration can be applied to other manifestations of public administration "being self-bound", classified – in a quite arbitrary manner – within a collective category of non-formalized promissory commitments.

Non-formalized promissory commitment is a manifestation of self-limitation of discretionary powers of the public administration that is not regulated in law, or regulated only in fragments. Due to the fact that promissory commitments of this type remain in between administrative law and administrative policies, doubts arise already at the stage of identifying the particular action of the body as an act of "self-binding", the non-exercise of which is sanctioned by the law.

Non-formalized promissory commitments can be used to direct the discretionary powers of the body of administration at both the stage of legal norm interpretation (interpretation of general clauses and indeterminate phrases), and at the stage of settlement (administrative discretion). There has been a years-long discussion among scholars about the features allowing classification of a particular action of an administrative body as falling into the category of administrative promissory commitments. It is necessary, however, to verify these views, especially in order to determine when the recipient of an action that may be perceived as a promissory commitment may seek protection before an administrative court.

It is beyond doubt that promissory commitment is a different thing than official information. It is in fact a declaration of intent, not a declaration of knowledge of the body. In practice, however, the distinction between these two categories may pose some difficulty[19]. In addition, certain official information (e.g. official information concerning interpretation of law or practice applied by the body) may have legal effects on the part of their recipients, in the same way as promissory commitments, which is discussed below.

Undoubtedly, a promissory commitment may be made only by a body to which the law confers the power to take the action (to allow the recipient to take the action) the promissory commitment refers to[20].

---

19 Cf. Judgement of SN (Supreme Court) of 5 August 1992, I PA 5/92, OSP 1993, vol. 7–8, item 142.

20 Therefore, this category should not contain zoning and land use decisions issued under the Act of 27 March 2003 on Spatial Planning and Land Development (consolidated

According to W. Taras, the recipient of a promissory commitment does not need to be precisely specified. It may be therefore addressed to all to whom it may concern and to those who submit the application within a specified time[21]. One must agree with that position, but one important objection must be raised. A body may grant a promissory commitment to an unidentified entity or group of entities, and this action can be classified as a public promissory commitment, but the recipients are not granted effective protection before administrative courts. It is hard to imagine administrative judicial protection when a promise of a body is directed to an unspecified recipient. Moreover, the recipient needs not to be a single entity. It is not about the number of recipients of a promise of the body in arithmetic terms, but rather the degree of individualisation of the promise. The lack of identification of the recipient of the promise of the body often makes this promise an act of policy that is not subject to jurisdiction of administrative courts. Hence, judicial protection may be effectively sought by a recipient of a promissory commitment identified as to forename and surname or business name (it must be sufficiently identified).

The possibility of granting a promissory commitment is not limited to cases concluded in the form of administrative decision[22]. It may be granted even if the final action of the body takes legal forms of activity, other than administrative decision, reserved for that body, (including resolutions of local government bodies, as well as other acts and activities, including those of a civil-law nature)[23]. However, one may seek administrative judicial protection only if the promised action is to take one of the forms that may be subject of judicial review, referred to in Article 3 paragraph 2 points 1–4, 5–6 of the Act of 30 August 2002 – Law on

text: Journal of Laws of 2015, item 199, as amended) or decisions on environmental constraints issued pursuant to the Act of 3 October 2008 on Provision of Information about the Environment and its Protection, Public Participation in Environmental Protection and Environmental Impact Assessment (consolidated text: Journal of Laws 2016, item 353). These decisions, issued, in principle, by executive bodies of local government (gmina), binds the entity which issues the building permit, usually a poviat Staroste (district governor). In addition, all the above-mentioned decisions are constrained decisions. These decisions represent some of many examples of situations where one administrative body is bound by decisions made by another administrative body, which does not make them administrative promissory commitments.

21 W. Taras, *Zalecenie, ostrzeżenie i przyrzecznie...*, p. 474.

22 Other opinion is expressed by W. Taras, *Przyrzeczenie administracyjne*, [in:] M. Chmaj (ed.), *Leksykon samorządu terytorialnego*, Lublin 1997, p. 214.

23 M. Stahl, *Szczególne prawne formy...*, p. 464.

the procedure before administrative courts[24]. In other cases, including when the promissory commitment concerns the conclusion of a specific future contract under civil law, the recipient is entitled to protection only in a civil court.

Admittedly, the very term "non-formalized promissory commitment" indicates that the law does not specify any particular form thereof, but for evidential purposes one should assume it should be given in writing. It is impossible to imagine effective judicial protection in the event of a promise made only verbally, even in the presence of witnesses.

In addition, the content of the promise may not be inconsistent with the provisions of applicable law. Administrative courts are guardians of the rule of law, their role is to control the legality of administrative actions, therefore in the event of a conflict between the principle of legality of these actions and the principle of citizens' trust in public authorities, the principle of legality prevails.

In addition, the recipient will be allowed to infer from the promissory commitment legal effects that are beneficial for him/her only if starting from the date of award of the promissory commitment to the date of issue of the final act (final activity) there will be no significant change in factual or legal circumstances.

A question arises here, whether a withdrawal from the promise may be justified by political changes, including a change in the leadership of the government, which usually entails personal changes at every level of administration. The rule is, after all, that those who take power from representatives of another political option, seek to change the policy line chosen by their predecessors.

On the other hand, it is obvious that certain decisions taken by people exercising functions of administrative bodies have long-lasting effects that go far beyond their term in office. Undoubtedly, it is a strong argument for the fact that personal changes in the administration do not nullify substantive legal implications of a public promissory commitment granted to an individual by the predecessor in a given office. In addition, one of inherent features of public administration is its impersonal nature, which means that from the point of view of a recipient of body's actions the person holding the particular office is irrelevant.

In the scholarly opinion in common law systems, an important role in the sphere of protection of legitimate expectations is attributed to the temporal horizon of the protection of expectations, i.e. whether the promise is of a short-term or long-term nature. If a promissory commitment of the body concerns a future one-off or short-term action, then the legitimate expectation of such action

24 Consolidated text: Journal of Laws of 2012, item 270, as amended.

is more likely to be granted protection than a promise for a future long-term action, including one that may extend beyond the term of office of the holder of the administrative body which granted the promise. However, the case law of those systems[25] permit exceptions to this rule, due to the specific individualized nature of the expectation, occurrence of a material loss/damage to the expecting party, or lack of paramount public interest that waives the protection[26].

A recipient of a public promissory commitment having all the aforementioned features may effectively appeal to the administrative court against an action of the body that is contrary to the earlier promissory commitment, by filing an appeal against a specific act or activity, if the content of either of them is contrary to the promissory commitment granted, or by a complaint against failure to act – if the body fails to issue any act or perform any action (of course, once all the administrative due course of instances is completed). The claim of the appeal may be then based on breach of one of the key principles of law and administrative procedure, namely the above-mentioned principle of citizens' trust in national authorities, expressed in Article 8 of the Code of Administrative Procedure.

This principle may also be invoked by an individual in a situation where the body acts contrary to earlier information provided to him/her, concerning the interpretation of a certain legal norm or practice used by this body. Neither interpretation of the law, nor the repeatability of a specific action (established practice) are administrative promissory commitments in the strict sense, but undoubtedly they cause a state of expectation of the recipient that the body will issue the final act pursuant to that interpretation or practice, especially in the sphere where the legislature granted the body some margin of decision. Therefore they constitute a special sort of guarantee for the compliance with the principle of citizens' trust in the state and law[27].

---

25 R v North and East Devon Health Authority, ex parte Coughlan [2000]2 WLR 622.

26 D. R. Knight, *Estoppel (Principles?) in public law: The Substantive Protection of Legitimate Expectations*, Vancouver 2004, p. 122 et seq.. In cases to seek substantive protection for an expectation caused by the granting a public promissory commitment, one should also take into account that there are certain areas of administrative activities in which individuals must consider frequent, rapid changes, and instability which is intrinsically inherent in their nature. In these areas, legal protection for the expectation should be granted after particularly careful examination. A. Ostrowska, *Ochrona oczekiwań w prawie publicznym*, [in:] *Sprawiedliwość i zaufanie do władz publicznych w prawie administracyjnym*, M. Stahl, M. Kasiński, K. Wlaźlak (ed.), Warszawa 2015, p. 243.

27 Z. Kmieciak, *Urzędowe interpretacje przepisów prawa podatkowego (nowe wyzwania)*, [in:] *Orzecznictwo w systemie prawa*, T. Bąkowski, K. Grajewski, J. Warylewski (eds.), Warszawa 2008, p. 123, referred to by M. Błachucki, *Urzędowe wyjaśnienia*

Apart from a few cases (e.g. individual interpretations of fiscal law) the procedure and effects of issuing official acts of interpretation of law are not regulated by legislation. The lack of regulation does not, however, entail an assumption that such actions of administrative bodies should be regarded as having no legal force. On the contrary, where in a particular case the individual has taken action in reliance of the information provided to him/her about the existing practice and application of the law, and this information was provided to him/her individually by specifying his/her name, and was individually related to his/her personal situation, it would be inconsistent with the principle of trust in the state and law, constituting a component of the constitutional principle of democratic rule of law, if the body acted towards this person differently afterwards. There is no obstacle to correct a practice or interpretation of law which is considered by the entity applying the law as inappropriate, but this should be done with effect for future cases, to persons with whom the authority has not yet established closer contact in the area of the preliminary decisions[28].

In administrative proceedings and administrative judicial proceedings, where the body has a certain decision margin, parties more and more often invoke promissory commitments or information provided by the body, concerning the interpretation of law or practice applied by the body. This is symptomatic that administrative bodies in its grounds for the decision – and even administrative courts – often completely ignore that circumstance invoked by the party. Also, administrative courts often deny the binding nature of non-formalized or not fully formalized promissory commitments[29], based only on the argument that the legislature did not determine the form of administrative decision or order for them, as well as by pointing out that there is a risk associated with the substantive defect of the promissory commitment[30]. This is one of the few

przepisów prawa wydawane przez organy administracji publicznej, [in:] *Źródła prawa administracyjnego a ochrona praw i wolności obywateli*, M. Błachucki, T. Górzyńska (eds.), Warszawa 2014, p. 125.

28 Judgement of SN (Supreme Court) of 5 August 1992, I PA 5/92, OSP 1993, vol. 7–8, item 142.

29 An example of such a not fully formalized promissory commitment is antiquities restoration recommendation issued on request of the owner or possessor of a historical monument pursuant to Article 27 of the Act of 23 July 2003 on the protection of monuments and care of monuments (consolidated text: Journal of Laws of 2014, item 1446, as amended).

30 Cf. Judgement of the Supreme Administrative Court of 25 January 2013, II OSK 1669/11, Judgement of the Regional Administrative Court in Warsaw of 6 April 2011, IV SA/Wa 140/11, Judgement of the Regional Administrative Court in Warsaw of 19

manifestations of the essential gap between the scholarly opinion and jurisprudence in administrative law.

The above presented position of the judiciary is not convincing, because the very form of a declaration of intent of a public body may not determine whether it is binding or non-binding. It suffices that the will of the body is appropriately communicated and recorded. In addition, as it was indicated above, only a promissory commitment, the content of which does not violate the law, is binding. Invoking risks associated with being absolutely bound by a defective promissory commitment as an argument is therefore baseless. The courts should pay due significance to promissory commitments granted to individuals by administrative bodies. Predictability, certainty and stability of activities of administrative bodies, seen as necessary components of good administration, are becoming an increasingly desired value in the process of application of law[31].

There is no doubt that the primary obligation of administrative bodies is to act under and within the limits of applicable law. But it is not difficult to notice that in the administrative type of application of law, the decision making entity and content of the decision issued by that entity is influenced by a number of extra-legal factors, including organizational and political ones, particularly in the absence of consequence selection criteria clearly formulated by the legislature. These factors, referred to among scholars of law as secondary directives for choice of consequences are a manifestation of actual binding, resulting from the operation of the body in a complex organizational and political system. Courts may not disable their binding effect in advance, unless they lead to a reduction or even elimination of the possibility of application of primary directives for choice of consequences, showing how to understand a particular phrase in a specific social context (linguistic, systemic and functional).

In the context of the development of the concept of protection of an individual against non-fulfilment of promises by public authorities in Poland, interesting results can be drawn from an analysis of the concept of "legitimate expectations" having the status of rule of law in Anglo-Saxon countries and in the EU law, as well as an analysis of the case law of the Court of Justice of the European Union, which many times invoked legitimate expectations of an individual. The rule of "legitimate expectations", both in *common law* systems

January 2015, VII SA/Wa 1317/14, available in CBOSA collection, https://cbois.nsa.gov.pl/cbois/query.

31 Cf. J. Zimmermann, *Prawo administracyjne*, Warszawa 2010, p. 354; J. Łukaszewicz, K. Kłosowska, *op. cit.*, sp. 103.

and in the EU law, concerns the relationship between the public administration and an individual. It is aimed at solving the fundamental conflict between the desire to protect certainty of expectations of an individual caused as a result of administrative actions (information provided by an administrative body or a particular practice) and the need to implement variable political goals by the body. This principle means that expectations that arose out as a result of administrative actions may have legal consequences. Thus, the administration must respect these expectations or provide substantial reasons why the public interest should be given priority.

Giovanni Pesce
(Administrative lawyer, Rome, Italy)

Discretionary power of public administration and control of public debt[1]

Abstract: The purpose of the article is to enquire whether the European and national rules on the government spending power, while at a first glance limiting discretionary power, may on the contrary result in an expansion of the administrative power.

Keywords: discretionary power, sustainability, EU rules, intergenerational equity

1. Introduction

Discretionary power is a central feature of administrative power, recognized since ancient times as a convenient tool of legal reasoning and defined by Aristotle as means of "*correction of the law*" (Eth. Nic., 1137, b).

In a narrower usage, discretionary power comes into play when the Administration is called to ascribe a meaning to a specific fact by choosing among several possible meanings.

Discretionary is the power of choice: it is a way of balancing between different interests (public and private) involved; it is a means to achieve the purpose intended by the law; it is a selection of an option between two or more solutions suggested by a preliminary activity.

The object of the choice can be "*an*" (whether or not to take measures), "*quando*" (when)," *quomodo*" (with such terms, conditions and loan covenants/ ancillary provisions) or "*quid*"(with what content).

Filling the gaps of law is an inevitable task. The legislator, however, sets up some constraints, such a reasonableness and proportionality test, coherence between choices, protection of legitimate expectations of the citizen, and punctuates the phases. Decisions have to be planned and to follow a due process of law. The authority is not entirely free: it exercises its power within the law and the public interest.

---

1 The paper had been prepared as a result of cooperation in the process of realization of the research grant DEC-2013/11/N/HS5/04212, entitled: "The influence of judicial decisions on the discretionary power of public administration in the law application processes" financed by the National Science Center (Narodowe Centrum Nauki).

The purpose of the article is to enquire whether the European and national rules, on the government spending power, while at a first glance limiting discretionary power, may __on the contrary result in an expansion of the administrative power.

Rules concerning the national public debt control affect administrative law, including discretionary powers as traditionally understood. "Sustainability" must be "secured" in the exercise of power of the public administration, and therefore not only at a legislative level, but also on a day to day implementation of national, regional and local policies.

Obviously also individual rights are affected: rights of first, second and third generation.

The liberal State, based on theoretical premises entirely acceptable, had to deal with a very different reality and with market failures. The State, in part because of the twentieth century industrial revolution and the wars that ensued, has abandoned the role of neutrality and indeed has significantly intervened in large sectors of the economy, often becoming a business enterprise. This phase, which started in the aftermath of Second World War lasted until the end of the twentieth century and in some ways it is still present. First, it has given rise to the entrepreneurial State and, later, to the Welfare State.

The issue has become more complex with the advent of the constitutions. Political communities which were born or resurrected after World War II have enacted constitutions which have created new rights and expanded existing ones.

At the same time, the tasks of the public administration have increased.

The State started to manage a greater share of public resources to support the growing demand for public goods and services, financed mostly through taxation.

Since taxation was not sufficient (which was common to all modern democracies), the State has resorted public deficit and public debt.

The result was a system that has grown inside a public organization whose social weight, politically and economically has become immense over the years.

The accession of several countries to the European project has complicated the already known scenarios.

Most state models, whether liberal or socialist carried out economic systems not open to global markets. Such a vision was in contrast with EU rules which, since the entry into force of the Treaty of Rome in 1958, have gradually replaced old economic models with new ones whose content was not clear at that time.

Such a situation has gradually led to the short circuit which we have today in many areas of Europe, including Italy.

While the weight of the government was increasing under the pressure of implementing constitutional provisions, Italy has willingly decided to join the single currency, which requires –today with urgency – reduction of that public organization and that same government which we have known for years.

New and more stringent rules such as (single currency, common rules on financial matters, parameters written for debt and the budget deficit) shall be added to the traditional rules of the Treaty of Rome (free competition, free movement of the goods and capital, prohibition of state aids).

The Maastricht Treaty of 1992, now incorporated in the Lisbon Treaty has signalled a new phase: a phase which concerns our present and our immediate future.

The fundamental mission of the State, that wants to be tied to the project of a single Europe, is to restructure public finances, which in turn implies a decrease of public spending, due to the high level of public debt and the interest burden on the debt itself.

The State, become unavoidably a State-finance, has committed itself to maintain a public deficit not more than 3% of GDP and a public debt below 60% of GDP. Although the convergence criteria are mainly political, their legal nature shall not be underestimated.

The Maastricht Treaty has provided for a complex process managed by the European authorities in order to monitor and sanction any negative deviations.

In this latter context, due to the serious economic crisis of 2008 and under the new international Treaty on the fiscal compact of 2012, Member States have introduced in their legal systems the principle that all public administration must keep the public debt within "sustainable levels" accepted by the financial markets.

The State should comply with the European commitments and manage the reduction of public spending through financial operations and extraordinary administrative measures.

Then, it becomes crucial to understand which sectors will be mainly affected by what appears to be a titanic task of the government.

The State, in fact, would reduce the benefits (in part stemming from the constitutionally guaranteed rights) until now mainly secured by an extensive spending power which has lasted more than a century. In some respects, this is a new situation and it raises several issues.

The EU Member States should, at the same time, restructure the public finances, maintain a balanced budget, reduce the debt up to acceptable levels, while securing acceptable levels the production of public goods and services, and dealing with vested rights resulting from already signed agreements.

Rights are concerned because the decision on how to use the resources, especially if they are scarce, depends not solely on government discretionary power but also on the interpretation of constitutional rights[2]. It follows that the debate on the sustainability of the government debt cannot be independent of the issue concerning the effects on the rights arising from the reduction of the debt.

The assertion of rights implies the need to examine the costs. From this point of view, there is no difference between the first and second generation rights[3]. All rights, including the future (third generation: Clean environment) must compete with the costs.

The costs are the burden for the public budget.

The rights are the important interests of individuals or groups, that can only be protected by the government intervention. The assertion of fundamental rights requires a very strong administration[4]: economic difficulties restrict their practical realization.

2. Role of administrative law in the new course of the debt reduction

The existence of the public administration is grounded of its ability to meet the needs of the community. The administrative law was created to regulate this phenomenon and to protect citizens from the abuse of authority or the failure to comply with the duties imposed by the Constitution for public policy.

There is therefore a close link between the organization of public administration and the use of public resources and between the government and economic model chosen by politics. There is also an immediate relationship between the expansion of debt and the affirmation of administrative law.

The continental European constitutions had drawn an administrative law model largely inherited from the past which put emphasis on ministries, local territorial authorities and public agencies. With the entry into force of European law, the system underwent a profound evolution that gradually led to a crisis of governmental entities and the advent of more complex administrative models aimed at pursuing the public interest in the functioning of market and free competition.[5]

Here a discussion on the systems which resulted and on whether the legislature has created the bases for an effective reduction of the public sphere will be omitted. In this context we would like to highlight that lawyers have drawn administrative

2 L. Ferrajoli, *Diritti fondamentali. Un dibattito teorico*, Roma-Bari, I Ed., 2001.
3 S. Holmes – C. R. Sunstein, *The Cost of Rights, W. W. Norton & Company, 1999.*
4 E.W. Bockenforde, *State, society, and liberty, Berg*, New York. 1991.
5 G. Corso, *Manuale di diritto amministrativo*, Torino, 2010, pp. 180 ff.

action models and suggested legislative reforms, on the assumption of the existence of a public power provided with discretionary spending power, which is a central element of administrative discretionary *tout court*.

It has been assumed that the public power had resources because spending power was reputed inherent to the essence of sovereignty.

The opportunity to rethink such models arises not solely from the desirable trend towards reduction of the public sector in social and economic relations, but also from the necessity of new analyses on the reduction of public power.

The watchword, today, is not an administrative reform, but the exercise of administrative powers that are compatible with the public debt. In this light shall be read the provision introduced in 2012 in the Italian Constitution (Art. 97), according to which public authorities have to ensure balanced budgets and public debt sustainability.

The intergenerational equity and the protection of creditors of the State have to find a reasonable compromise.

3. Looking backwards and looking forward

It is possible to examine two scenarios: the future and the past of public debt.

The future is entrusted to the automatic reduction of public debt to the level required by the EU Treaty and, most recently, by the Fiscal Compact.[6]

While the Treaty limits itself to setting the rules known to admit the deficit up to 3% and the debt up to 60% of GDP, the Fiscal Compact establishes in Art. 6 that "with a view to better coordinating the planning of their national debt issuance, the Contracting Parties shall report ex-ante on their public debt issuance plans to the European Commission and to the Council".. The numerical and control constraints should ensure a more orderly recourse to debt.

The various principles introduced in EU countries will always look to the future, especially the balance of the budget. They fix the rule for which the recourse to debt is allowed only in order to consider the effects of economic cycle "[7]. In addition, these principles introduce some institutional controls to cover any overruns of spending targets set by the Union.

Within a framework even further away, the Stability Bonds will also enter into force. They are intended to replace national issuance with joint sovereign bonds

---

6 The Treaty "on Stability, Coordination and Economic and Monetary Union governance", establishes for the Contracting Parties with a debt to GDP ratio over 60% laid down for the Maastricht Treaty, the obligation to reduce by at least 1 / 20th year.

7 The balance "*over the cycle*".

among Member States of euro area: this remedy would be effective, but it requires a shift to a common European fiscal policy[8].

For the future, the age-old question of the conditions and the limits for debt seems to be properly addressed, in a context of greater responsibility the European institutions which are called to set the spending limit and to monitor the developments in government debt of the Member States. Therefore, the recourse to the financial market must be considered physiologic, appropriate and necessary, just in case of emergency or to correct a negative economic cycle.

Conversely, the use of public debt cannot be justified to cover current expenses or to cover higher costs that could undermine the balanced budget, to avoid a serious anomaly in the financial management as well as the violation of the Treaties and the constitutional rules.

The past however looks very different. There is a mountain of public debt which has been accumulated for half a century and over in a large part EU countries, thanks to which many States have mortgaged Nations and with them – this generation and the next.[9]

To ensure the sustainability of public debt, it also means striving to look retrospectively and therefore using all the tools to reduce the burden of debt and the interests accumulated deriving from the past. These instruments may result even by administrative law. In fact, the attempt to reduce the public debt with the proceeds of privatization of state assets can be considered ineffective. These are operations that, particular as regards beneficial effects on free competition, recall the parable of the spoon which empties the sea.

It is useless the old ploy of recourse to inflation, which is now under the direct control of the European Central Bank. Finally, it is also difficult to achieve the goal of reducing the debt burden through tax increases or other extraordinary tax systems.

The road is to honor the debt, upon different conditions. This road could become mandatory in the near future. Its aim is to renegotiate the debt in accordance with the European law, so the public administration could reduce the mass

---

8 See paper on the feasibility of *stability bond* European Commission Green Paper "Feasibility of introducing Stability Bonds", COM(2011) 818 definitive.

9 According to data from Eurostat 2014 the average debt of EU countries is 87% of GDP. Bearing in mind the situation, it is clearly evident that all the countries finally aggregates to European project lower the average level. The following list represents the most indebted countries: Greece: 175.1%; Italy: 132.6%; Ireland: 123.7%; Portugal: 129%; Cyprus: 111.7%; Belgium: 101.5%; Spain: 93.9%; France: 93.5%; United Kingdom: 90.6%; Germany: 78.4%.

of securities in circulation, the duration of them and especially the measurement of the interest rate.

Contrary to this view there is the thesis of intangibility of the agreements signed by the State, that is, the inviolability of public debt. Such a thesis, whose value shall not be underestimated, could, however, now be balanced with other interests and especially considering that a fair balance must be found between the rights of creditors and the rights of present and future generation. So basically, the public administration must ensure the sustainability of public debt and, at the same time, the rights of creditors.

The European law is, therefore, intended in the coming years to affect the administrative law for profiles related to the reduction of public debt and so on a different side from the one known so far and with the related effects on the notion of administrative discretionary known until now.

While the law founded on free market, as the European law, had reduced the areas of administrative law, the law that must deal with the public debt sustainability and intergenerational equity requires a strong public administration and the use of the tools of administrative law.

In this sense, we could predict a future where the administrative law will be again in charge of the regulation of public authorities, society and economy; as well as we can imagine that public officials will perform such tasks with greater competence, foresight and knowledge of the responses to the requests of citizens.

4. The future of the public debt

The contemporary jurist strives with difficulty to comment on rules and analyze legal cases relating to acts, such as the massive accumulation of public debt and its impact on future generations, that occurred decades ago. Today, "the current generation" wears the uncomfortable clothes of the "future generation" at the time those decisions were made, that have brought the level of debt to unsustainable levels.

In other words, the discussion about the sustainability of the public debt concerns those who are suffering the consequences of any facts dated over time, hoping to give an answer that can solve the problems of the present and the future. We do not know whether the question has actually been taken over by those who, for example, have issued debt securities with a maturity of 15 to 30 years or more since the issue date; or by those who have constantly renewed over time remunerated short-term securities with high interest rates and hedging with derivatives.

The answer is probably negative if it is true the opinion that only actual and present interests have a voice and demand consideration. To quote Hans Jonas, the future is not represented by any collegiate body nor it is a force that can throw their weight on the scale: a thing that does not exist, it can have no lobby.[10]

A solution "for the past and the future" which, however, follows the economic theory, it is to try to understand the meaning, rather than to formulate their theories that can influence public spending powers.

This solution certainly is not made easier by the vast and arcane rules governing public finance, dotted with various level sources (EU Treaties, the Constitution, international Treaties, laws, regulations and directives; decisions of the ECB and the IMF; ministerial decrees; circular; banking instructions), as well as decisions of the internal and European Courts).

The reality has shown that any cure or theory has not produced, at the time, the desired results: not only the level of debt is not decreased but it also increased, despite high taxation and policies aimed at automatic reduction of public levels. Moreover, even the tightening of balance budget principle in itself is capable of resolving the issue, resulting in more rules to prevent excessive budget deficits and to apply for the future, as a remedy for the burden accumulated in the past.

It is one thing, in fact, to say that the necessary way forward for the consolidation it is to create primary budget surpluses, in order to use them for the gradual coverage of interests and deficit and, in the long run, for cancelling the debt. Another thing is to apply in practice this measure without creating recessionary effects that end up undermining to the eyes of the markets the credibility of the adjustment strategy.

5. The primacy of the Treaties on public debt and failure of European law

With the full opening of markets and the introduction of the single currency, the European Union has significantly affected the administrative power[11]. National public interest has lost the relevance it had in the past.

The phase which started with the Maastricht Treaty and culminated in the single currency, has resulted in a relative legal and financial impossibility for EU Member States to achieve the goals concerning the debt set forth in the Maastricht Treaty. On the other hand, precisely because of community constraints, the State has been deprived of any significant room of maneuver and debt management according to the previous rules: in this way it has been impossible to maintain the

10 H. Jonas, *Das Prinzip Verantwortung*, Frankfurt, 1979, p. 30.
11 S. Cassese, *Lo spazio giuridico globale*, Bari, Laterza, 2003.

debt to sustainable levels and to reduce the weight of administrative organization and the related management of goods and services of constitutional significance.

However, the action of European law has not proven fully effective for this purpose either.

The supervisory and control proceedings of the European institutions set forth in the Treaty, have not been translated into concrete actions.

Yet, the Union is intended to be a guidance for the policies concerning the public finances of individual States. The concept of healthy public finances is a fundamental pillar to the survival of the single currency and the European Union. The relevance of such a pillar is testified by the fact that Treaties have included provisions concerning the levels of deficits and debt considered "sustainable" for the presence of the State in Monetary Union[12]; while proceedings for monitoring compliance with the financial provisions and, in severe cases, to impose a sanction of State in breach (Art. 126, formerly 104, TFEU) has been set forth. Although the infringement proceedings are intended to be brought against Member States for failure to comply with the excessive deficit prohibition, the citizens are the immediate beneficiaries. The infringement proceedings may constitute an opportunity given to the citizens of the State in breach to hold politicians accountable and to pressure for a political turnover.

Beyond its political importance, Article 126 is the legal basis for EU actions towards Member States' public debt, while, at the same time, limiting the powers of the EU institutions and the governments of Member States[13].

Unlike what happened in the past, when the Member States maintained monetary discretionary, the single currency management is, indeed, within the Union's exclusive administrative jurisdiction (Art. 3 TFEU).

The Union monetary policy may not be independent of or even in contrast with other European law provisions, such as those that require the Union to Union to promote the welfare of EU citizens (art. 3, ex 2, the EU Treaty), full employment and social progress.

In other words, the monetary Union shall be interpreted as instrumental to the main goals set forth in the Treaty. Arguing otherwise would mean interpreting each provision of the Treaty as totally unrelated with other provisions and with the main and whole European project.

On these premises, we may argue that the Union itself could be held accountable for the negative results of Member States with a deficit in excess. With a view

12 Protocol (No 12) annexed to the Treaty.

13 J. Ziller, *Le basi giuridiche per un debito pubblico europeo*, 2012, p. 135.

of better coordinating the planning of their national debt issuance, Article 6 of the Fiscal compact provides that the Contracting Parties shall report *ex ante* on their public debt issuance plans to the Council and the European Union. Such a provision supports our view that national debt issuance shall be coordinated with the Council and the Commission and that a collective liability arises.

It follows that Contracting States with excessive deficit are not the only parties to blame. Excessive deficit implies that the Union coordinating role has not properly functioned.[14].

6. Self-sufficiency or failure of the public law?

If, as Hume argued, we should really consider the possibility of a "violent death" of public debt[15], we shall conclude for a voluntary bankruptcy of the State, whose effects would be as disastrous as useless for the citizens. Is it really necessary to go so far? Certainly not.

While waiting for positive results produced by the complex mechanism of the Treaties, some answers could come from the public law and the correct use of discretionary power.

Public law currently offers stronger legal protections to public debt holders compared to common law or private law. While in case of bankruptcy of private companies, creditors may be compelled to renounce to a portion of debt and debt restructuring is a common remedy, public debt holders are immune from such events. Yet, the administrative law and the administrative judge are considered a significant safeguard of private citizens in their relationship with the government. For more than a century Italian administrative justice has given the opportunity to private citizens to bring claims against the government and to question the validity of administrative acts. Administrative law is intended as a barrier on administrative power.

When public debt is involved, we have a three party relationship: on the one hand, the creditors, i.e. the debt holders; on the other hand the government (the debtor); and thirdly the citizens. While citizens are formally the debtor, they do not have any contracting power. It results that it is the government which has to act as an agent in the interest of its principal. While public law usually provides for a flexibility of government action especially when public interest is involved, in the case of public debt, a different solution seem to prevail. In the relations between

14 ECJ case law13 july2004 (C-27/04).

15 D. Hume, Essay VIII "*Of Public Credit*", *Political Discourses,* Fleming, 1752.

citizens of that State and creditors, creditors are stronger than the citizens and the State. The inequality is clear in this matter.

However, public law may suggest a different conclusion. It is possible to argue that the power of the government to renegotiate the debt does not contrast with EU provisions and fulfils the aim of the Treaty. It is even further possible to argue that both European law and the Italian Constitution do not allow for a an absolute and preferential treatment of creditors.

7. New role of administrative law in the reduction of public debt

Now that the principle that requires the debt sustainability has been constitutionalized in order to protect present and future generations, the main issue is how to balance between the different interests at stake.

It is not enough to provide for a decrease of the public debt in times of crisis, only through containment maneuvers in government spending without affecting the interest on the debt and the time of enforcement of the past debt capital[16].

The decline of the level of public debt must therefore be reflected in the adoption of administrative measures aimed at the renegotiation of already issued bonds, even when they are derived from signed contracts. In any case, if there is a contract there is also the administrative act that starts "upstream" the entire administrative procedure, for which the public administration retains all powers of review by all standards dictated by law and jurisprudence.

Renegotiation may involve both interests and the length of the debt, extending the deadline.

The State shall not only ensure the vested rights of property of the credit holders, but shall meet the commitments made to citizens and the EU. According to this perspective, market confidence, based on consistency of State behavior, shall be balanced with other principles, among which firstly the suitability of solutions in line with the canons of administrative action. Indeed, because of the recipes to contain the debt have proved ineffective until now, the same markets may take a positive view of measures that, in the medium to long term, are resolved in the stabilization of the debt and the country's system. In other words, the sacrifices must apply to everyone.

16 F. Merusi, *Il sogno di Diocleziano. Ruolo del diritto pubblico nelle crisi economiche*, in *Riv. trim. dir. dell'econ.*, fasc. 1/2013 p. 2.

It may be argued, in other words, that public interest shall be realized through renegotiation. It follows that the public administration has not only the power but also the duty to ensure the sustainability of public debt.

If we go back to the question of the relationship between the government/citizens on the one hand and the creditors on the other and ask: why the latter must prevail? The most common answer is: the latter prevails because they are stronger. But we know that law is essentially meant to balance among different power situations and resolve conflicts. The most appropriate solution is to balance with reasonableness among the vested rights of creditors and the legitimate expectations of the majority.

In general terms, the administration has the power and the duty to remove the instrument adopted previously, each time it is in conflict with the interest to debt reduction and to intergenerational equity. And of course, the measure would be in compliance with the public interest.

8. The renegotiation of the public debt within the framework of the Treaties

There are other arguments, arising from European law, in favor of the duty to renegotiate public debt.

One of the Union's founding principles, indeed the central, is the single market, which is an economic instrument in order to achieve a political project[17]. To ensure the unity of the market it is necessary to create competition between States[18]. The latter is a pre-condition required to apply the competition between EU businesses by the rules laid down by the Treaty[19]. Both monetary policy and the definition of competition rules are exclusive competence of Union and the States cannot adopt rules in contrast with such provisions (Art. 2 TFEU). The conditions, through which the action of the public authorities performs within the single European area, must be as uniform as possible.

If one of the States is weak because of the debt, the companies of that State will be in worse position than companies from other countries with sustainable debt, because on them it will be reversed the burden (higher taxes, lower incentives,

---

17 M. Cartabia- J.H.H. Weiler, *L'Italia in Europa*, Bologna, 2000, pp. 18, 243.

18 Among many, Court of First instance, 28 February 2002 (N-86/95-General Shipping companies).

19 Please refer to Title VII of Chapter I TFEU (Section I – Rules on competition; Section II Aids granted by states), Chapter II (Tax provisions), Chapter III (Approximation of laws, Regulations and administrative provisions of the Member States).

infrastructure investments insufficient). If a Member is heavily in debt, the issue is outside the narrow political sphere of relations between individual State and citizens of it. Therefore, one of the fundamental objectives set out in Art. 3 of the TFEU (ex 2 TEC) is threatened. The Article provides that, in order to establish an internal market, the Union "shall work for the sustainable development of Europe, based on economic growth "balanced and with stable price", on social market economy that is highly competitive, aiming at full employment and social progress, and based on an high level of protection and improvement of environment quality. It shall promote scientific and technological progress.

There is a close parallel between this programmatic provision and the other one much more concrete, that regulates the parameter of debt and public finances of the Member States (Art. 119 of the TFEU), which lays down the principle of coordination of Member States' economic policies. Once the single currency is introduced, this action should include the definition and conduct of a monetary policy and a unique exchange rate policy, with the primary objective of maintaining price stability and to support the general economic policies of Union in accordance with the principle of an open market economy with free competition. These actions of Member States and the Union shall involve also the respect of the principle of "sound public finances and monetary conditions". The declination of these principles is entrusted in particular to the provisions of the TFEU concerning the Union's economic and monetary policy[20], including specific provisions relating to the parameters of public debt and deficit[21].

How can the individual State achieve all the objectives laid down of the Article 3 of the Treaty, if it devotes huge resources to repay the past debt? The ECJ stated that the purposes enunciated in this provision "are linked to the existence and functioning of the Community" and that their achievement "must be the result of the establishment of the common market." Therefore the link between the existence of sound finances and basic objectives of the Union is confirmed.

The State has to eliminate any internal factor that could limit the equality in the European legal space and undermine the implementation of economic freedoms and fundamental rights under European law.

The result is to strengthen the idea that the reduction of domestic debt may be obtain by resorting to extraordinary administrative instruments and not only by focusing on the containment of public spending. The limitation of property rights of the creditors of the State could be justified by the general interest to comply with

20 Title VIII, chapter I-II-III-IV.
21 Art. 126 (ex 104 TCE).

the Community provisions. According to the Community system, the exercise of property rights may be restricted, if the Member States believe it "necessary" for the protection of the citizens[22].

To argue otherwise would lead to a unreasonable asymmetry. European States have been constrained recently with more and more radical provisions for the control of public finances and the level of debt, to the point where the budget law must receive every year the prior authorization of the Commission. These requirements are intended to protect the sovereign debt and to reassure creditors.

It would be impossible, taking into account this vast program, to deny citizens, which have to bear the burden of austerity policies, the benefits arising from being EU citizens and namely the existence of a legitimate expectation of compliance with rules that expand their legal rights implicit in the fundamental objectives of the Treaty, among which the "promotion of a high level of employment, the guarantee of adequate social protection "(Art. 9 TFEU).

There is another argument in favor of this conclusion. Article 12, paragraph 3, of the Treaty that establishes the European Stability Mechanism (ESM), entered into in Brussels on 2 February 2012 provides that "Collective action clauses shall be included, as of 1 January 2013, in all new euro area government securities, with maturity above one year, in a way which ensures that their legal impact is identical". The Collective Action Clauses allow a supermajority of bondholders to agree to a debt restructuring that is legally binding on all holders of the bond, including those who vote against the restructuring. These clauses are included in prospectuses or in newly issued government bond regulations and they allow a State in difficulty to restructure its debt, for example by extending maturities, reducing rates or proposing the exchange with other bonds, through a fixed procedure that is able to arrive in the easiest and fastest way to an agreement with the majority of creditors at the expense of the unruly minority. The system of collective action clauses confirms that the reduction of public debt can also occur through extraordinary measures that are placed on a parallel plane with respect to the reduction of public spending[23].

9. Debt sustainability in a theoretical perspective

Constitutions and laws contain a new provision: the sustainability of public debt to meet future generations. It is the solidarity ethics applied to public accounts. It is important to ask yourself what it means in theory "sustainability", of which up to

22 ECJ case law December, 13, 1979, (C- 44/79-Hauer).
23 ECJ, case law11 June 2015 (226/2013 – Fahnenbrock).

now we have heard in other areas and particularly with respect to environmental policies[24].

The two major moral theories to the political phenomenon, namely utilitarianism of Bentham and Mill, and "the contract" of Kantian ancestry, were inadequate to respond to the ethical problem that sustainability aims to address: the duties towards future generations. This also is to be referred to the financial sustainability in the economic field and therefore for debt sustainability. The idea of holding the debt can disagree with utilitarian precept to pursue wellness[25]. First of all there are different opinions in the literature on the relationship between the debt level and the sound economy of a country.

Second, even if the reduction of public debt in the long term may prove to be a winning strategy from an economic point of view, for utilitarian could still face the problem of justifying the strong suffering of populations waiting for future benefits. The case of Greece could be exemplary.

Even contract theory does not offer a good crutch to the principle of sustainability. The original contract, assumed by many political theories (such as John Rawls[26]), would hardly be possible as a pact between the generations present and future.

In order to understand the principle of sustainability is, rather, useful the thesis of Hans Jonas[27] about the imperative of responsibility. Jonas moves from inadequacy of utilitarianism and contract theory to answer moral questions raised by this scientific technique and internationalization of ethics and law, and in particular: (a) the attitude against those who are far from us (not part of Rawls' contract); (B) the requirements of future generations.

The principle of responsibility, applied to public ethics, implies the possibility of an authentic and free life. Freedom, however, generates responsibilities. Only those who are truly free can predict and calculate the future consequences of their actions, and only those who are free can alter them. The principle of responsibility therefore requires caution. This attitude is reflected in the legal political precautionary principle.

This thesis can justify better, in terms of the general theory, the legal and political debate on the sustainability of public debt. In fact, the principle of sustainability cannot be understood with the traditional criteria taken from the utilitarian and contract theories. On the one side, the globalization and the full opening of the

---

24 C. Pugh, *Sustainability, the Environment and Urbanization*, New York, 1996.

25 R. Hare, *Moral Thinking: Its Levels, Method, and Point*, Oxford, 1981.

26 J. Rawls, *A Theory of Justice*, Harvard University Press, 1971.

27 H. Jonas, *Das Prinzip Verantwortung*, op. cit.

markets are not able to ascribe liabilities, for example, for speculative maneuvers that may cause difficulties for the economy of a country. On the other side, the same financing of the economy creates a situation where actions are disconnected from consequences. Instead, the sustainability associated with the principle of responsibility is a concept that is based on the exhaustion of resources. It allows to establish a connection between the consequences of actions -in this case level of debt – and the future political dimension.

John McClellan Marshall
(The Honorable Senior Judge, Fourteenth Judicial District of Texas, Honorary Professor of the Maria Curie-Sklodowska University in Lublin, Poland)

Stare Decisis and Judicial Review of Public Administration in American Common Law System[1]

Abstract: The publication focuses on the *stare decisis* principle and its influence on the formation of precedent and later judgements, including the courts control over public administration in the American constitutional order. The article also shows a model of judicial review of public administrative action in the context of American jurisprudence.

Keywords: precedent *stare decisis, common law* legal culture, judicial control over public administration

Stare decisis is a principle of judicial decision-making that promotes efficiency, fairness, and legitimacy through consistency[2]. As such, it enhances both consistency and finality internally within the judicial system because it requires that in a given case the lower court must take notice of the decisions of a higher court that have been made on the same or similar matters. It is the definition of "higher" and "lower" that can sometimes lead to confusion when looking at the United States. Because the American state system is a component of the federal Constitutional structure, in addition to the federal court system each state has a judicial branch of government that includes several levels of trial courts and usually two levels of appeal, most often called the "court of appeals" and the "state supreme court." Within this system, the decisions of the courts of appeal or the state supreme court normally are the rules of decision for all of the trial courts of the state. In effect, there are fifty-one court systems in the United States that are in simultaneous operation, each of which employs *stare decisis* as a component of its decision-making process.

---

1 The paper had been prepared as a result of cooperation in the process of realization of the research project (UMO-2013/11/B/HS5/03821) "The Potential of Precedent Argumentation in the Polish Legal Order (A Theoretical and Comparative Approach)", granted by the National Science Center (Narodowe Centrum Nauki).

2 See *Weiner v. Wasson*, 900 S.W.2d 316 (Tex. 1995).

Precedent in the common law system can, however, be overruled by the court at any level if the reasons for doing so are sufficiently weighty from a public policy perspective. Among these factors are: 1) the original rule or decision was simply flawed; 2) the application of the prior rule can lead to and has led to inconsistent results, thus belying one of the underlying justifications for *stare decisis* in the first place; 3) the rule conflicts with other precedent in some respect, especially if there is a newer and better reasoned case; 4) that the rule regularly produces an unjust result unanticipated by the original decision or that places an unnecessary burden on the system; 5) the reasons that support the precedent no longer exist because of the passage of time[3]. One of the unarticulated factors is, quite simply, politics, in the sense that the courts historically have been very much in tune with public opinion on many thorny topics. This has meant that, from time to time, they have seemed to "legislate from the bench", when in fact they have merely assisted the law in moving with the times to meet the needs of society. It should be noted that normally the longer a precedent has been in place, the less likely it is to be overturned and the higher the court that is likely to be required to overturn it. This is in addition to the process by which a precedent can be overturned in some cases by the Legislature or by amendment of the Constitution.

It has long been considered desirable in American jurisprudence that in addition to having consistency with prior judicial decisions, the judgments of courts be "final" as early as possible in the process. The reasons are quite simple in that finality serves to conserve both the economic resources of the parties and the judicial resources of the state while at the same time resolving the dispute at hand. In this context, there are three doctrines that, as particularized extensions of the doctrine of *stare decisis,* reinforce the requirement of finality of judgments as a function of consistency. This is true both internally as to the case at bar and externally as to other cases that might be brought before a court, and they are: *res judicata*, collateral estoppel, and "law of the case."

Res judicata translates as "the thing has been adjudicated," and it focuses on the claims asserted by parties to a case that are attempted to be reasserted in a second case by the same parties. Simply put, in American civil law, this is not permitted, and, in effect, there is an internal operation of *stare decisis* that determines the outcome of the second case before it can ever get started. For example, in the context of a summary judgment, *res judicata* or claim preclusion, operates as a

3 *Ex parte Lewis*, 219 S.W.3d 335 (Tex.Crim.App. 2007).

matter of law as to limitations only after the cause of action has clearly accrued[4]. Similarly, *collateral estoppel* prohibits someone with interests identical to a party that *was* present at a prior proceeding from bringing issues or defenses in a second case when that party *might have* appeared or those issues or defenses *should have* been brought by the similarly situated party in the first case. Though the burden of proof is slightly different in these two doctrines, the principle is the same in that the law discourages multiple lawsuits on the same topic between the same or related parties.

Res judicata involves the dual principles of *merger* and *bar*. If the plaintiff should prevail, then all of its causes of action are *merged* in the judgment, but if the defendant should prevail, then the plaintiff is *barred* from bringing another action based on claims actually litigated or which could have been litigated. The defense requires proof of the following elements: 1) a prior final judgment on the merits by a court of competent jurisdiction; 2) identity of parties or those in privity with them; and 3) a second action based upon the same claims that were raised or could have been raised in the first action[5]. When used defensively, the burden on the party asserting the defense is to establish privity or identity of parties in the previous action[6]. It is axiomatic that *res judicata* cannot apply to causes of action that have not come into existence as of the time of the prior suit[7]. The principles that apply to *res judicata* apply to a final divorce decree to the same extent that they apply to any other final judgment[8].

The doctrine of *res judicata*, or *claim* preclusion, prevents the relitigation of a claim or cause of action that a court has finally adjudicated as well as relitigation of related matters that, with the use of diligence, a party should have litigated in the first suit[9]. A party may not pursue a claim determined by the final judgment of a court of competent jurisdiction in a prior suit as a ground of recovery in a

---

4 *Little v. Air Force Village Foundation, Inc.*, 974 S.W. 88 (Tex.App. – San Antonio 1998, pet. denied).

5 *Amstadt v. U. S. Brass Corp.*, 919 S.W.2d 644 (Tex. 1996).

6 *Fiallos v. Pagan-Lewis Motors, Inc.*, 147 S.W.3d 578 (Tex.App. – Corpus Christi 2004, pet. denied [2 pets]).

7 Genecov Group, Inc. v. Roosth Production Company, 144 S.W.3d 546 (Tex.App. – Tyler 2004, pet. denied).

8 *Nelson v. Williams*, 135 S.W.3d 202 (Tex.App. – Waco 2004, pet. denied), *citing Baxter v. Ruddle*, 794 S.W.2d 761 (Tex. 1990).

9 *Barr v. Resolution Trust Corp. ex rel. Sunbelt Federal Savings*, 837 S.W.2d 627 (Tex. 1992); see also *John G. & Marie Stella Kenedy Memorial Foundation v. Dewhurst*, 90 S.W.3d 268 (Tex. 2002).

later suit against the same parties[10]. In the case of the assertion of *res judicata* as an affirmative defense to a compulsory counterclaim, the movant must satisfy each element of *res judicata* and that the counterclaim is a compulsory one[11]. For this doctrine to support a judgment, there must be the same claims and same parties in the prior litigation; otherwise, at the most there may be collateral estoppel on some, but not all, issues[12]. Privity of parties may also be a factor in the defense[13]. It should be noted, however, that a judgment or determination of fact in a justice court is not *res judicata* and is not a basis for estoppel by judgment in a proceeding in a district court, except that a judgment rendered in a lower trial court is binding on the parties thereto as to recovery or denial of recovery[14].

The assertion of claim preclusion in divorce cases can be applied to tort claims[15]. Typically, the attorney for one side or the other intervenes for his or her fees, and the party obligated to pay the fees sues the attorney for malpractice. In such an instance, the failure to assert malpractice as a counterclaim to the intervention in the original action will operate as *res judicata* in favor of the attorney[16]. In a case of this type, as in any requiring an expert affidavit, the attorney may offer his or her testimony under the same terms as any other expert affidavit.

In the event that the original judgment was entered in a federal court, then federal law governs whether *res judicata* will bar the later state court proceeding[17]. Under the transactional test applied by the Fifth Circuit in civil cases, a prior judgment's preclusive effect extends to all rights of the plaintiff with respect to all or any part of the transaction or a series of connected transactions out of which the original action arose[18]. In criminal matters, the concept of *res judicata* is of Constitutional origin in the provisions of the Fifth Amendment that prohibit a

10 *Igal v. Brightstar Information Tech. Group, Inc.*, 250 S.W.3d 78 (Tex. 2008).

11 *Ingersoll-Rand Co. v. Valero Energy Corp.*, 996 S.W.2d 203 (Tex. 1999).

12 *Collins v. Guinn*, 102 S.W.3d 825 (Tex.App. – Texarkana 2003, pet. denied). See *Compania Financiara Libano v. Simmons*, 53 S.W.3d 365 (Tex. 2001) and *Quinney Electric, Inc. v. Kondos Enter., Inc.*, 988 S.W.2d 212 (Tex. 1999).

13 *Dennis v. First State Bank of Texas*, 989 S.W.2d 22 (Tex.App. – Fort Worth, 1998, no pet.); *Traweek v. Larkin*, 708 S.W.2d 942 (Tex.App. – Tyler 1986, writ ref'd n.r.e.).

14 *Lopez v. Sulak*, 76 S.W.3d 597 (Tex.App. – Corpus Christi 2002, no pet.).

15 *Twyman v. Twyman*, 855 S.W.2d 619 (Tex. 1993).

16 *Goggin v. Grimes*, 969 S.W.2d 135 (Tex.App. – Houston [14th] 1998, no pet.).

17 *San Antonio Independent School District v. McKinney*, 936 S.W.2d 279 (Tex. 1996); *Geary v. Texas Commerce Bank*, 967 S.W.2d 836 (Tex. 1998) ["transactional test"]; *Drago Daic v. Nauru Phosphate Royalties*, 27 S.W.3d 695 (Tex.App. – Beaumont 2000, pet. denied).

18 *Test Masters Educational Services, Inc. v. Singh*, 428 F.3d 559 (5th Cir. 2005), *cert. denied*, 547 U.S. 1055, 126 S.Ct. 1662, 164 L.Ed.2d 397 (2006).

person from being placed twice in jeopardy in a criminal matter. This is commonly referred to as "double jeopardy," and, with some technical exceptions prohibits a person from being tried twice for the same criminal offense if he is acquitted in the earlier case, even if later evidence should come to light that establishes his guilt. In a proceeding that involves claims that were also part of a Chapter 13 bankruptcy proceeding, the final order of the bankruptcy court operates to preclude litigation of the state court claims that could have been raised in the bankruptcy court[19]. Of course, a part of the summary judgment proof in such a case could well involve proving up the federal law as an exhibit to the motion in order to establish what the claims were in the federal action. Similarly, if the judgment should be from a sister state, the introduction of the judgment into evidence in proper form creates a *prima facie* case for its recognition and enforcement under the Full Faith and Credit Clause[20].

It should be noted that in the absence of a "judgment" there is no issue of *res judicata* that can raise an issue of fact or law sufficient to defeat a summary judgment[21]. For example, *res judicata* does not apply when the initial tribunal lacks subject matter jurisdiction over the claim[22]. From the point of view of a civil law jurisdiction, this concept would find ready application in the case of administrative bodies, as the doctrine also applies to the relitigation of claims previously determined by an administrative agency[23].

Collateral estoppel, or *issue* preclusion, is designed to promote judicial efficiency, protect parties from multiple lawsuits and prevent inconsistent judgments by precluding relitigation of issues[24]. The party asserting collateral estoppel must establish that the facts to be litigated in the second action were 1) fully and fairly litigated in the first action, 2) essential to the judgment in the first action, and 3) the parties were cast as adversaries in the first action[25]. Normally, collateral estoppel arises as a defense that must be asserted in detail. It should also be noted

19 *Blum v. Restland of Dallas Inc.*, 971 S.W.2d 546 (Tex.App. – Dallas 1997, no writ).

20 *Centre Equities, Inc. v. Tingley*, 106 S.W.3d 143 (Tex.App. – Austin 2003, no pet.).

21 *Montemayor v. San Antonio Fire Department*, 985 S.W.2d 549 (Tex.App. – San Antonio 1998, no pet.).

22 See *Citizens Insurance Co. of America v. Daccach*, 217 S.W.3d 430 (Tex. 2007).

23 See *Tricon Tool & Supply, Inc. v. Thumann*, 226 S.W.3d 494 (Tex.App. – Houston [1st] 2006, pet. denied).

24 *Sysco Food Services, Inc. v. Trapnell*, 890 S.W.2d 796 (Tex. 1994).

25 *SWEPI, L. P. v. Camden Resources, Inc.*, 139 S.W.3d 332 (Tex.App. – San Antonio 2004, pet. denied).

that an earlier judgment may be considered "final" for purposes of collateral estoppel even if an appeal from that judgment should be pending.

An ancillary doctrine applicable to both *res judicata* and collateral estoppel is evidentiary in nature, and it is "judicial estoppel." In its simplest form, the doctrine prohibits a party or a witness from contradicting in a subsequent proceeding statements made under oath in an prior proceeding, regardless of whether the prior case is "final." This is particularly applicable in cases that have multiple parties that are tried in a sequence, rather than all at once. The key issues in whether judicial estoppel will apply are who gave the evidence in the earlier proceeding and whether it is in fact a prior proceeding to which *res judicata* or collateral estoppel could apply. Obviously, the doctrine does not apply if the factual situation has changed or if new evidence has come to light so as to require an honest alteration of testimony. Again, the intent of the doctrine is to maintain the integrity of the judicial process by preventing a party or a witness from altering testimony to meet the exigencies of the moment.

As a general rule, *res judicata* also applies to the outcome of administrative proceedings. Fundamentally, this is a result of the rule-making process within the administrative system. For an administrative rule to take effect, it first must be formally proposed to the agency. Once it has been gone over to insure that there is no conflict with other agencies or rules of the proposing agency itself, the rule is published to allow for public comment on it. This often results in the revision of the rule, based upon input from those persons or entities to be affected by the new rule. The time allowed for comment can extend for several months, depending upon the number and substance of the revisions that are offered. Once that time has expired, assuming that there be no additional comments or proposed changes, the rule is published in its final form in the *Federal Register*, or the state equivalent publication, and then added to the Code of Federal Regulations in the proper location. At that point, the rule, now a regulation, has the force of law, assuming that it is within the scope of the responsibilities of the agency that promulgated it. Of course, one of the bases for challenging the validity of a rule is that it was not within the competence of the agency, though that is very rare in the modern world.

Normally, a complaint involving an administrative agency originates within the agency itself. It is filed before an administrative law judge who has special competence in the field of that agency's responsibilities. This is a function of the doctrine of "primary jurisdiction" and reflects the reality that the administrative agencies are in fact part of the executive branch of government. The administrative law judges are appointed normally for a term of years, not for life, though many in fact serve for extended periods of time. That is important since the Article III federal courts are reluctant to interfere in the day-to-day operations of the other two branches of government. In hearing a complaint, the agency proceeds complaint in accordance with procedural rules that are designed to provide "due process" while focusing on the agency responsibilities as the basis of the decision. That said, however, the initial hearings are often quite informal as compared with a conventional courtroom setting. It should be noted that the agency is presumed to be more competent at interpreting its own regulations than is the court on appeal, so the standard is very much in favor of the administrative determination. The agency engages in fact-finding and then issues its ruling. Once a final determination of an administrative agency that is otherwise competent to hear the matter has been made, *res judicata* principles apply in a subsequent lawsuit[26]. This notion is reinforced by the principle that, unless otherwise provided, the Administrative Procedure Act contested-case and judicial-review procedures apply to agency-governed proceedings[27].

If the complainant should lose in the agency hearing, it is possible to appeal to the district court [or court of similar jurisdiction], as provided by the rules of most states and the federal courts. The appeal consists of a review of the administrative decision, specifically the regulation that was at issue and the evidence supporting the decision. If there should be "substantial evidence" [any evidence of probative value] supporting the decision, then the court upholds the administrative agency and dismisses the appeal. If, however, the agency should have disregarded its own decisions and regulations, or if there should not be sufficient evidence, then the court would vacate the decision as being "arbitrary and capricious" and send it back to the agency for a rehearing. Further, if the complainant still disagrees with the decision, the principal of *res judicata* likely will operate to defeat a subsequent lawsuit on the subject. In the absence of a specific statutory authority in an administrative agency to interpret and enforce a contract or to perform other functions as to issues routinely heard and decided by trial courts, that is, inherently judicial in nature, then the administrative agency does not have primary jurisdiction and would not necessarily be "otherwise competent"[28]. Obviously, in such a situation, *res judicata* might or might not be applicable.

The interaction between the doctrines of *res judicata* and *stare decisis* demonstrate that they common law system has one other, very important, aspect to

26 *Igal v. Brightstar Information Technology*, 250 S.W.3d 78 (Tex. 2008).
27 *Marble Falls Independent School District v. Scott*, 275 S.W.3d 558 (Tex.App. – Austin 2008, pet. denied).
28 See *In re Cano Petroleum, Inc.*, 277 S.W.3d 470 (Tex.App. – Amarillo 2009, no pet.), citing *Amarillo Oil Co. v. Energy-Agri Products, Inc.*, 794 S.W.2d 20 (Tex. 1990).

its operation: a limitation on the discretion of the trial judges, indeed on judges at any level in the system, to decide a case without any guidelines to serve as a reference. It is quite rare in modern common law jurisprudence to have a judge confronted with what is a true case of "first impression", that is one that has never come before a court, either because of the factual setting or the legal requirements that would drive the decision. In such a case, obviously, these two principles would have little application, but even so at the very least a judge would have to consider such things as the public policy that his or her decision would be articulating and whether that was consistent with the Constitution and historical concepts of "due process". The concepts of *res judicata* and *stare decisis*, in such a case would require the judge to look to the future development of the law and so be instrumental in framing the law as it may be. To that extent, these two doctrines form that circle of "experience" to which Holmes was referring, linking the past with the future and so preserving the commonality of the common law.[29]

29 Holmes, *The Common Law* (1881), 1. "The life of the law has not been logic; it has been experience…"

Studies in Politics, Security and Society

Edited by Stanisław Sulowski

Vol. 1 Robert Wiszniowski (ed.): Challenges to Representative Democracy. A European Perspective. 2015.

Vol. 2 Jarosław Szymanek: Theory of Political Representation. 2015.

Vol. 3 Alojzy Z. Nowak (ed.): Global Financial Turbulence in the Euro Area. Polish Perspective. 2015.

Vol. 4 Jolanta Itrich-Drabarek: The Civil Service in Poland. Theory and Experience. 2015.

Vol. 5 Agnieszka Rothert: Power of Imagination. Education, Innovations and Democracy. 2016.

Vol. 6 Zbysław Dobrowolski: Combating Corruption and Other Organizational Pathologies. 2017.

Vol. 7 Vito Breda: The Objectivity of Judicial Decisions. A Comparative Analysis of Nine Jurisdictions. 2017.

Vol. 8 Anna Sroka: Accountability and democracy in Poland and Spain. 2017.

Vol. 9 Anna Sroka / Fanny Castro-Rial Garrone / Rubén Darío Torres Kumbrián (eds.): Radicalism and Terrorism in the 21st Century. Implications for Security. 2017.

Vol. 10 Filip Pierzchalski: Political Leadership in Morphogenetic Perspective. 2017.

Vol. 11 Alina Petra Marinescu: The Discursive Dimension of Employee Engagement and Disengagement. Accounts of keeping and leaving jobs in present-day Bucharest organizations. 2017.

Vol. 12 Jacek Giedrojć: Competition, Coordination, Social Order. Responsible Business, Civil Society, and Government in an Open Society. 2017.

Vol. 13 Filip Ilkowski: Capitalist Imperialism in Contemporary Theoretical Frameworks. 2017.

Vol. 14 Leszek Leszczyński / Adam Szot (eds.): Discretionary Power of Public Administration. Its Scope and Control. 2017.

www.peterlang.com

www.ingramcontent.com/pod-product-compliance
Ingram Content Group UK Ltd.
Pitfield, Milton Keynes, MK11 3LW, UK
UKHW011005120926
8556IPUK00027B/44

9 783631 674680